# Turning Points in Middle Eastern History

Eamonn Gearon, M.A.

PUBLISHED BY:

THE GREAT COURSES
Corporate Headquarters
4840 Westfields Boulevard, Suite 500
Chantilly, Virginia 20151-2299
Phone: 1-800-832-2412
Fax: 703-378-3819
www.thegreatcourses.com



Printed in the United States of America

## Eamonn Gearon, M.A.

Professorial Lecturer
Johns Hopkins University,
School of Advanced International Studies

Eamonn Gearon is a Professorial Lecturer in African Studies at Johns Hopkins University, School of Advanced International Studies, in Washington DC. Having graduated with an undergraduate degree in Theology from the University of Southampton, England, Mr. Gearon moved to Egypt, where he taught at the American University in Cairo. He received his M.A. in Near and Middle Eastern Studies and Arabic from the School of Oriental and African Studies (SOAS) at the University of London.

Mr. Gearon is the cofounder and managing director of The Siwa Group, a specialist consultancy firm that works with both the U.S. government and the private sector. Mr. Gearon is responsible for training U.S. Department of State officials, Department of Defense workers, and other U.S. government employees whose work takes them to, or is concerned with, North Africa and the Middle East. He is a noted analyst and researcher into military affairs and Islamist-inspired terrorism across the Middle East for organizations such as Jane's.

A camel expert, Mr. Gearon also spent years living in, traveling, and exploring the Sahara, both with the Bedu people and on a number of solo, camel-powered expeditions. These days, he enjoys his role as a public speaker, whose presentations combine elements of Middle Eastern history and contemporary affairs. He is a distinguished speaker on Cunard's flagship *Queen Mary 2* and other vessels.

Mr. Gearon has published extensively on Middle Eastern history, culture, and contemporary politics. A regular reviewer for *The Times Literary Supplement* and other prestigious publications, he is also the author of *The Sahara: A Cultural History*. He has contributed to numerous other titles, including the *Encyclopedia of African History* (edited by Kevin Shillington), *Meetings with Remarkable Muslims: A Collection of Travel Writing* (edited by Barnaby Rogerson and Rose Baring), and *Sahara Overland: A Route and Planning Guide*. ■

## Introduction



## Lecture Guides

## Supplemental Material

# Turning Points in Middle Eastern History

Scope

The Middle East is one of the most fascinating and important regions on earth. This course examines the history of that region from the dawn of Islam, in 622, until the final end of the Ottoman Caliphate, in 1924.

By looking at some of the most important events that took place during this period, this course not only reveals a series of occurrences but explains how these events shaped the region's political, military, social, and religious history. Each of these stories also introduces us to a fascinating cast of people and places, many of which remain of enduring importance.

Like history the world over, the history of the Middle East is often seen solely through the lens of violent conflict, but as this course will make clear, the region's history is much more vibrant and nuanced than this. As well as looking at those conflicts which have shaped the region's religious, political, and social makeup, we will also consider a much broader selection of events to provide a more balanced picture of the Middle East's history.

Many of the turning points in this course might come as a surprise, such as the pilgrimage made by the richest man who ever lived, Mansa Musa, who journeyed from his kingdom in the Sahara to Cairo and Mecca, then back again. Another character we'll meet is Fatima al-Fihri, a wealthy widow from Tunisia who lived in Morocco. Although not a household name, she deserves to be: She was the woman who established the world's first university, in the city of Fes, two centuries before a similar establishment was created in Europe.

We will also meet some more familiar faces, including Richard the Lionheart and Saladin from the period of the Crusades. During this era, we'll consider both the crusaders' conquest of Jerusalem, in 1099, and the city's recapture by Saladin's Muslim army a century later.

There are also numerous periods of greater peace, prosperity, and progress, as we will see. Among them is the flourishing of Cordoba, in Spain, when Muslim monarchs eagerly employed the best available talents, regardless of whether they were Muslim, Jewish, or Christian.

The fall of Granada in 1492 marked the end of almost 700 years of Muslim rule in much of that part of Andalusia. When we learn about this event, we will see how events in the Muslim Middle East have, and continue to have, more long-term and wide-reaching impact than is first obvious.

Other great cities this course visits include Baghdad and Cairo. In both of these cases we will discover why they were founded when they were, why, by whom, and what impact these foundational moments had both then and for centuries to come.

Together, this course's 36 lectures offer a comprehensive survey of 1,300 years of Middle Eastern history, reaching up to the early 20th century. That period included the discovery of oil, the dramatic Arab Revolt led by Lawrence of Arabia during World War I, and the postwar peace settlements that created the modern Middle East out of the pieces of a shattered Ottoman Empire. ■

# Muslim Empires: Land, Language, Religion

Lecture 1

Basic relationships are central to stories about even the biggest names in history. Each event turns on the capacities and limitations of human beings, and so they may be expressed in relationships—some of which worked very well, and some that went badly. This lecture examines one set of relationships—the Saud-Wahhab pact—which shows how the past informs the present. The lecture also defines what exactly the Middle East is for the purposes of this course, and identifies themes and characters which will guide it.

## Language and Countries

- This course will explore a 1400-year period from the rise of Islam—and the life of Muhammad, Islam's most important prophet—to the fall of the Ottoman Empire, and the end of the last caliphate in Islamic history.

- A *caliph* can be understood as Muhammad's earthly successor, and the caliph's domain—or *caliphate*—was intended to combine the Muslim political and spiritual realms under his sole authority.

- In Islamic history—from the moment Muhammad died, and his successor was chosen, in 632 AD—some political entity in the Muslim Middle East always laid claim to that title, until shortly after World War I. Matters are very different today, for reasons that'll become clear as we move through the course. Consequently, no contemporary group has much success claiming the title (which doesn't mean that they won't try).

- The point here is that language—and how we use it—matters, as we see from the continuing relevance of a word such as *caliphate*.

- Another important term is the *Greater Middle East*. Although this geo-political identifier only recently has come into our lexicon, it

Cairo, Egypt

is useful in describing a loose geographical area. By referring to the Greater Middle East, we're signalling that in addition to covering the Arabic-speaking countries of the Middle East, we're also going to take into account Turkey and Iran (or Persia), as they relate to the Arabic-speaking countries of the region.

- Turkey and Iran transact life and politics in languages other than Arabic, principally. They have distinct cultural traditions of their own. But they also share a great deal of common cultural and religious heritage with the Arabic-speaking world.

- The Middle East in this course will include North Africa from Morocco to Egypt; as well as Iraq, Jordan, Lebanon, Syria; and the whole Arabian Peninsula, from Kuwait in the north to Oman and Yemen in the south. It will include Jerusalem, but not the post–World War II state of Israel, as the tale before us will end just after World War I.

**Turning Points**

- What kinds of turning points will we be looking at in the history of the Middle East? The answer is: exactly the same sort of things you'd expect to find in a study of any other part of the world. In other words, it's the history of humanity in a particular geographical location, over a certain period of time. And there are plenty of surprises, including the story of the richest man who ever lived. We'll see war and peace, and everything in between. We'll witness invasions and conquests. And we will examine the social and intellectual flowering coincident with scholarship and tolerance.

- We'll see manifestations of genius and humanity at its best, as well as displays of human folly, ignorance, and stupidity. To highlight a couple of watershed events, we will revisit, in detail, the sack of Baghdad, in 1258, by an invading Mongol horde. We will also study the French invasion and conquest of Algeria, which began in 1830.

- We're also going to consider such turning points as the foundation of Cairo, by the Fatimids, in 969. Among the less-known episodes that upturned the Middle East and the West alike, we will highlight the Battle of Talas. It is the one time in history that Arab and Chinese military forces met in battle. One unintended result of this hostility—fought in 751, on the border between their empires—was the transfer of paper-making technology from China to the Middle East, and then from there into Muslim Spain, and on through Europe.

- Moving from events to individuals, we're likewise going to come across familiar faces, including such men of action as Muhammad, Saladin, Suleiman the Magnificent, and Lawrence of Arabia.

- But it's not just men of action who make a mark in history; thinkers too have an indispensable role to play. In this group, we will meet al-Ghazali, who lived in the 11th century, and whose importance to Islamic theology is substantial. And although men dominate the headlines of early history, we're also going to meet a woman by the name of Fatima al-Fihri, who had the vision, and the financial means, to found the world's first university

- Another favourite character from world history is the 14th-century scholar Ibn Khaldun, from the city of Tunis. While there have been any number of brilliant scholars in history, few may lay claim—as Ibn Khaldun can—to pouring the intellectual foundations for least four different disciplines of learning: sociology, historiography, modern economics, and demography.

- Ibn Khaldun trained his mind to recognise turning points, so much so that he charted three such moments in his own lifetime: the Mongol invasions, in the 1250s; the Black Death, which struck Europe and the Middle East in the 1340s; and the rising power of European states in the 14th century.

- Religion is a defining theme in many of the turning points in this course. Judaism and Christianity brought monotheism—the belief in one God—to the forefront hundreds of years before Muhammad. But with Islam, Muhammad united and transformed a people into a religious empire that today is the world's second largest faith, representing 1.5 billion people. His language, Arabic, became another unifying force for the religion and the region.

- Another defining theme is the idea of empire, or at least of territory. Piece by piece, the Muslim faith and its predominant language transformed continents (and the peoples who inhabited them) into a more unified force and face. Even with the demise of the Ottoman caliphate after the First World War, we see a continuing transformation of many of these properties into modern Turkey, Saudi Arabia, and other modern states in the Middle East.

### The Saud-Wahhab Pact

- The past informs the present. Ibn Khaldun himself said, "The past resembles the future more closely than one drop of water resembles another." Another of Ibn Khaldun's big ideas was about how dynasties and empires rise and fall over time.

- This leads us to the story of the Saud-Wahhab pact of 1744. The story starts in a remote corner of the Arabian Peninsula, at the happy wedding of a young couple, which involved two families from unremarkable, out-of-the-way villages.

- One family was led by minor chieftains, who ruled a small oasis. At the head of the other family was a radical religious reformer who had already been expelled from own village, for stirring up trouble.

- While the couple was uniting in matrimony, the wedding also marked a political pact that fused two families. The minor local ruler is named Muhammad ibn Saud, and the controversial religious reformer is Muhammad ibn 'Abd al-Wahhab.

- Examples of marriage contracts between ambitious and prominent families are found throughout history. The hope of each family is that it will prosper, and grow stronger, through the common bond. In our example, that's exactly what happened.

    - Ibn Saud was keen to increase his political reach in Arabia, and saw the potential in protecting—and working with—the missionary zeal of this religiously conservative Muslim preacher.

    - At the same time, 'Abd al-Wahhab, in criticising everyone around him for not being religious enough, had made enough enemies that he needed sanctuary—the very refuge Ibn Saud could offer him.

- The two men agreed that the Saud family would help promote al-Wahhab's religious reforms, and that 'Abd al-Wahhab would support the Sauds' dream of conquering Arabia, thereby legitimising each other's ambition. Today's Kingdom of Saudi Arabia—and the Sunni line of Muslim faith known as Wahhabism—demonstrates the strength of this alliance, which persisted through good times and bad.

- In terms of political governance, the central point of the Saud-Wahhab agreement was the combination of political and religious institutions into a single ruling body, to be headed by a king. These state leaders would come from the Saud side of the family. But in religious terms, the union meant the promotion of 'Abd al-Wahhab's own view of Islam. As it happens, that line is one the most uncompromising—least tolerant—forms of the Muslim faith.

- While contemporary Saudi Arabia represents a very conservative society, by and large, it's important to note that only about 23 percent of the native population ascribe to the ultra-conservative, Wahhabi interpretation of Islam.

**Cycles**

- Petroleum wealth changed not only Saudi Arabia and the Greater Middle East, but also the entire world around it. The global oil shock, in 1973, was among of the first external signs of this transformation, followed by wars in Iran, Iraq, Kuwait, and elsewhere.

- The promotion of religious intolerance against the backdrop of concentrated wealth and shallow political institutions has done a great deal to propagate much of the violence we see in the region today. It is an example neither perpetrated by, nor even supported by, anything like the majority of Muslims.

- The net result of such polarization is the emergence of terrorism, carried out in the name of Islam. As we'll see, when we explore the Crusades—and several intra-Muslim wars—religiously inspired violence isn't a new phenomenon. Nor is it by any means limited to the Middle East. But hopefully this shadow will pass.

- During Ibn Khaldun's lifetime, in the 14th and early 15th century, it took just three generations for a new power to emerge on the fringes of an old empire, then reach its apogee, and begin its almost inevitable decline. That is just one of many stories, and cycles, we will examine in this course.

- Some time after the relatively recent discovery of large oil reserves in Dubai, in 1966, the Emir Rashid bin Sa'id al-Maktoum was asked for his views on the country's unexpected financial windfall. He offered the following thought: "My grandfather rode a camel, my father rode a camel, I drive a Mercedes, my son drives a Land Rover, his son will drive a Land Rover, but his son will ride a camel."

**Suggested Reading**

Gearon, *The Sahara.*

Hitti, *History of the Arabs.*

Hodgson, *The Venture of Islam*, volume 1, book 1.

Lapidus, *A History of Islamic Societies.*

Ruthven, *Islam.*

Yergin, *The Prize.*

**Questions to Consider**

1. Although the dawn of Islam in the Middle East brought about many profound and lasting changes across the region, is it perhaps more accurate to think of history since Islam, rather than Islamic history?

2. How much of the history of the Middle East has been driven by individuals versus more impersonal factors, such as sudden fluctuations in population, internal or external economic factors, or resource insecurity in a typically arid or semi-arid environment?

# Muhammad and the Dawn of Islam—622

Lecture 2

The subject of this lecture is the dawn of Islam—Muhammad's first revelation—and the events that followed during the remainder of his lifetime. In any discussion of the 1,400 years of Islamic and Middle Eastern history, Muhammad's first revelation is peerless—a turning point among turning points. Without Muhammad's account of his mysterious revelation in a mountain cave, there would have been no prophetic mission, no preaching to the masses, no converts, no Islam, and an impossible-to-imagine alteration in global history, from that moment until the present day.

## Muhammad's Life

- Muhammad was born in the city of Mecca in or around the year 570. He lived in Mecca for the first 52 years of his life, according to most sources. Because of the central importance of certain divinely inspired revelations to the story of Muhammad's life, this first chapter is often divided into the years before his first revelation, when he was 40, and the dozen years following the first revelation. After that, he fled Mecca for Medina, 200 miles to the north. He was based there for the last 10 years of his life.

- Muhammad's father died before he was born, and his mother passed away when he was about six. Consequently, the youth was raised for the most part by a paternal uncle, Abu Talib. Abu Talib was a successful merchant and the head of the Banu Hisham clan, which was part of the larger Quraysh tribe.

- Once Muhammad was old enough, probably about 13 years of age, he started to work for his uncle, and accompanied him on trading trips to different parts of Arabia.

- Before Muhammad, Arabia was primarily a polytheistic society. Although there were Jews, Christians, and some indigenous

Kaaba in Mecca

Arab monotheists, the majority of locals worshipped one or more of hundreds of local, tribal and regional deities.

- Muhammad's message of monotheism was a challenge not only to the local religious beliefs that predominated on the Arabian Peninsula, but also to the economic basis of the locals who attended to them.

- Mecca was an important pre-Islamic destination of monotheistic pilgrims, or those who travel to sacred places for religious reasons. The *kaaba*, a large black cuboid, was the pilgrims' final destination in the center of Mecca. Muhammad was the member of a tribe, the Quraysh, that was responsible for protecting the kaaba in Mecca, an important center of polytheistic pilgrimage.

- However, after Muhammad converted Arabia to Islam, he ordered destroyed the 360 statues of idols housed in the kaaba. It was then co-opted—or adopted—as Islam's physical focal point on earth.

**Muhammad's First Revelation**

- In the year 610, Muhammad received his first revelation. Forty years old, and happily married to a successful businesswoman named Khadija, Muhammad was already in the habit of walking out from the city, to spend nights alone in contemplation—meditating in a small cave on a mountain just outside of the city.

- Gebel an-Nour—or the Mountain of Light—is a prominent peak, about three miles from the center of Mecca. Muhammad would rest in a small cave on the side of the mountain. It was there, according to the tradition, that the Angel Gabriel appeared to him.

- Moses is said to have spent 40 days and nights on Mount Sinai before encountering God and receiving the Ten Commandments. In the Jewish, Christian, and Muslim traditions, both Elijah and Jesus spent 40 fasting in the wilderness. In the Muslim tradition, Muhammad also spent 40 days alone, fasting and in contemplation, before he received the first of the prophetic revelations that eventually would comprise the Quran, Islam's holy book.

- The first word that Gabriel is said to utter is *Iqra*, which means "read" or "recite." Muhammad replies that he's unable to read, at which Gabriel grabs hold of Muhammad and again orders Muhammad to read, saying:

    > "Read: in the name of thy Lord Who created, Created man from a clot. Read: and thy Lord is the most Generous, Who taught by the pen, Taught man that which he knew not."

- Returning from the mountain, Muhammad spoke to his wife Khadija. As the first person to hear and believe Muhammad's message—and to accept him as prophet—Khadija is recognized as the first Muslim convert. For that, she maintains a special place in Islam.

- Most traditions agree that Muhammad didn't receive another visitation from Gabriel for three more years, during which time he became depressed and worried about what might happen next.

- But then Muhammad received his second revelation, and shortly thereafter he started to publicly preach his message of monotheism, including the urgent need for people to mend their ways, to repent, and to submit to the will of God. The oneness of God is absolutely central to Islam, as is the idea of subordinating themselves to God's will. The Arabic word for *submission* is *Islam*.

**Muhammad's Enemies**

- Muhammad attracted very few converts in the first years of his preaching Islam. Nevertheless, he did make plenty of enemies, including from his own tribe and those of other prominent merchant families, who relied on pilgrims for much of their income.

- Traditionally, in pre-Islamic Arabian culture, retribution in a blood feud could be extended to any family member, which, for practical purposes, extended to any member of the extended clan. Once started, blood feuds could easily get out of control, and often lasted for generations.

- Despite the offenses Muhammad provoked, he remained more or less safe from physical attacks, because he was still a member of the powerful Banu Hashim clan. And so long as his uncle, Abu Talib, was head of the clan, Muhammad's guardian protected him from fellow tribesmen and others, and urged them to forgive the errant nephew's religious zeal.

- Such protection was good only up to a point. In the year 619, Abu Talib died, as did Muhammad's beloved wife and confidant, Khadija. Ominously for Muhammad, leadership of the clan passed to Abu Lahab, one of Muhammad's paternal uncles. An implacable foe of Muhammad, Abu Lahab withdrew the clan's protection.

- Now if an enemy now killed Muhammad, it would not lead to a blood feud. Abu Lahab was opening the door for Muhammad's murder. And so, after 12 years of contentious preaching in Mecca, word reached Muhammad that he was the subject of an assassination plot.

**Muhammad's Flight**

- The conspiracy to kill Muhammad brings us to the flight of Muhammad and his Muslim faithful away from Mecca and away from danger. During the pilgrimage season, Muhammad met with a group of men from Yathrib, an oasis town 200 miles north of Mecca.

- Later, Yathrib would be renamed The City of the Prophet—or Medina an-Nabi—in Muhammad's honour. Over time, the words *of the prophet* were dropped from common usage, which is why today it's simply called Medina.

- In June 622, Muhammad departed Mecca in the dead of night. This moment of exodus, or *hijra* in Arabic, marks the start of the Islamic calendar; the birth of a new religion; and a radical upheaval of the entire region's existing political order.

- Even after he became safely settled in Medina, Muhammad remained an outsider. Under certain circumstances, this could be a disadvantage. But it was useful in Medina, as it meant he was called on to settle disputes in which he had no personal stake.

- As he came to be trusted by the heads of all the major tribes in Medina, Muhammad's arbitration skills marked the start of his political leadership there, soon to be formalized in what became known as the Constitution of Medina.

- Apart from creating an alliance between the main Medina tribes for the first time, the constitution offered specific protections to the "people of the book," which is to say Jews and Christians.

- Meanwhile, the Meccan authorities—having been thwarted in their goal of killing Muhammad—seized all property and possessions of the Muslims who'd fled the city.

- Now living in exile, penniless, and without other means of financial recourse, they started launching armed raids against the pilgrim caravans en route to Mecca. Looting the caravans obviously enraged the Meccan authorities and harmed their economy. Open warfare broke out.

- A turning point in this armed conflict occurred at the Battle of Badr in March 624. In the traditional account of the battle, about

300 Muslims fought a Meccan army of almost 1,000 adversaries. In spite of being outnumbered by more than 3 to 1, the Muslims won an easy victory, and killed many of the Meccan leaders in the process.

- Taking this victory as evidence of God's favor shining on them, the Muslims found their reputations greatly enhanced. They attracted many new followers, and secured their positions in Medina.

- The Muslims weren't always so lucky, however. In coming years, they suffered a number of military defeats at the hands of the Meccans.

**Muhammad, 630–632**

- Eventually, in 630, Muhammad decided that his army had grown strong enough to risk an all-out attack against his former hometown of Mecca. It's said that Muhammad now led some 10,000 people.

- The Muslims easily routed the enemy upon arriving at Mecca. Resistance was somewhat muted, and the city surrendered with little bloodshed.

- With the new religious and political Muslim entity firmly in charge—and Muhammad at its head—most of the city accepted the new order, not least because of the amnesty the prophet extended to his erstwhile enemies.

- In 632—10 years after he had first fled from Mecca to Medina—Muhammad performed what's properly considered the first Islamic pilgrimage in the city of his birth. In this way, he established the religious obligation on all Muslims—their health and financial resources permitting—to perform the *hajj*, or "pilgrimage," to Mecca, at least once in a lifetime.

- Upon performing the first *hajj*, Muhammad returned to Medina. Shortly afterward, he developed a fever and a headache—the result of a poisoning, according to many sources. After a few days of illness, Muhammad died on June 8, 632, at the age of 62.

**Muhammad as a Turning Point**

- Muhammad's mission brought about profound changes that make his life, particularly the last 22 years of it, a turning point that set in motion world change on an incalculable scale.

- Muhammad's message impacted the religious, political, and social life of the era he inhabited. It demonstrates his view that religion couldn't be a private matter, removed from the real world in which people live and operate.

- In political terms, virtually the entire Arabian Peninsula was united as a single political realm for the first time in its history, at the time of Muhammad's death.

- In societal terms, Muhammad's introduction of the concept of personal accountability, superseding tribal law, was radical.

- Examples of practical changes that Muhammad, or the Quran, insisted on, are numerous. They include outlawing the practise of female infanticide, and providing women with legal rights, to property, to divorce, and to remarry. These rights were far in advance of those enjoyed in most of the world during the 7th century. As the historian Bernard Lewis has written, Islam "denounced aristocratic privilege, rejected hierarchy, and adopted a formula of the career open to the talents."

- In religious terms, polytheism had all but disappeared from the Arabian Peninsula by the time of Muhammad's death.

### Suggested Reading

Armstrong, *Muhammad*.

Bulliet, *The Camel and the Wheel*.

Esposito, *Islam*, chapter 2.

Hitti, *Makers of Arab History*, chapter 1.

Lapidus, *A History of Islamic Societies*, chapter 2.

Lings, *Muhammad*.

Ruthven, *Islam*.

### Questions to Consider

1. Given that the three great Abrahamic religions were conceived in desert places, what, if anything, do you think might be the connection between geography and prophecy?

2. Although Muhammad said Islam was only the completion of the earlier monotheistic prophetic tradition, in what ways is Islam distinct from Judaism and Christianity? In what areas are these three faiths similar?

Lecture 3

# Arab Invasion of North Africa—639

After the introduction of the camel, the 7th-century Arab invasion of North Africa was easily the most profound and permanent change ever to hit the region. Starting in 639, Arab armies would conquer the whole of North Africa in just 70 years, and institute a new order such as the region had never seen before. This conquest, from the Red Sea to the Atlantic, was more widespread—and more complete—than anything achieved by previous invaders. The changes were permanent.

## Setting the Stage for Invasion

- It was in 639 that the Arabs invaded North Africa. In the eastern Mediterranean region, a decades-long war between two of the ancient world's superpowers—the Eastern Roman Empire of Byzantium and the Persian Sassanian Empire—had left each side exhausted, impoverished, and disorganized.

- Periodic outbreaks of bubonic plague and divisive succession battles further weakened these empires. The timing couldn't have been better for the emergence of a new conquering force, especially one coming out of the city-free—and thus plague-free—deserts of Arabia.

- Many of the Arabs' earlier attacks were little more than armed raids designed to seize loot. These smash-and-grab runs were carried out by relatively small numbers of men, and made possible by the Arabs' use of camels—which had evolved to live in desert places—as cavalry.

- By the time we come to the Arab invasion of Egypt, we're entering a new phase in the early history of the Arab Empire. This was the period when opportunistic raids were swapped for a more systematic, planned approach.

- At the time, the Muslim Empire was led by its second caliph: Umar al-Khattab. Umar ruled for 10 years, from 634 to 644. Initially reluctant to risk an invasion of Byzantine Egypt, Umar was eventually persuaded to do so by his military governor in Palestine: Amr ibn al-‘As.

- Before his conversion to Islam, Amr had been a trader who knew Egypt's highways and byways, and, so, the best invasion route. Having previously won military victories in Palestine and the Levant, Amr persuaded Umar that now was the perfect moment to invade Egypt. Egypt was a great prize: the breadbasket of Byzantium.

### Amr's Moves

- After Amr set out, Umar had second thoughts, and wrote to Amr ordering a halt. Umar believed that the 4,000-strong force he'd assembled was too small to be an effective invading army. Amr saw the caliph's messenger galloping towards him just as he was approaching the Egyptian border at Rafah. Amr said he'd review the message at the end of that day's march, by which time he and his army would have crossed the Egyptian frontier.

- While the caliph's letter ordered Amr home, it also contained the following postscript, according to the Arab historian Ibn Abd al-Hakam: "If you receive this letter when you have already crossed into Egypt, then you may proceed. God will help you and I'll send you any reinforcements you may need." The wily Amr was free to push on, and execute his dream of conquering Egypt.

- Amr first took the fortified town of Pelusium, near the Egyptian coast, east of Port Said. The Arabs marched on to Babylon, a well-fortified town. After some initial skirmishing, Amr pulled back and sent a request to Umar for reinforcements. He got 8,000 extra men, many of them veterans from campaigning in Syria.

- Now, with a force-strength of 12,000, Amr launched a night-time attack and, using siege ladders to scale the walls, routed the defenders. With no practical alternative, the general Cyrus handed over sovereignty of Egypt to the caliph Umar. But When Heraclius learned of Cyrus's surrender, he was furious and refused to accept the terms.

- Faced with this, Amr had little choice but to march on Alexandria. The Arab army arrived in March 641, and set about laying siege to the walled city. Alexandria was heavily forified and could be supplied by sea, which was to the Byzantines' advantage. But Heraclius died while preparing to lead a force in the defense of his city. The promised reinforcements melted away, and the garrison at Alexandria was left to its fate.

- The defenders held out for six months until they were overwhelmed by the Arabs. The fall of Alexandria marked the end of any serious resistance to the Arabs invasion of Egypt.

### After the Capture

- Instead of putting the city's defenders to the sword, Amr gave them a year during which they could leave—taking their possessions with them—or stay and live under the new political reality of Arab-Muslim rule. Amr deliberately kept in place the city's tax collectors and other administrators. As these officials knew best how to run the city, it was a wise decision indeed.

- If Amr had his way, Alexandria would have remained the capital. The Caliph Umar thought otherwise, telling Amr that the city's maritime setting made it vulnerable to future attack from Constantinople.

- Legend has it that before setting out for Alexandria, Amr found a bird nesting in his tent, and ordered that the bird. He ordered that it should be left undisturbed until its chicks had hatched and flown. Returning from Alexandria, Amr ordered that Egypt's new capital would be founded where his tent stood.

- The city of Fustat—whose name comes from an Arabic word for *tent*—continued to grow on the banks of the Nile. Nearly 1,400 years later, it's still the center of Old Cairo.

- With Egypt secured, Amr turned his attention to the west, and marched into Libya. Amr marched 1,000 miles along the southern Mediterranean coast, from Alexandria—via Barca—as far as Tripoli and Sabratha. And he took these cities with little effort.

- In Barca he established a permanent base, appointing Uqba bin Nafi governor, before being relieved of his command and ordered to pull back to Fustat. This wasn't conquest as such, but raiding on an extraordinary scale.

### Further Raids and Invasions

- The first serious invasion of North Africa beyond Egypt's borders was launched in 647 by the third caliph, Uthman. Uthman dispatched an army of 10,000 men—some sources say 20,000—from Fustat on a campaign that was to last 15 months.

- Uthman's army moved rapidly through Libya and into southern Tunisia, where it easily defeated a Byzantine force. Afterwards, the Arabs fought the indigenous Berber tribes for loot, but for the next 20 years they did little to secure more land. Instead, they seemed content to limit their activities to profitable smash-and-grab raids.

- Meanwhile, away from North Africa, tensions were growing back in the center of the Arab world. The murders of Uthman in 656, and his successor Ali in 661, led to a war for the caliphate that was more pressing than the expansion of the Arabs' empire in North Africa.

- However, once the new Umayyad caliph, Mu'awiya, had established himself in Damascus, he decided to consolidate and expand this empire. Mu'awiya appointed Uqba, a loyal Umayyad general and nephew of Amr ibn al-'As, governor of all North Africa.

- Uqba, with his deep knowledge of the region, was able to ensure that this second Arab invasion made rapid progress back across Libya, and into modern-day Tunisia—or Ifriqiya, as the Arabs knew the Roman province.

- When he got within 80 miles of Carthage, Uqba decided that he'd be in a stronger position if he had a permanent military base in the region. In 670, he founded the city of Kairouan on the site of an established camp and crossroads.

- From there, Uqba pressed on to his ultimate goal of Morocco. In Arabic, Morocco is called *al-Maghreb*, which simply means "the west." As Uqba had said before he set out, he wanted to conquer lands that no Muslim had previously seen. Uqba reached Tangier before heading south and, crossing the Atlas Mountains, west to the coast.

**The Berbers**

- It wasn't until 694 that another Arab army—effectively the third Muslim invasion of North Africa—settled the question of who would control Ifriqiya. After decades of apparently ignoring the Byzantine presence in Carthage, the Arabs now attacked the city, expelling its denizens and razing its walls.

- The removal of Byzantine influence did not mark the end of opposition to Arab rule, however. For years, Berber revolts continued to trouble the Arabs. The Roman term of opprobrium for any non-Roman—*barbarian*—had now morphed into an Arabic proper name, creating a Berber identity that saw them as a united people.

- The most serious Berber uprising started in the 680s, and was led by the legendary female warrior al-Kahina. Al-Kahina was likely a Jewish or Christian Berber. Through her desire to remain free of foreign domination, she inspired others in a series of ultimately doomed revolts.

- Described as a beauty with the gift of prophecy, Al-Kahina seemed to understand that her resistance movement would ultimately fail, as she gave her sons to her Arab enemies for safekeeping.

- Al-Kahina died fighting the Arabs in around 700, marking the end of organized Berber resistance. Ever since her death, al-Kahina has been adopted as an inspiration by an array of disparate groups, from Berber nationalists to Maghrebi feminists, Arab nationalists, and even French colonists.

**After the Invasions**

- By this time the Arabs had conquered virtually the whole of North Africa. They proceeded to divide the region into the provinces of Egypt, Ifriqiya and the Maghreb, with provincial capitals at Fustat, Kairouan, and Fes, respectively.

- In time, they founded new provincial capitals that allowed them to securely rule over the much larger, native populations while living apart from them. In all three instances, those who selected these new capitals ignored earlier maritime bases, preferring instead the security of inland locations.

- Arab forces took the city of Tangier in the spring of 710, completing the conquest of North Africa. In less than 70 years, the armies of Islam had now advanced from Egypt to Tangier. It was a remarkable feat, especially when one considers the harsh terrain they traversed.

**The Consequences**

- By and large, as the British-American historian Bernard Lewis put it, the conquered peoples of North Africa found "their new masters less demanding, more tolerant, and above all more welcoming than the old." For one thing, the new Muslim overlords were far more religiously tolerant than had been the Byzantine emperor Heraclius.

- Where the reaction to the conquerors was not positive, it was often neutral. What did it matter to most peasants if they were ruled by an Arab, a Byzantine, or an Iranian?

- The Arabs now ruled these lands but were usually happy to rely on locals to administer their new territorial gains. Indeed, Caliph Umar forbade Arabs from owning agricultural land in the newly conquered territories, insisting instead that they restrict themselves to living in the new military garrisons.

- By the eighth century, however, these garrisons would themselves grow into cities, as the Arabs moved from occupiers to settlers. We see this in Fustat for Cairo, Qairouan in Tunisia, and with Fes in Morocco.

- Finally, it's important to understand that the Arab invasion of North Africa was about Arab conquests much more than it was about converting locals to Islam. Over conversion, the Arab invaders preferred the payment of a tribute by non-Muslims, the *jizya*.

- While the conquest of North Africa was swift, conversion to Islam and the adoption of Arabic as the state language was much slower. But when it finally happened, it was permanent.

**Suggested Reading**

Al-Tabari, *The History of al-Tabari*, volume XIII.

Brett and Fentress, *The Berbers*, chapter 3.

Bulliet, *The Camel and the Wheel.*

Gibbon, *History of the Decline and Fall of the Roman Empire*, volume 5; chapters 51 and 52.

Hitti, *History of the Arabs*, chapter 14.

Kennedy, *The Great Arab Conquests*, chapters 4 and 6.

**Questions to Consider**

1. To what extent was the success of the Arab invasions of North Africa dependent on the waning influence and growing unpopularity of the Byzantine Empire? Does this explain what would become the absolute and lasting conquest of the region?

2. Subject to payment of *jizya*, or religious tax, the tolerance of the Arab invaders for other "religions of the book," notably Judaism and Christianity, is often cited as one of the keys to their success. How does this compare with our own time, and how and why might this be the same or different?

Lecture 4

# Umayyad Caliphate in Damascus—661

At first glance, there might seem to be nothing controversial about choosing Damascus for the capital of an Arab-Islamic empire. After all, Damascus is today the capital of Syria, a strategic Arabic-speaking country, where more than 90 percent of the population is identified as Muslim. But that's now. In this lecture, we're going to consider something that took place in the year 661, when the newly founded Umayyad caliphate established its own capital in Damascus. Believe it or not, this was one of the most controversial decisions ever taken in the Middle East.

## The Umayyads

- The Umayyads' decision to move the capital of the Islamic Empire from Medina to Damascus, 650 miles to the north, was the most important political turning point in early Muslim history. When the Umayyads decided to make Damascus their capital, the city was an important trading center.

- As a prominent family from Mecca, the Umayyads understood soon after Muhammad started preaching that if Islam took hold, they could lose a great deal of prestige and influence. It was for this reason that the Umayyad family converted, and did so only at the last minute, after virtually every other important family in Mecca already had.

- Opponents of the Umayyads, already angered by their resurgence in power, were furious when the first Umayyad caliph, Mu'awiyah, announced he was introducing a system of dynastic succession, so that his son would take over when he died. This system of dynastic succession would become the norm for all caliphates for the next 1,300 years.

- Supporters of the Umayyads point to their legacy as a sign of greatness. Under their rule, the Islamic empire grew to its greatest extent. Indeed, when the Umayyad conquests came to a halt, their empire was the largest the world had ever seen, and it remains the fifth-largest empire in human history.

- The Umayyads' empire covered the whole of the Arabian Peninsula, the Levant (which refers to an extensive area in the eastern Mediterranean), modern Iran and Iraq, parts of Afghanistan, Pakistan, and northwestern India. It ranged across North Africa to the Atlantic. And it covered virtually the whole of the Iberian Peninsula, eastern Anatolia, the Caucasus, and parts of Central Asia.

**Damascus as the Capital**

- The fateful decision by Mu'awiyah, the fifth caliph, to make Damascus his capital was not met with universal approval. A civil war broke out with further, periodic outbursts of unrest marking the whole 90 years of Umayyad rule.

- The eminent historian of the Middle East, Philip Hitti, neatly sums up the Umayyads' move to Damascus: "Henceforth, the history of Arabia begins to deal more with the effect of the outer world on the peninsula and less with the effect of the peninsula on the outer world." In other words, the political caravan had moved on, leaving in its wake numerous unhappy Arabian interest groups.

- Some of the loudest critics were former companions of Muhammad, including many of his own family members and other early converts to Islam. They had enjoyed special status during the early days of Islam. They objected loudly to any move away from Arabia, rightly seeing that they were, in the process, losing political power.

- Aside from such personal objections, many native Arabians were wary of Damascus in and of itself. This major cosmopolitan center was, after all, among the most important cities in the

Byzantine Empire, richer and worldlier than anywhere in Arabia. There was a fear that temptations lay in large cities—people and ideas that could lead one astray.

- A Muslim army had conquered Damascus 26 years earlier, in 635, but even now Muslims remained a small minority among the total population. Damascus was largely made up of Byzantine-Christians.

- Apart from the everyday immorality associated with cities, there was a worry that foreign ideas would corrupt the purity of Islam and Islamic rule—ideas such as dynastic succession. For Arabs, dynastic succession would, in all but name, turn caliphs into kings. In hindsight, this was an astute, and not inaccurate, assessment.

**Mu'awiyah**

- After being installed in Jerusalem as the fifth caliph, one of Mu'awiyah's first announcements was that he was now "first among his peers." In the process, he abandoned any pretense of being a religious leader, which was anyway only one part of the role played by the first four caliphs.

- What Mu'awiyah now made clear was that his right to rule was based not on religious authority, but on his position as a tribal chief and governor, plus the collected swords and cavalry of the army in Syria who stood by him.

- The logical conclusion of his announcement was this: If he were ruling as a tribal leader, and not as the religiously approved choice of the companions of Muhammad, what was to stop him from handing power over to his son? The answer was nothing, and this is exactly what he announced three years before his death.

- While he managed to win the support from some quarters, opposition from others was just as strong. That opposition would pursue all 14 Umayyad caliphs throughout their 90 years of power in the region. The most serious troubles the Umayyads faced were during periods of civil war.

- Mu'awiyah's rise to power marked the end of the first Muslim civil war, or *Fitna* in Arabic, the "time of tribulation." Under the Umayyads, there would be another two periods of serious tribulation and a number of other revolts challenging Umayyad authority in different parts of the empire.

- As for Mu'awiyah's feelings towards the Persians, it seems they were right to be resentful. As he wrote to one of his Arab governors during one period of unrest: "Be watchful of Persian Muslims and never treat them as equals. ... As far as possible give them smaller pensions and lowly jobs. In the presence of an Arab, a non-Arab shall not lead prayers, nor are they to be allowed to stand in the first row of prayer." Such a view hardly tallies with what Muhammad had in mind when he said that all Muslims, regardless of race, were equal before God, and should be treated as such.

**Citizenship and Religion**

- The sharp rise in the size of the Umayyad empire, the subsequent increase in non-Arab converts, and the often shoddy treatment of these converts led to a great deal of resentment, which would become an important contributing factor in the Umayyads' eventual fall.

- By the year 750, and the end of Umayyad rule in the Middle East, there were more non-Arab than Arab Muslims, a statistic that has never been reversed. Today, it's reckoned that less than 15 percent of the world's Muslims are Arabs.

- Mu'awiyah himself is usually regarded—by the standards of his day—as a religiously tolerant individual. However, the judgment of history suggests that this was probably due more to politically rather than religiously enlightened views.

- Toward the end of his reign—around the year 675—Mu'awiyah banned non-Muslims from entering the cities of Mecca and Medina. Mu'awiyah's ban on non-Muslims entering Mecca and Medina appears to have been part of a broader policy to sideline these cities, as they were centers of opposition to his rule as caliph. Without visits from non-Muslims, Mecca and Medina were unable to flourish as mercantile centers.

**Ummayad Territory**

- In terms of conquests, the Umayyads were in possession of two-thirds of what had been the Byzantine Empire. They extinguished serious resistance among the Berbers and completed the conquest of North Africa, before invading Europe. There, they quickly conquered Spain and pushed north into France, getting within 120 miles of Paris before their advances faltered, most famously at the Battle of Tours, also known as the Battle of Poitiers.

- In Eurasia, they pressed into the Caucasus region and beyond, establishing a presence at the mouth of the Volga River on the shores of the Caspian Sea. In Central Asia, they took city-states such as Ferghana and Samarqand and pressed up to the borders of Tang China, while in the south and east they made important inroads through Afghanistan and into modern Pakistan and India.

- Unprecedented in scale, these conquests would have been fleeting had it not been for the organizational infrastructure that underlay them. And this, again, is why the move to Damascus was vital. Arguably, had Mu'awiyah not established the Umayyad capital in Damascus, he wouldn't have obtained the insight and administrative know-how that proved essential in making his empire a functioning entity.

**Abd al-Malik**

- Mu'awiyah's later successor, the fifth Umayyad caliph and master administrator, was Abd al-Malik. The administrative genius of

Abd al-Malik saw the introduction of two important innovations. First, he made Arabic the official state language, and second, he introduced a single, empire-wide, distinctively Islamic currency.

- As Arabic took over from Persian and Greek as the languages of local government, anyone who wanted to get ahead in the Umayyad world would learn Arabic in order to do so. Among other benefits, it released Abd al-Malik and future caliphates from relying on their conquered subjects to provide most of the educated workforce.

- As for coinage, until this point the Arabs had been happy to use pre-existing coins, as minted by the region's older empires, namely the Byzantines and Sasanians. But this style eventually changed to coinage that featured a Quran verse alongside the name of the Muslim ruler. Abd al-Malik used coinage to make it clear that his Islamic empire was here to stay.

**The Dome of the Rock, Jerusalem**

- As for Damascus, it would remain a majority Christian city until the 9th century. In fact, much of what we think of as the Muslim Middle East and North Africa would remain Muslim-minority countries for another century or more.

- Through the Arabic language and a distinct Islamic currency, Abd al-Malik put the non-Arab city of Damascus firmly at the center of his global empire. This wasn't just a process of nationalizing but Arabising. It wouldn't happen overnight, but when it did take it would stand in the vast majority of North Africa and the Middle East until the present day.

- Mu'awiyah, Abd al-Malik, and other of the Umayyad caliphs instigated innumerable grand building projects. The most famous of these included the magnificent Grand Mosque in Damascus, and the al-Aqsa Mosque complex, which includes the Dome of the Rock, in Jerusalem. These two spots are held to be Islam's third and fourth most sacred sites, respectively.

**Suggested Reading**

Bennison and Gascoigne, *Cities in the Pre-Modern Islamic World*.

Crone, *God's Rule*, chapter 3.

Esposito, *Islam*, chapter 2.

Hitti, *Makers of Arab History*, chapter 3.

———, *Capital Cities of Arab Islam*, chapter 3.

Hourani, *A History of the Arab Peoples*, chapter 2.

Kennedy, *The Prophet and the Age of the Caliphates*.

Lapidus, *A History of Islamic Societies*, chapter 4.

Lewis, *Islam in History*, chapter 23.

**Questions to Consider**

1. What was the primary driving force behind the Umayyads' decision to establish their capital in the non-Arab city of Damascus? Consider how different the subsequent Islamic history of the Middle East might have been if their capital was founded elsewhere.

2. How valid do you consider the Umayyads' claim to political and religious legitimacy, or their opponents' counter-claims, during this seminal period in the creation of the first Islamic empire?

Lecture 5

# Battle of Karbala—680

The Battle of Karbala in the year 680 cemented a division that still exists between Islam's two main branches. The majority Sunni and the minority Shia initially began to split over a succession dispute. Broadly speaking, this lecture is going to cover three topics: how that succession dispute came about in the first place, the individuals behind the dispute, and what happened during the Battle of Karbala. After covering those areas, this lecture describes the political and religious fallout that followed.

## Defining Shia and Sunni

- Although the the terms *Shia* and *Sunni* weren't really in use at the time of the Battle of Karbala, defining them will help make the dispute between the two sides easier to understand.

- The Arabic word *Shia* means a "follower" or "partisan." Originally, the Shia were better known as *Shiat Ali*, or the "party of Ali"—those who sided with Ali. The word *Shiite* is derived from *Shia*, and can be used as either a noun or an adjective.

- The term *Sunni*, to describe Islam's main confessional branch, comes from an Arabic word meaning "custom," "habit," or "tradition." Implicit in the label is that a Sunni Muslim is considered a follower of the *Sunnah*, or the traditions, of Muhammad.

- Today, it's estimated that as many as 90 percent of the world's Muslims are Sunni, while the remaining 10 percent are Shia.

## The Succession Dispute

- The root of what would become the Sunni-Shia divide was anticipated at the very moment of Muhammad's death, in 632. Muhammad did not explicitly appoint as a successor. The Sunni-

Shia split started out as a leadership question, more a matter of power and politics than anything else.

- In the Shia view, Muhammad *did* appoint a successor: Ali, who was Muhammad's son-in-law and cousin, a blood relative. Ali was also the first male to accept Islam, responding to Muhammad's message at the age of 12.

- The Shia view that Ali was the rightful successor to Muhammad is based on their interpretation of numerous *hadith*, or sayings, of Muhammad. However, Sunni Islam contends the hadith only allude to this. In contrast, Shia tradition holds that the appointment of Ali as the successor to Muhammad is explicit.

- And so two camps appeared in the leadership struggle: those who favoured a direct descendant of Muhammad, the Shia; and, those who believed Muhammad's successor should be chosen on merit and consultation by leaders, the Sunni.

**Abu Bakr, Umar, and Uthman**

- Muhammad's successor had to be appointed quickly, if there was to be stability in the new empire. This urgency was particularly acute because many Arabian tribal leaders believed they'd sworn allegiance to Muhammad during his lifetime, rather than to his successors, or to the religion that lived on after him.

- With this is in mind, a small group of influential men from Mecca chose Abu Bakr as Muhammad's successor. Abu Bakr was Muhammad's father-in-law and came from an elite family. In the Shia tradition, Abu Bakr's selection was done deliberately fast so that Ali, who—with other members of his family—was preparing Muhammad for his burial, was not present to argue his own case.

- Abu Bakr was relatively elderly at the time of his appointment, and he ruled for just two years before he died. His successor, the second caliph in the Sunni tradition, was Umar, who ruled from 634 to 644. Like Abu Bakr, Umar was also from an elite Meccan family.

- After Muhammad, Umar is probably the most important person in the development of Sunni Islam. Umar was responsible for starting to organize the expanding Islamic empire, which was ongoing when a discontented Muslim slave from Persian murdered him. Before he died, Umar rejected the idea of appointing his successor. Instead he drew up a list of six names, and asked that his followers settle the matter by consultation.

- While Ali's name was on the list, he was not selected to become the next caliph. Instead, that was a man named Uthman. Unlike Abu Bakr and Umar, Uthman's time in office was controversial, with disputes breaking out over his apparent favouritism towards members of his own tribe.

- After 12 years in power, disaffected Muslims from Egypt and Iraq assassinated Uthman. This was the first serious, bloody and public rupture in Islam. Now, Ali's supporters at last saw him become caliph.

**War**

- Ali's five years as ruler, from 656 to 661, marked Islam's first civil war, and the battle for political supremacy, which pushes us forward to that fateful day at Karbala.

- Ali had nothing to do with Uthman's murder, but certain Uthman supporters felt that Ali had failed as a leader by not bringing the killers to justice. One of Uthman's supporters was his cousin and governor of Syria, Mu'awiyah. Mu'awiyah issued a direct challenge to Ali, who was based in his own capital, the Iraqi city of Kufa, about 100 miles south of modern Baghdad.

- Either Ali would produce Uthman's killers, or he would be held accountable as an accomplice to his murder. Ali was assassinated while at prayer in the Great Mosque in Kufa during the course of the first Muslim civil war.

- With Ali dead, the Shia decided that his eldest son, Hassan, should succeed him. However, Hassan almost immediately signed a peace treaty with Mu'awiyah, which ended the civil war and saw Hassan go into retirement in Medina.

- But Mu'awiyah broke the terms of his treaty with Hassan. In an incendiary move, Mu'awiyah announced that his son, Yazid, would succeed him as caliph. The supporters of the late caliph Ali were enraged by the announcement, and the very public way in which Mu'awiyah had broken his word.

- Many non-Shia were also shocked. Hadn't Umar confirmed the consultative tradition by appointing a council to decide on his successor? And if there were going to be dynastic succession in Islam, surely it was only fitting that the successors should be members of Muhammad's family?

- Mu'awiyah's family, the Umayyads, had opposed Muhammad's message of Islam until the last possible moment. It was Mu'awiyah's father who forced Muhammad and his early followers to run from Mecca to Medina in the first days of Islam. That this family would now become the first Islamic dynasty upset many.

**Behind the Dispute**

- When Mu'awiyah died after nearly 20 years in power, his son Zayid did indeed become the sixth caliph, and the second Umayyad caliph. This is not a state of affairs that Ali's surviving son, Hassan's younger brother, Hussein, could accept. Nor did the older families from Medina or Mecca, who continue to see the Umayyads as overreaching their authority.

- Another group that was unhappy about Yazid's succession were the rulers of Kufa. Having enjoyed a brief period as the capital of the Muslim world, during Ali's time as caliph, they now saw an opportunity to regain this prestige and power. With this in mind, the authorities in Kufa wrote to Hussein, asking him to leave Mecca for Kufa, and to lead a rebellion against the Umayyad caliphate. Thus the stage was set for the Battle of Karbala.

- By the time Hussein was en route, the Kufans had switched sides, in response to being threatened by Yazid's governor in the city, a man named ibn Ziyad. Suddenly the prophet's grandson, with his family and a small band of men, were riding towards an unfriendly, enemy city.

**The Battle Itself**

- Two days outside of Kufa, Hussein's caravan of about 150 people found themselves confronted by the army of ibn Ziyad. Orders were handed down that Hussein and his family, trapped on the desert plain, were to be forced to surrender. To ensure this, they were to be stopped from getting water, right in sight of a river.

- After four days without water, the battle took place on the 10th day of Muharram, the first month in the Islamic calendar. As dawn

The Battle of Karbala

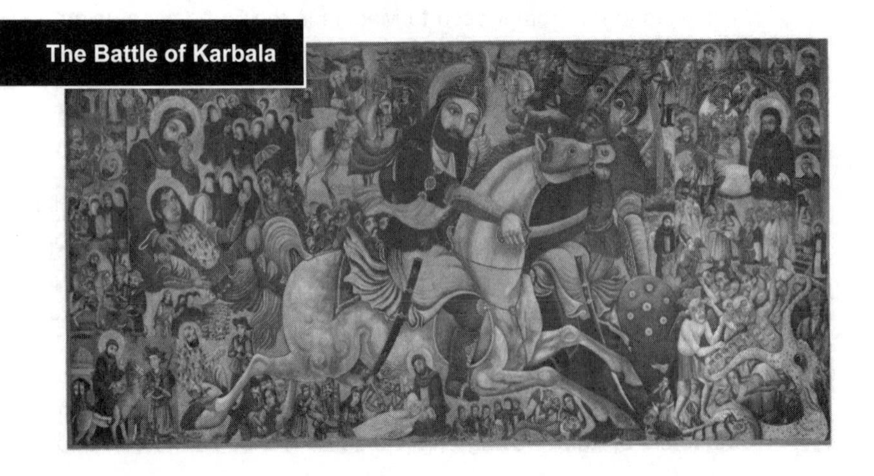

broke, Hussein and the other men readied themselves to fight. They consisted of 40 men on foot and 32 on horseback. They confronted an Umayyad army of between 5,000 and 25,000.

- Ibn Ziyad's army opened the combat by showering Ali's small camp with arrows. Fearing for the safety of their women and children, Ali and his men asked for the right to meet ibn Ziyad's soldiers in single combat. This was accepted. One by one, Ali and his men went out to meet their enemies in hand-to-hand combat, fighting and dying.

- The outcome was never in doubt. If Ali's band of 72 managed to cause 88 enemy fatalities, the result at battle's end was still that Hussein and his companions lay dead. After ibn Ziyad's army left the battlefield, some locals buried the dead, marking only Hussein's grave. The day after the battle, the captive women and children—including Hussein's younger sister Zaynab—were loaded onto camels, and taken to Kufa.

**The Aftermath**

- The feast of Ashura—the annual commemoration of the martyrdom of Hussein—is noted for the dramatic wailing on the part of many participants, as well as self-flagellation in some cases. After more than 1,300 years, the sense of guilt for failing to defend Hussein seems to remain as powerful as ever among some Shiites.

- The annual commemorations are possible, in part, because Zaynab and other family members retold the story of the battle, even during captivity in Damascus. One especially poignant incident forms a central part of the traditional narrative: that Hussein's infant child was struck and killed by an arrow fired by ibn Ziyad's men.

- On the orders of ibn Zayid, every one of vanquished party, now consisting of 72 bodies, was beheaded, with individual heads being given to the various tribal leaders. Hussein's head was mounted on a lance, and marched the more than 500 miles to Damascus. What happened next is a matter of debate—and faith.

- The Shia believe that Hussein's head eventually was returned to Karbala and interred with the rest of his remains. However, there remain a number of other pilgrimage sites across the Muslim world that claim to be the keeper of Hussein's head. As a result, one can travel to Karbala, Cairo, Damascus, or the city of Ashkelon in Israel and find shrines claiming to contain the head of the last of Muhammad's grandsons.

- Eventually, the story of Karbala was written down. The differing accounts of the battle make clear that embellishment and error crept in over time. Regardless, while Hussein and his companions failed to beat the caliph's army on that day, accounts of the battle—and the unnecessary cruelty carried out by the caliph's men—saw the dead win more sympathy than the victors.

- In time, the battle would be the defining moment in the split between the two main branches of Islam. Both branches see the battle as tragic, but its religious significance and impact is much greater for Shi'i, whose annual Ashura commemoration is an important point in their religious calendar.

- For the Shia, Karbala remains of central importance not only on the matter of authority in Islam, but also for their view of themselves and the world at large. As one traditional Shia saying goes, "Every day is Ashura and every land is Karbala." The sense of sacrifice for God and one's community remains paramount, and Hussein's martyrdom at Karbala is the best example of such an attitude.

**Suggested Reading**

Dabashi, *Shi'ism*, chapters 1, 2, and 3.

Daftary, *A History of Shi'i Islam*, chapter 2.

Donner, *Muhammad and the Believers*, chapter 4.

Esposito, *Islam*, chapter 2.

———, ed., *Oxford History of Islam*, chapter 1.

Kennedy, *The Prophet and the Age of the Caliphates*.

**Questions to Consider**

1. Bearing in mind the Battle of Karbala was about political power and influence, rather than questions of Islamic theology in any real sense, is there any possibility of reconciliation between these two main strands of Islam after so long, and considering they have now developed different doctrinal views of their common faith?

2. How might the development of martyrdom and persecution in the Shia religious narrative have impacted their place in society, both under Sunni Abbasid and Ottoman caliphates, and in our own time?

3. Iran's 1979 revolution ushered in a theocratic Shia state. How might that country's religious-political authorities view their political "success" against more traditional views of loss and persecution?

# Lecture 6 Arab Invasion of Andalusia—711

It was during the rule of the Umayyad caliph al-Walid ibn al-Malik I that the Arab invasion of Spain took place. Al-Malik's reign would mark the last major advances in the history of this—or any subsequent—Islamic empire. This invasion marked the start of almost 800 years of Muslim rule in the Iberian Peninsula. But this lecture examines whether the "Arab invasion of Spain" can properly be called that at all. It then looks at the key figures in the event, and what happened after.

## Tariq ibn Ziyad

- In spring of the year of 711, a man stood in thought, staring at a mountain that dominates the landscape. The locals still knew the mountain by the Roman name: Hollow Mountain.

- The man was Tariq ibn Ziyad, and he was about to sail into history. Once Tariq reached this imposing signpost, the peak, and the body of water over which he would sail, would both be known by his own name: Tariq's Mountain. In Arabic, that is *Jebel Tariq*. In English, it's *Gibraltar*.

- Tariq was a native of North Africa, probably from the area of modern Libya. He was a proud Berber, who are the indigenous people of North Africa. But many years earlier, Tariq was taken prisoner during a losing battle against Arab invaders. Tariq was the property of the Arab governor of the Roman province of Ifriqiya, or modern Tunisia. He spent years living as a slave.

- But Tariq's master, Musa bin Nusayr, recognized his bravery, and his talent for leadership, and granted him freedom—making him a general in his army.

Tarik.

- Tariq's life had already taken some dramatic turns, and the most dramatic was yet to happen. Here he stood, a general and his army—a recent convert to Islam—preparing to invade Spain.

## Accounts of the Invasion

- In the case of the Arab invasion of Spain, the sole surviving contemporary account is a document called the Chronicle of 754. Compiled by an anonymous native Iberian Christian who lived under Arab rule, the chronicle gets its name from the fact that the year 754 is the last year covered in the text.

- The Chronicle of 754 is frustratingly vague on many important points, such as the numbers of combatants involved and the location of certain clashes. But in terms of contemporary accounts, it's all we've got to go on.

- For Arab narratives, we're even less well served. The earliest account we have is by Ibn Abd al-Hakem, a generally careful writer, but one who clearly relies on earlier accounts that we have no way of judging. And while Abd al-Hakem provides us with far more detail than the Chronicle of 754, he's writing 3,000 miles from the scene, in Cairo, and 150 years after the fact.

**Arab Invasion of Spain or Not?**

- There is good reason to challenge the three central planks of the idea of an Arab invasion of Spain. Those planks are the event's Arab-ness, the Spanish-ness of the place that was invaded, and the whole event's status as a deliberate invasion.

- The man who led the assault, Tariq ibn Zayid, was a native North African Berber, not an Arab. The vast majority of the troops that accompanied Tariq from Africa to Europe were Berbers, about 7,000 of them. Without the Berbers, there might have been no invasion of the Iberian Peninsula at all.

- The Berber-Arab army attacked, and eventually took over, what we now call Spain. But Spain would not exist in the sense of a nation state for centuries yet. What was in its place was the Roman designation Hispania.

    - Hispania covered most of the Iberian Peninsula, that is to say, both Spain and Portugal. And the name *Iberia* predates the Romans.

- After the Berber-Arab invasion, the term *Hispania* fell into disuse, and was replaced by the more familiar *al-Andalus*, or in its Westernised form, *Andalusia*.

- It seems likely that the whole affair started out with a few disorganized raids, undertaken by Berbers intent on grabbing loot. Tariq and his Berber kinsmen were locals and had long had trade links to the Iberian Peninsula, which was less than nine miles from the coast of North Africa.

  - The Berbers knew about the fertility of the land and the potential wealth of trade there.

  - Whether Tariq thought he was leading a raiding party or a full-blown invasion, we'll never know.

- For the sake of ease, this lecture will talk about "Arab armies" and the "invasion of Spain," with the stipulation that the reality is rather more nuanced and complicated.

**Tariq's Campaign**

- While the exact date of the invasion is still in dispute, we're fairly sure it took place in the year 92 in the Islamic calendar. Most commentators agree on April 711 as the western date of Tariq's landing.

- There was at least one smaller approach a year earlier, when Tariq sent 400 infantry and 100 cavalry on a preliminary raid. It was partly the success of this raid that led Tariq to prepare a bigger, bolder attack the following spring.

- Tariq's invasion force consisted of about 7,000 Berber troops, later reinforced by an additional 5,000-strong Arab force.

- According to legend, Tariq was helped to sail to Spain by a local vassal of the Visigoths who ruled Andalusia at that time: Julian, Lord of Ceuta. The story goes that when Roderic had become king of the Visigoths a year earlier, Julian agreed to remain a loyal subject of this new, controversial king. Julian sent one of his daughters to King Roderic's court, in order for her to be educated.

- But Roderic raped Julian's daughter, who then became pregnant. Outraged, Julian contacted Tariq; they made peace, and Julian decided to get his revenge through helping the ambitious Berber by providing ships to transport him and his army to Andalusia.

- According to the Chronicle of 754, Roderic violently usurped the throne in 710. He possibly murdered the incumbent king, an act that led to anger and dissent among those who were in line to the throne.

- It was at this moment—when Visigothic Andalusia was in the midst of, as the chronicler puts it, "internal frenzy"—that Tariq and his army landed. Roderic was forced to march out and confront the invading Berbers. He had cobbled together an army, but he was far from certain where their loyalties lay.

- The fateful encounter was the Battle of Guadalete. It took place in July 711 somewhere on the Guadalete River. Exaggerated reports say Roderic's army consisted of as many as 100,000 men. More circumspect estimates place this figure at 40,000, but even this sounds overly large. In many early histories, when tens or hundreds of thousands are mentioned, it's often meant to indicate a very large force, rather than a literal or accurate number.

- There's not much to say about this battle beyond the fact that it was a rout. The chronicler tells us that Roderic was betrayed by some of his rivals for power, and that the army of the Visigoths was annihilated. Thus ended not only Roderic's life, and his one-year reign, but also the Visigoths' empire in Andalusia.

- By the end of that summer, Tariq found himself in control of close to half of the peninsula, and the rest of it would fall in the following year.

- At this point, some accounts say that Musa, the Arab governor in Tunisia, had become both angry and jealous at the runaway success being enjoyed by his former slave. Remember, it's far from clear that Musa had ordered Tariq to invade.

- In any event, when word got back to the Umayyad caliph, Abd al-Malik, he *was* initially angry, and ordered Tariq and Musa to Damascus to explain what they meant by launching this unauthorised war.

- By the time the caliph's orders reached Tariq, he'd already destroyed the opposition and taken Iberia for the distant Umayyad caliph, so he could at least hope to be received as the conquering hero. In any event, neither Musa nor Tariq ever returned to North Africa or Andalusia. They quietly disappeared from the story, apart from Tariq's now-eponymous mountain and body of water.

**The Next Stage**

- Moving northward, the Arabs crossed the Pyrenees, in 717, and marched into Gaul, what we now call France. The Arab-Berber attacks and invasion of Gaul didn't see the invaders establish any permanent footholds north of the Pyrenees. And even south of the mountains they started suffering setbacks and territorial losses.

- In about the year 722, a small but significant battle took place in the region of Asturias, on Spain's northern coast. Since the Berber-Arab invasion and conquest of the Iberian Peninsula, bands of refugees—including the surviving Visigoths—had retreated further and further north, until they found themselves in this remote and mountainous region.

- Being so remote encouraged the refugees and locals to put up some resistance. That was much easier here than it would have been for anyone living closer to the Arabs' capital in Andalusia, the city of Cordoba.

- The resistance movement, which started when the locals refused to pay taxes to their Arab masters, grew until the Arabs were forced to take action. The Arabs met the Spanish-Visigothic resisters at the Battle of Covadonga, and, alas for the Arabs, were roundly beaten. The importance of this battle in the history of the Arab invasion and conquest of Spain is that it was the first time they'd lost such an encounter.

- The Arabs never managed to re-take the Asturias region. As a result, many historians see the Battle of Covadonga as the start of the *Reconquista*, that is, the nearly 800-year process of—from the perspective of European chroniclers—re-taking Andalusia for Christendom. Before long, other northern regions would be wrested away from the Muslim empire.

- The Iberian Peninsula settled down into two distinct zones: the prosperous Muslim lands in the southern two-thirds, with their capital at Cordoba; and the northern portions, made up of a number of small Christian-ruled states.

**Consequences**

- The Arab invaders were not universally welcomed by the locals. There most certainly was bloodshed, murder, destruction, looting, and all the rest. That's typically the way with conquests.

- On the other hand, we should not allow ourselves to fall into the trap of seeing the Arab invasion of Spain as especially bloody or disastrous, for the region or its peoples. It was not much different from countless other conquest events in the east and west throughout human history, and it was a great deal less bloody than many.

- The early days after the conquest didn't usher in a golden age of learning, culture and peace in Andalusia; that came later. What did happen was unrest and infighting between the Arabs and the Berbers, and among them.

- The Berbers were unhappy at the loot and lands that their Arab overlords gifted to them. The Arabs, who still saw themselves as the natural superiors of the North Africa natives, felt otherwise.

- It would be 40 years before a greater degree of peace and stability prevailed in Andalusia. This followed the arrival of Abd ar-Rahman, the sole surviving member of the Umayyad family, after the slaughter of his family by their Abbasid rivals. The tribes settled down under his centralized rule, and he established a dynasty that lasted for nearly 300 years.

**Suggested Reading**

Brett and Fentress, *The Berbers*, chapter 3.

Collins, *The Arab Conquest of Spain*.

Hitti, *History of the Arabs*, chapters 34 and 35.

Kennedy, *Muslim Spain and Portugal*, chapter 1.

———, *The Great Arab Conquests*, chapter 9.

**Questions to Consider**

1. How far should one see the events of 711 as a deliberate, Arab-Berber invasion of the Iberian Peninsula, as opposed to a series of raids in search of booty, which then developed into an invasion proper for want of any serious opposition?

2. With communication difficulties inevitable over large distances in the Eighth century, consider the various possible reactions from the caliph in Damascus on learning that one of his governors had conducted a successful, albeit unsanctioned, conquest of a new territory?

Lecture 7

# Battle of Talas—751

Try, for a minute, to conceive a world without paper. Imagine not just how limiting that would be to our everyday lives, but also how much slower we would find it to share information. This was the situation in the Middle East before the Battle of Talas, which took place in modern-day Kyrgystan, in July, 751. After this event, papermaking quickly spread west, and the Arabs became engaged in a frenzy of literary production. A strong case can be made for the Battle of Talas being an event that would witness the birth of the Islamic Golden Age.

## Talas and Tours

- The Battle of Talas is named for a nearby town, and saw the first—and only—occasion when Arab and Chinese armies opposed one another. It ended in a clear victory for the Abbasid Arab force.

- Talas is a long way from Western Europe, and the steppes of Central Asia are also very remote, for the West, at least. Many Western historians, as a result, ignore the event.

- They also ignore it because of the Battle of Tours, which took place in the year 732. In the battle, Charles Martel beat an Arab army just 120 miles south of Paris. That is close to 3,500 miles west of Talas, so it's not surprising which event got more attention from European scholars.

- In the past, most Western historians saw Tours as a turning point in European history. It was the moment, they argued, when the Arab-Islamic tide was turned back. But a very real question is whether the Arabs, had they won the Battle of Tours, intended to continue their northward march. Given accounts of their clothing, which was ill-suited for cold weather, it's far from certain that they were a conquering army.

Papermaking

**Focusing on Talas**

- The Battle of Talas marked the furthest reaches of the Islamic world to the northeast of the Middle East—beyond Persia—as well as the maximum extent of western Chinese expansion.

- Neither side particularly wanted to fight. As often is the case with major empires, they were—apart from covering a lot of territory—ruling over a variety of subject peoples and political entities, including vassal states and protectorates.

- The Chinese and the Abbasid Arabs alike found themselves caught up in smaller-scale disputes between local rivals, and were forced to make use of mercenaries when it came to joining battle.

- If either side ignored the various appeals for help—putting in place a puppet ruler here, or putting down a rebellion there—the distant borders of the Chinese and Arabs' respective empires could become vulnerable to more serious threats in the future.

- Neither the Chinese nor the Abbasid Arabs were really familiar with the local geography. They were both a very long way from their heartlands and moved hesitantly toward one another.

- The site of the battlefield has never been definitively identified. But after picking apart Arab and Chinese sources, we can be sure it wasn't far from Kyrgystan's modern-day city of Talas, near the country's northern border with Kazakhstan.

- On the Muslim side, the best available accounts were written in the early 13th century by the Kurdish historian Ibn al-Athi, and in the 14th century by Damascus-born al-Dhahabi. Where there are facts that can be checked, the work of both men generally agrees with the main Chinese account of the battle, which can be found in the History of the Tang Dynasty, an official Chinese record of events.

- Arab and Chinese sources agree that the battle took place in the summer of 751, and that the fighting was spread out over a period of five days, and that the Chinese were soundly beaten.

- After Talas, the victorious Arabs and the defeated Chinese alike wrote accounts of the battle. Not surprisingly, the Chinese account says that the Arabs had a force of as many as 200,000. Now, the typical size of armies of this period was between 10,000 and 30,000 men, and there is no reason to think that the Battle of Talas was unusual in this regard. So we can say that the Chinese number was a massive exaggeration.

- The Arab sources say they were confronted by 100,000 Chinese troops, but this, too, is almost certainly an example of chroniclers embellishing the truth. The sides were likely fairly evenly matched.

- Both sides employed and relied on large numbers of foreign troops at Talas. The Abbasids employed Tibetans, who were already involved in a fight against Chinese domination. The Chinese, led by Gao Xianzhi, had as many as 20,000 Karluk mercenaries in their ranks, or as much as two-thirds of their army.

- The Karluks were Turkic, nomads who made up part of a large, prominent, nomadic confederacy that hailed from Central Asia. Their descendants are the modern-day Uighers and Uzbeks. It was the Chinese reliance on Karluk mercenaries that would lead to their defeat.

**The Fighting**

- Five days is an awfully long time to fight in hand-to-hand combat. Both sides competed with swords and spears, and each made some use of chain-mail armor and metal helmets.

- Both civilizations also made use of cavalry, and the Arabs employed camels, although it was more commonplace for these animals to carry troops and supplies to the battlefield before the men dismounted and fought on foot.

- The two sides became exhausted, and the outcome would naturally depend on who could hold out longest.

- According to both versions of events, the Karluk mercenaries employed by the Chinese simply changed sides, and attacked their former paymasters from behind, while the Abbasids pressed on from the front.

- Chinese sources claim the Karluks had been planned this act of wanton treachery even before the battle began. On this point, surely the Chinese sources are wide of the mark. Why, if you had decided for whatever reason to change sides, would you endure four full days of fighting before doing so?

- The Arab chroniclers offer no explanation for the Karluk turncoats, although it must have been the Abbasids who were responsible for persuading these nomadic people.

- Ultimately the Chinese—seeing that they could not possibly prevail while being simultaneously attacked from the front and the rear—escaped from the battlefield as best they could, among them the commanding general, Gao Xianzhi.

- While Xianzhi lived to fight another day, best estimates suggest he fled with no more than 2,000 surviving Tang Chinese soldiers.

- We're unlikely ever to know the truth of the matter, but it seems most likely that the Karluks were bought off by the Abbasids. Promises of money or other forms of booty, such as horses and camels, seem most likely.

- Animals would be highly prized by Central Asian nomads, whereas promises of land would hold far less appeal. The Karluks roamed where they liked and would likely take what they liked, too, in terms of land for grazing. They were obviously bold enough to fight against two of the region's biggest empires during the course of a single battle.

**After the Battle**

- The Battle of Talas didn't mark the start—or the end—of a dynasty or an empire. Only 18 months earlier, the Abbasids had seized power from their Muslim rivals, the Umayyads, to become the Islamic world's ruling power. And the Abbasids would go on to rule for 500 years more. In China, the Tang dynasty lasted for another 150 years.

- Very much like the Battle of Tours two decades earlier, the importance of the Battle of Talas is more symbolic than practical. That said, in practical terms it would prove to be the easternmost expansion of the Abbasid Arab Empire, and the westernmost expansion of the Tang Dynasty—or for that matter any subsequent Chinese dynasty.

- Four years after the Battle of Talas, a major rupture emerged in the political life of the Tang Dynasty. This was the An Lushan Rebellion. It almost certainly played a part in there being no further westward push by the Chinese.

- It might be difficult to fathom in the context of the recently completed Battle of Talas, but during the course of the An Lushan Rebellion, the Tang Chinese asked for—and got help from—the Abbasid Muslims. This is a good example of how quickly political and military interests and allegiances can shift.

- However, neither side attempted to establish permanent diplomatic links in the immediate aftermath of Talas. The ruling Arab caliph and the Chinese emperor remained largely ignorant of one another.

- Another 40 years would go by before a subsequent Abbasid caliph established proper ties with China. And that man, the fifth Abbasid Caliph, was the justly famous patron of learning, Harun al-Rashid. It was his founding of the House of Wisdom in Baghdad that one day would do much to spur the Islamic Golden Age.

### Talas as a Turning Point

- The Battle of Talas was a major turning point in the history of the Middle East and Europe. Thousands of Tang Chinese and Abbasid Arabs were killed over the course of five days of fighting, and thousands more were taken prisoner.

- Among the captured were two men who brought with them—and were forced to reveal—the technological expertise of papermaking.

- Critics of this story will say that it's just too easy, and too convenient, of an explanation for how paper and papermaking came to the Middle East.

  - But before the battle, paper was barely known in the Middle East, and certainly not produced there.

  - Furthermore, the first known paper mill in the Islamic world was founded in Samarqand, just 300 miles from Talas, in the very same year the battle took place.

  - Large-scale paper production is then recorded in Baghdad in the year 793, in Cairo in 900, and in Morocco by 1100.

- In Baghdad, the invention of machines allowed stronger paper to be made in bulk. It was the creation of this sturdier form of paper that saw an explosion of use in the city that was not only the capital of the Muslim world, but was growing into one of the largest, most sophisticated cities on earth.

- Simply put, the introduction of paper to the Islamic Middle East was a revolutionary moment for the Muslim world, and eventually for wider Western civilization.

- Later, during the Islamic Golden Age, paper became the means for Arab scholars to write, translate, disseminate, and store the tremendous wealth of knowledge for which they became known the world over.

- Without access to multiple copies of the same document, a single event—such as the fire that destroyed the Great Library at Alexandria—could otherwise have proven devastating for human knowledge.

- By the year 850, a century after the Battle of Talas, the cultural, literary, and scholarly life of the Middle East had undergone a transformation. From the middle of the 8th century until about the middle of the 12th century, the Arabs were easily the most cultured people on earth. That, to a very large degree, was due to the availability of paper.

### Suggested Reading

Al-Hassani, *1001 Inventions*, chapter 4.

Kennedy, *The Prophet and the Age of the Caliphates*.

Twitchett, ed., *Cambridge History of China*.

### Questions to Consider

1. While the result of the Battle of Talas is undisputable, how does the lack of detail about many other facts limit our understanding of this event, or any other important historical occasion for which we have limited reliable sources?

2. Had paper not become so widely available in the Middle East in the years following the Battle of Talas, how different might the intellectual history of the region looked? What impact might a delay of a century or more have had on literature and learning there and in Europe?

Lecture 8

# The Founding of Baghdad—762

In this lecture, we're going to look at the story of the founding of Baghdad. The decision to build any new city is consequential. But in the case of Baghdad, it was especially so because this city was conceived, and built, to be the capital of an empire. We're going to start by looking at all of those details: the bricks and mortar. But what makes the founding of Baghdad a turning point in the history of the Middle East is the all-important human factor, and that's what sits at the heart of this lecture.

## Baghdad's Background

- The decision to build Baghdad was made by the second Abbasid caliph, known as al-Mansur. In the year 762, al-Mansur issued the order to build the new capital. Mansur's decision, and choice of site, was a shrewd political move that signalled two things: greater inclusion of recently converted Persian Muslims, and the fact that his empire needed Persia—modern Iran—and its people.

- The Abbasids took their name from Muhammad's youngest uncle, Abbas ibn Abd al-Muttalib, who died 100 years before the dynasty was founded. Al-Mansur was the second of the Abbasid caliphs, but, because of his importance in consolidating the new empire—and for founding Baghdad—he is widely regarded as the dynasty's true founder.

- Al-Mansur surveyed other places before settling on Baghdad. As the historian al-Tabari wrote in the $10^{th}$ century, Mansur's decision was based on its suitability for a military camp, access to the Tigris and Euphrates rivers, and access to food products.

- The rich alluvial plain where Baghdad is located, between the Tigris and Euphrates Rivers, is at the center of perhaps more cultural and geographic capitals than any other region in the world. Just 160 miles to the south, the Sumerian city of Uruk—home to the legendary king and demi-god Gilgamesh—was built around 4000 B.C., and is likely the first recorded city in history.

- Ancient Babylon lies 50 miles south of where Baghdad would be built. Even closer by was the Persian city of Ctesiphon, imperial capital to both the Parthian and Sasanian Empires. From the year 570, Ctesiphon was the largest city in the world, and remained so until the Arabs conquered it in 637.

- Building Baghdad almost in the shadow of the Sassanians' former seat of power was the Abbasids' clear attempt to demonstrate domination over the older Persian Empire while, at the same time, showing a certain regard for the civilization.

- Instead of Baghdad, Mansur decreed that his capital would be called *Dar as-Salaam*, which translates as the House, Home, or Abode of Peace. Regardless of what Mansur wanted, the city unofficially became known by the more descriptive and prosaic name: the Round City, because of Baghdad's circular design.

- But it was Baghdad's official name—*Madinat al-Salam*, or City of Peace—that appeared on all official documents, coins, and other items of state business, even while the ordinary citizens held onto the older, pre-existing, village name. It wasn't until the 11th century that *Baghdad* would be universally, and exclusively, adopted as the name for the Abbasid's capital.

**Building Baghdad**

- The circular design Mansur laid out for Baghdad was identical to one already commonly used in Persia. This was in contrast to Greek and Roman urban planners, who favoured cities laid out in on a grid system. In ancient Persia, on the other hand, cities were typically arranged in a series of concentric circles, with avenues radiating outwards from the palace and government buildings at the center.

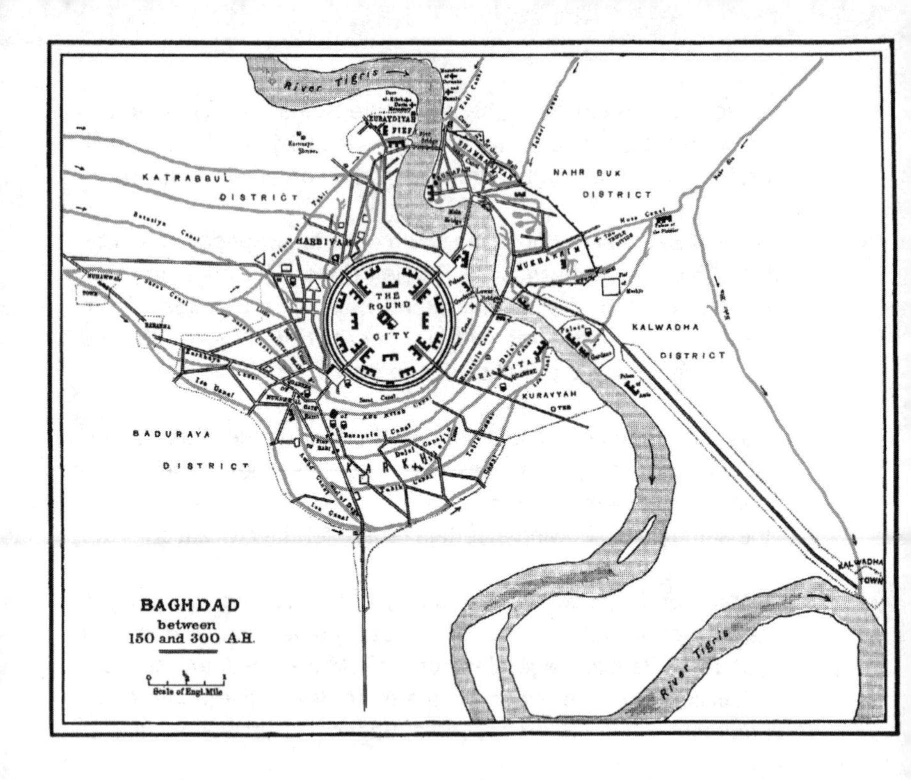


- The caliphal palace along with mosque and housing for Manur's family and concubines—and a garrison for his personal bodyguard—lay at the center of the city's innermost circle, and covered about an eighth of a mile. Its gilded entrance would be known as the Golden Gate Palace. It was to the Golden Gate Palace that ambassadors, scholars, and other VIPs from around the known world would come to parlay or negotiate.

- Like anyone designing his or her dream home, Mansur wanted the best men on the job. He hired the services of two foreign architects. One was a Jew named Mashallah, from Khorasan in Persia, while the other was a Zoroastrian named Naubakht.

- The palace ceilings were a series of domes, the highest of which was 130 feet. Apart from grandeur, the palace's domes gave inhabitants unrivaled, 360-degree visibility for miles around.

- In order to get the job done, Mansur employed 100,000 workmen. One of the first jobs was the construction of two massive defensive walls, one inside the other. Extra protection came in the form of a water-filled moat.

- When finished, the inner wall was 90 feet tall and had inclined paths running along its interior, allowing cavalry to ride swiftly to the top, which was itself 40 feet wide. The outer wall was pierced with four massive, evenly spaced gates.

- Each of the four gates was named for the city, or region, towards which it was oriented.

  - The gate facing southeast was the Basrah Gate, after Iraq's great port city.

  - The southwest-facing gate was named after the city of Kufah, which is a little over 100 miles from Baghdad. Not only does Kufah remain an important pilgrimage site for Shia Muslims today, being the place where the fourth caliph, Ali, was murdered, but it was also the Abbasids' capital before the founding of Baghdad.

  - The wall's northwest gate was the Syrian Gate.

  - The northeastern entrance to the city was called the Khurasan Gate. In another sign of the growing importance of the Persian world for the Arab empire, this northeastern entrance was named after a formerly very important, and powerful, province of eastern Persia and Central Asia that supplied the caliph with his imperial bodyguards.

**The Human Factor**

- The story of Baghdad isn't just about geography, but rather encompasses a series of long-term political, social, and economic factors. The empire's fast-growing, non-Arab Muslim populations were critical.

- The administrative center grew rapidly so that two further settlements were quickly tagged on to the main center circle. To the north, there was a large military camp, while in the south a town took shape that housed increasing numbers of workers.

- In the city itself, one could find craftsmen as well as as thousands of construction workers, drawn for work from across the Middle East and beyond. There were also grocers and other merchants who catered to the workers' needs, as well as workshops that produced the workers' tools and clothes.

- With such growth, excitement grew around the building of Baghdad. In turn, such expanding expectations attracted other nobles to the site, keen to be in closer proximity to this new magnet of power. Baghdad grew larger and wealthier every year. And as more grand palaces were planned, these too needed more builders, and more shops and industry to provide for the needs of those workers in turn.

- By the start of the 9th century—that is, within three generations of its founding—not only was this the largest metropolis that had ever existed in the Middle East, it was quickly becoming the largest in the world. Just 60 years after its foundation, Baghdad was out of all proportion to anything the original city planners could have envisioned. It measured 25 square miles and had a population of between 300 and 500,000.

- Historians estimate that by the year 900 it had a population of 900,000, and that it passed 1 million around the year 925. At that time, only China—the world's other great civilization—had an urban center that was larger.

- Libraries proliferated in Baghdad, with countless books and manuscripts coming in from Persia and India in the east, as well as from as far away as Egypt and the Mediterranean nations to the west. Mathematics, science, and medicine made great advances in Baghdad, and the ancient Greek works of philosophy and astronomy were translated and preserved.

**The Abbasid Reign**

- It was in 750 that the Abbasids had overthrown the Umayyads. Forces that rose against the Umayyads came from a mix of nationalities, including the Persian Muslims in Khurasan, who came to supply Mansur's bodyguards. The Abbasids also successfully appealed for help to the disgruntled Shia and disaffected Iraqis. The Umayyads, it seems, failed to realize that not only had the balance in their empire shifted, but so, too, had the center of gravity, in terms of population.

- Having won over the Persian aristocracy, not least by employing them and many of their ideas, the Abbasids also did their best to combine the authority of the Arab tribes with the imperial—and administrative—structures used by the Persians. Thus, they satisfied two very different camps.

- The Abbasids began their long period in power with a show of Islamic piety, and the promise of reforms to better represent all Muslims—not just Arab Muslims. This gained them time to win over the cultured—and sophisticated—Persian population, who'd been rather sidelined, and patronized, by the Umayyads.

- Whereas the Umayyads had derived much of their support from the Syrians, the Abbasids now drew much of their strength by relying increasingly on Iraqis and Persians. Moreover, when recruiting army officers, the Abbasids were clever enough to register these men based on their current places of residence, rather than by any tribal or ethnic affiliation.

- In this way, the Abbasid authorities reduced the importance of tribal and ethnic solidarity, replacing these concepts with a of common interest. This guaranteed greater inclusion for non-Arabs.

- It wasn't only in the army that the existing social structures were challenged. Across the board, the old Arabian aristocracy found itself being sidelined by an entirely new social order that included merchants, craftsmen, scholars, and administrators.

- In the midst of these radical social changes, the only institution that remained essential to rule was the state's official religion, Islam, along with ruling society's language, Arabic. In most other respects Baghdad soon became an almost entirely Persianised city. Characteristics of its nature included the presence of fine wines, non-Arab styles of dress, and concubines for those at court.

**Challeges to Baghdad**

- The glory that was Baghdad—with its wealth and proximity to the royal court—wasn't able to stem the rising ambitions of governors in the caliphate's remote corners. The first piece of the Abbasid caliphate to go its own way was the westernmost extremity. The Abbasids, in their overthrow and slaughter of their rivals in Damascus, had failed to kill every member of the Umayyad family.

- The sole surviving male member of that line fled first to Egypt, before making his way across North Africa to Spain, where he set up an Umayyad court in exile, in the city of Cordoba. From there, a new dynasty put down roots. This "shadow caliphate" harried the Abbasids, and eventually took part of their empire in northwestern Africa, modern Morocco, and beyond.

- But not all of the challenges to Baghdad's power were so distant. Local struggles saw more than one caliph move his official residence from Baghdad to Samarra, another city on the banks of the Tigris, some 80 miles north of Baghdad.

- Baghdad would remain the capital of the great Abbasid dynasty for most of the next 500 years, but its sublime first century of existence would always be remembered as the most secure, peaceful, and perhaps glorious period.

## Suggested Reading

Al-Tabari, *The History of al-Tabari.*

Bennison, *Cities in the Pre-Modern Islamic World*, chapter 3.

———, *The Great Caliphs*, chapter 2.

Hitti, *Capital Cities of Arab Islam*, chapter 4.

Hourani, *A History of the Arab Peoples*, chapter 2.

Kennedy, *When Baghdad Ruled the Muslim World.*

Lapidus, *A History of Islamic Societies*, chapter 4.

Lyons, *The House of Wisdom.*

## Questions to Consider

1. Consider the importance of pre-Islamic, Persian administrative skills and wider scholastic knowledge for the success of the Abbasid Caliphate. Would they have been able to supplant the Umayyads without this help?

2. Access to a reliable source of clean water is obviously central to urban planning, but apart from this and similar considerations of physical geography, how far do questions of human geography, including proximity to allies and enemies, trained and unskilled workers, impact the decision of where to build? As well as Baghdad's location, think about other cities in the Middle East, and the wider world.

Lecture 9

# Islamic Golden Age Begins—813

The Abbasid Caliph al-Ma'mun (r. 813–833) was instrumental in elevating the Abbasid Empire, and its capital in Baghdad, to among the world's most important centers of learning. The Islamic Golden Age neither began nor ended with Caliph al-Ma'mun. But under his reign, it flourished—with the means to continue after his death. It's no exaggeration to say that in the person of al-Ma'mun, we're looking at a man whose love of learning provided the patronage for scholarship, and a vital foundation for the European Renaissance about six centuries later.

## The Middle Eastern Framework

- From the first man to succeed Muhammad in 632, to the last Ottoman caliph, when the title was abolished in 1924, the four major caliphates produced some 85 caliphs between them. When we add in rival—or shadow—caliphates, such as the emirs of Cordoba and the Fatimids, the total rises to over 100.

- Out of these more than 100 caliphs—who span almost 1400 years of history—there's a case to be made that al-Ma'mun was the most important of them all.

- Abu Ja'far Abdullah al-Ma'mun ibn Harun—to give him his full name—was born in Baghdad in 786. His father was the fifth Abbasid caliph, Harun al-Rashid, and his mother a Persian slave.

- Six months after al-Ma'mun's birth, a half-brother was born. This mother, rather than being a concubine, was Harun's wife, Zubaida, a member of the ruling Abbasid family. It was understood that the half-brother, al-Amin, would be first in line to succeed the boys' father.

- Sure enough, when al-Amin was five years old, his father, Harun al-Rashid, designated him as the next caliph. Within a few short years, however, Harun recognized that his lower-born son, al-Ma'mun, was superior both in terms of intellect and in potential.

- While trying to reach an equitable solution, Harun issued a decree that sowed the seeds for an inevitable clash between the youths. Al-Amin would remain first heir, while the concubine's son, al-Ma'mun, now 13 years old, would be his second. Thereby, al-Ma'mun would be entitled to inherit the title of caliph in the event his half-brother al-Amin died before him. Al-Ma'mun was also named governor of the Persian region of Khurasan.

- While both sons agreed, the moment Harun died in the year 809, al-Amin—advised by his Arab viziers—started to renege on the deal. The role of *vizier*, or caliphal advisor, had grown in importance under the Abbasids. In the examples of al-Amin and al-Ma'mun, their viziers represented different worldviews, and were responsible for fomenting the dispute.

    - On one side, al-Amin and his senior adviser represented the older Sunni Muslim order with—as they would see it—undiluted Arab bloodlines.

    - On the other side, al-Ma'mun—with his Persian mother, his Persian vizier, and his Persian power base—had more support from Shia Muslims, as well as what we might call more generally non-Arab Muslim converts.

- Al-Amin made several announcements that foreshadowed his intention to undo the terms of the succession agreement. Specifically, he planned to allowing his own son to inherit the caliphate after his death instead of his half-brother, al-Ma'mun. Naturally, al-Ma'mun—advised by his Persian viziers—was not going to stand for this. And so a civil war broke out.

- Known as the Fourth *Fitna*, or period of tribulation, this conflict would last until 827. For the purposes of our story, the most important phase of the war ended in 813, when al-Ma'mun sent an army from his Persian base to attack Baghdad, and removed al-Amin from power.

- After this victory, al-Ma'mun's army went on to besiege Baghdad. Al-Amin, while suing for peace, was then caught fleeing from the city and killed. This is the moment, in September 813, when al-Ma'mun's caliphate starts. But because many al-Amin loyalists still occupied the Abbasid capital, it would be six years before al-Ma'mun would make his triumphal entry into Baghdad in 819.

**Al-Ma'mun's Baghdad**

- With peace assured, trade into and out of the city on the Tigris mushroomed, and agriculture on the surrounding plains bloomed again. Apart from becoming famous as a city of scholarship, Baghdad became a major industrial city and center of innovation and manufacturing, with a global reputation.

- As al-Ma'muun received tax and other revenues on a previously unimaginable scale, he was able—and willing—to lavish more patronage on scholarship than any caliph before him. As a result, scholars started coming to Baghdad in increasing numbers.

- Worthy of attention is the development of three broad areas of scholarship in al-Ma'mun's Baghdad: literature, the sciences, and religion—specifically Islamic theology.

- All three subject areas received much of their source material from a massive push to translate works of scholarship from languages other than Arabic and from other traditions. In fact, the very tradition of translation was already well established in Persia.

- The center of translation and original scholarship in al-Ma'mun's Baghdad was Bayt al-Hikma, or the House of Knowledge. Established by his father, Harun al-Rashid, the House of Knowledge grew under al-Ma'mun to become the greatest single seat of learning the world had ever seen.

- Ma'mun also sent scholarly missions out to collect texts from beyond the borders of his empire, including more than one delegation travelling to the Byzantine emperor in Constantinople.

- By the end of his reign, Ma'mun's scholars had translated into Arabic virtually the complete medical works of Hippocrates and Galen; the mathematical treatises of Archimedes; Euclid's geometry; and every extant work by both Plato and Aristotle. And where earlier works had existed, the scholars in the House of Wisdom were, in almost every instance, responsible for producing new, improved translations.

## Literature and Prose

- One of the most famous works of Arabic literature is actually a translation of an earlier Persian text. Known in Arabic as *Kalila and Dimnah*, it's a beautiful set of fables that features anthropomorphic animals discussing various scenarios.

- Comparable with Aesop's Fables, Kalila and Dimnah is still taught to Arab schoolchildren, and for centuries was far better known than *One Thousand and One Nights*.

- The use of animals allowed the storyteller to make a point without having to identify the human subject of the story. In the "Tale of the Rabbit and the Elephant King," for example, the supposedly wise elephant king is made to look foolish when the rabbit shows him the reflection of the moon.

- Although translated from the Persian, the tales of *Kalila and Dimna* have their origins in an even earlier Sanskrit text from India—just another example of cross-cultural borrowing.

## The Sciences

- The terms *science* and *scientists* weren't in use at the time, and wouldn't be coined for more than a thousand years in the future. But there was work being done on mathematics, chemistry, physics, biology, medical science, and astronomy, which incorporated astrology.

- Astronomy held a place of importance. Muslim scholars were first and foremost concerned with astronomy for religious reasons, which is why the subject was so important.

- When Muslims pray, they are expected to face the Kaabah, the black cuboid sanctuary, in the city of Mecca. Being able to orientate oneself in the right direction—aided by astronomical observation—is obviously very important.

- In addition, the Islamic calendar is based not just on astronomical calculations, but also on lunar observation and the sighting of a new moon, which marks the start of the next in the 12-month, annual cycle. A result was the development of astrolabes—astronomical measuring devices—to predict sunrises and the position of the fixed stars.

- Scientists in Ma'mun's Baghdad also devoted a great deal of time to the study of astrology. While contemporary Islamic scholars are almost universal in their rejection, and even condemnation, of astrology as un-Islamic, it was a very different story when Ma'mun was caliph.

- One of the most famous astronomers working in Baghdad at this time was a Persian scholar named Abu Ma'shar. His book, *An Introduction to Astronomy*, was not only eagerly studied in the Middle East, but, again, after arriving in medieval Europe via Muslim Spain, it was central to the revival of interest in—and the study of—astronomy and astrology.

- Abu Ma'shar also applied his astrological studies to medicine, adopting the earlier Greek idea of the human body being composed of different humors.

- After astronomical works, Ma'mun's Baghdad gave great emphasis and importance to the translation into Arabic of mathematical treatises. The most important source with regards to mathematics was India, with the ancient Greeks close behind.

- One of the most important names in the history of mathematics of any age was working for Ma'mun at this time. He was another Persian, whose name was Abu Abdallah Muhammad ibn Musa al-Khwarizmi, usually referred to al-Khwarizmi. The Latinised form of his name, Algorithmi, spawned the term *algorithm*.

- One of al-Khwarizmi's more important works is the elegantly entitled *Compendious Book on Calculation by Completion and Balancing*. It presented algebra as a distinct branch of mathematics, complete with a system of solving quadratic equations.

- Al-Khwarizmi's second work, *The Book of Addition and Subtraction According to the Hindu Calculation*, introduced the Indian system of numerals, (1, 2, 3, etc.) to the Middle East.

**Religion**

- The third area of scholarship undertaken in Ma'mun's court was the most controversial: religion, specifically Islamic theology.

- Dabbling with Shia Islam for a time, Ma'mun eventually settled on a radical school of thought whose members were known as *al-Mu'tazilah*, or "those who secede." Ma'mun built on earlier Christian and Ummayad Muslim debates about the role of free will and a just God. This opened the door to the possibility of individuals questioning otherwise inviolable theological concepts.

- Ma'mun and the al-Mu'tazilah attacked the doctrine of the eternal nature of the Quran, arguing that such a belief challenged the more vital concept of the oneness of God.

- When Ma'mun decided to elevate his own rather radical views to the level of official state religion, he was almost guaranteed a violent response from the more conservative adherents of Islam.

- Ma'mun declared that the Qu'ran, rather than having been eternal—as in existing through all of time—had instead been a creation of the Muslim faith, so as to articulate it. He insisted that his governors and judges across the empire sign a declaration agreeing with him. Ma'mun then instituted the first inquisition in Islamic history to enforce his views.

- Among the four main schools of Islamic legal thought, the strictest, most conservative of them is the Hanbali school, named after its founder, Ahmad ibn-Hanbal. Hanbal refused to sign the caliph's decree. Hanbal eventually died in prison without having signed on. By all accounts, his funeral was one of the largest ever seen in Baghdad. The Hanbali school of Islam still exists today.

- While Ma'mun's more rationalist approach to his faith did not win the day, the scholarship he promoted in the House of Wisdom had an enormous, positive impact on global learning. Under Ma'mun, Baghdad became the intellectual and scientific capital of the world, and the learned men working there were recognized as great translators and originators of an astonishing body of new knowledge.

- Without the Greek scholarship, the Renaissance wouldn't have been possible. Without the work of Arab and Persian scholars of all faiths, that Greek scholarship would not have survived, and been improved upon, before being passed on in turn to the West.

**Suggested Reading**


Al-Khalili, *The House of Wisdom.*

Bennison, *The Great Caliphs*, chapter 5.

Hitti, *Makers of Arab History*, chapter 5.

Kennedy, *When Baghdad Ruled the Muslim World.*

Lyons, *The House of Wisdom.*


**Questions to Consider**

1. Caliph al-Mamun is remembered for his attempt to reconcile the Sunni and Shia branches of Islam. Had he been successful in this goal, what practical outcomes might have resulted in the Islamic world and beyond?

2. In forcibly imposing his own, rationalist form of Islam on his subjects, al-Mamun's damaged his otherwise good reputation for tolerance. That aside, how far do you think his belief in free will and human responsibility drove the Islamic Golden Age?

Lecture 10

# Qairouan University—859

In this lecture, we'll look at the founding of the world's first university, including where it was built and whose idea it was. We'll meet a woman who was responsible for changing the face of higher education forever. We'll also examine the life and work of one of this university's most influential graduates, who stands out as being responsible for a revolution in European scholarship and education. Finally, we'll conclude by considering the influence of this first university in the Middle East and beyond, to include the West.

## Fes, Morocco

- Fatima al-Fihri was a wealthy Muslim widow who was keen to spend her inheritance on something that would make a difference. It was the year 859, in the Moroccan city of Fes, that she received permission from the local ruler to set up a university.

- At that moment, the world of learning was about to change forever. The University of Qairouan in Fes is the world's first, and thus oldest, degree-granting institution, according to both UNESCO and the book *Guinness World Records*.

- Fatima was a native not of Fes, but of the city of Qairouan, in modern-day Tunisia. Qairouan was the first major center of Islamic learning in Africa. Fatima's father, Muhammad al-Fihri, was a prosperous trader who was likely forced to move his family the more than 1,000 miles overland, from Qairouan to the city of Fes in Morocco.

- This family wasn't alone. In 818, a rebellion erupted in Qairouan against the Aghlabid rulers who had been installed by the Abbasid caliph, in distant Baghdad. The attempt to remove the Aghlabid family failed, and the Aghlabid ruler responded by expelling about 2,000 families from his domains. Like Fatima's family, many of these exiles were welcome in Fes.

- Morocco had recently been taken over by a new ruling dynasty known as the Idrisids. The Idrisids were Shia. Because of the Sunni-Shia power struggle raging in the Arabian Peninsula at the time, the Idrisids fled, establishing themselves in the far northwest of Africa.

- Fes, Morocco—like Fatima al-Fihri's home city of Qairouan—was a new town, at the time, established in two stages: first by Idris I in 789, and later by his son and heir, Idris II, in 808.

- When Idris II made Fes his capital, the city's future prosperity was ensured. Fes's location, like Qairouan's, was also ideal for a trading center. It sits on a plain that leads west to the Atlantic, and north to the Mediterranean, and it was built in a pass that runs through the Middle Atlas Mountains.

**Fatima al-Fihri's Wealth**

- Fatima's father—having settled in Fes just 10 years or so after it became the Idrisids' new capital—continued to prosper. And when he died, Fatima and her siblings inherited a substantial fortune.

- What to do with this new wealth? Fatima's father had raised his daughter—and her sister, Mariam—to get the best possible educations. Fatima and Mariam both decided to spend their inheritances on building a mosque and school for their local community. The complex soon became known as the Qairouan mosque and school because it was built in that part of Fes where most of the refugees from Qairouan, Tunisia, lived.

- Initially, Qairouan had the same religious function of any mosque and madrasa, namely the teaching of the traditional and most important subjects in any course of Islamic theology. The three main areas of study for anyone reading Islamic theology

Al-Qarawiyyin University

were as follows: one, *tafsir*, or Quranic exegesis, or scriptural interpretation; two, a study of the *hadith*, or the sayings of Muhammad; and three, *fiqh*, or Islamic jurisprudence.

- However, Fatima's school also offered non-Islamic subjects as part of a broader education, including mathematics, astronomy, astrology, physics, poetry, and literature. This was critical to Qairouan becoming more than solely a religious establishment. It was also a turning point in the history of the University of Qairouan—and for the future of higher education around the globe.

- No longer would education be limited to religious instruction, such as seminarians or others embarking on spiritual lives. The field of advanced education was now technically thrown open to anyone with the means to study. Ultimately, that would prove to be a revolutionary moment for human society, extending well beyond the 9th century in North Africa, and the wider Muslim Middle East.

**Famous Alumni**

- Any number of great names passed through this venerable institution: Maimonides, the Jewish polymath from modern-day Spain; the Tunisian writer and theorist Ibn Khaldun; and the Berber traveller and writer Hassan ibn Muhammad al-Wazzan al-Fasi, known in the West as Leo Africanus, or Leo the African.

- But perhaps Qairouan's most influential student was the man who introduced the decimal system and Arabic numerals to Europe. This replaced the earlier, more cumbersome system of Roman numerals that had been in place for more than 1,000 years.

- This same individual also re-introduced the abacus and the armillary sphere into European circles. And if that weren't dramatic enough for one lifetime, he also went on to become the first French pope. Born Gerbert d'Aurillac, in southern France—around the year 946—Gerbert took the name Sylvester II when he became the Holy Father a little more than a half century later, in the year 999.

- Gerbert's talent for learning was spotted soon after he entered a monastery in his native France, around the age of 17. Four years later, he was sent to study in another monastery in Barcelona.

- Gerbert, a Christian monk, was welcomed to study at the Muslim-founded University of Qairouan. Religious tolerance had long been the norm in Muslim North Africa, with anti-Jewish and anti-Christian factions constituting a very small minority.

- As a Shia dynasty in a Sunni-majority Muslim world, the Idrisids found it in their best interests to be more accepting of the beliefs of others. For another thing, Morocco was situated on the western fringes of the Muslim world. This geographical reality meant that Morocco, under the Idrisids, became an attractive location for those wishing to remain beyond the reach of the Abbasids. So the arrival of Gerbert to study in Fes wouldn't have been all that remarkable.

- What was remarkable were Gerbert's own scholastic abilities, which enabled him to absorb a great deal of what was unarguably the most advanced scholarship of its day, anywhere on earth. Gerbert's literary output was significant, especially after his time studying in Morocco. He wrote books about arithmetic and geometry, as well as on astronomy and music. In addition, appropriately enough for a pope, he wrote several notable ecclesiastical works.

**Pope Sylvester II**

- Had Gerbert remained a remarkable—but unheralded—scholar, there's every reason to believe that the transfer of knowledge of Islamic mathematical and astronomical knowledge would have been delayed, at the very least. What made all the difference is that Gerbert became the Catholic pontiff as Pope Sylvester II, putting him in a position to make an enormous difference.

- It was on his instructions as pope that Arabic numerals replaced the older Roman numbering system in the church. There had been enormous resistance to this from vested interests—merchants and churchmen alike—who favoured the status quo over innovation, especially when that innovation meant adopting tools that many thought highly suspect, coming as they did from Muslim hands.

- Regardless, Pope Sylvester II realized the power of the Islamic numbering system and pushed the changes through. As the vast majority of Europe was illiterate at the time, the initial impact might have been slight. But the long-term impact was enormous. Gerbert's discovery of Arabic—which is to say Indian—numbers also allowed him to re-introduce the abacus to Europe.

- According to a letter from one of his pupils, Gerbert's abacus was divided into 27 parts, with nine number symbols. His calculating machine, therefore, didn't include zero, which instead was represented by an empty column.

- Gerbert's student described the speed with which Gerbert was able to use the machine, doing relatively complicated arithmetic calculations with ease. These calculations were extremely difficult for people who were stuck with Roman numerals. Thanks to Gerbert, by the 11th century the abacus was once again in widespread use throughout Europe.

**The University's Effects**

- By the time of Sylvester II's death in 1003, another university-mosque complex, al-Azhar, had sprung up in the Arab world. Its reputation would eventually eclipse that of Qairouan. Founded by the Shia Fatimids in Cairo in 970, al-Azhar became a center of Sunni Muslim jurisprudence and scholarship after the end of the Fatimid Caliphate in 1170. Today, al-Azhar remains arguably the foremost center of religious orthodoxy and authority in the Sunni Muslim world.

- Meanwhile, more than 80 years would pass after Sylvester II's death before the first university in Europe was founded, in 1088, in the Italian city of Bologna. Just about a decade after that, we have the first solid evidence of teaching taking place at the University of Oxford.

- By the early 20th century—by which time Morocco was a French protectorate—Qairouan's glory days as a center of learning were behind it. Competition—from a proliferation of Muslim world universities—was partly to blame, as was the tendency of Moroccan elites to send their children to complete their educations in Europe, which offered more modern instruction and greater prestige.

- After the independence of Morocco from France in 1956, Qairouan was integrated into the state education system. By the late 1980s, it once again had a broad, multi-disciplinary syllabus, offering Islamic and non-Islamic studies.

- More broadly, Morocco in the 20th century found itself on the fringes of the Muslim Middle East. It was far from bigger, more powerful cultural centers such as Cairo or Beirut, and remote from the emerging oil-rich nations of the Arabian Peninsula. Once, its sultans had exercised domain across the Atlas Mountains, which were at the leading edge of encounters and relations with the great powers of Europe. Now, it was something of a backwater.

- Some scholars might argue that the University of Qairouan—and later, that of al-Azhar in Cairo—had little, or nothing, to do with the development of universities in Europe. But this is being contrary for the sake of it: Nothing travels quite like learning.

- The royal founders of Christendom's great centers of learning in Bologna, Paris, and Oxford might be somewhat wary of heaping praise on great ideas from their ostensibly rival, Muslim powers overseas. But the establishment of the University of Bologna in 1088, at a time when it was an important city of southern European trade, fits a likely timeframe for the transfer of knowledge from the universities of North Africa.

- We owe a large debt, of course, to Gerbert d'Aurillac, or Pope Sylvester II. But it's a good idea also to remind ourselves about the philanthropy of Fatima al-Fihri, the woman whose vision and wealth changed the story of education in the Middle East, and the entire world.

## Suggested Reading

Brown, *The Abacus and the Cross*.

*Encyclopaedia of Islam*.

Ibn Khaldun, *The Muqaddimah*.

## Questions to Consider

1. The founding of the world's first university is obviously a moment of supreme importance in the history of formal education. How significant or otherwise do you think it is that this institution, the Mosque-University complex of Qairouan in Fes, Morocco, was established and privately funded by an educated woman rather than, for the sake of argument, a king or other male head of state?

2. What are some possible reasons for the decline in standards of education, particularly higher education, in today's Middle East, relative to comparable educational establishments found in North America and Europe?

3. How important might the Islamic nature of Morocco have been in the promotion and success of the University of Qairouan? Factors to consider might include its being part of a wider, united Islamic Empire; the movement of traders and scholars across this empire; the use of Arabic as a lingua-franca in Islamic scholarship; proximity to Europe, and other, alien ideas and forms of knowledge.

Lecture 11

# The Fatimids of Cairo—969

The founding of Cairo by history's sole Shia caliphate is the focus of this lecture. To grasp how important the founding of Cairo was, we must have some understanding of the people responsible for building it—and why they thought it necessary to build a new city on the Nile. To do so, this lecture is built around the following three questions: Who were the Fatimids? How did they rise up to challenge the Abbasid caliphate? And why did their capital, Cairo, become one of the most important cities in the Islamic world?

## The Fatimids

- The Fatimids were the only Shia caliphate in Islamic history. They're also the only caliphate in Islamic history that originated in North Africa, and then spread east towards the Arab heartland, rather than spreading west from Arabia.

- At the height of its power, the Fatimid empire covered the whole of North Africa, Sicily, the Levant in the eastern Mediterranean, and both shores of the Red Sea. And they controlled all of this from Cairo.

- In speaking about the Fatimid caliphate, it's actually more accurate to speak of a *shadow caliphate*, established, in political and religious opposition to the ruling power of the day—the Baghdad-based Abbasids. And while the Fatimids' parallel—or—caliphate would end in the year 1171, the Abbasid caliphate existed in one form or another for a further 350 years.

- In claiming to be the legitimate heirs of Muhammad, the Fatimids were not just saying that they had the right to rule over lands they'd already conquered. They were also asserting their right to rule over the entire Muslim world. Such a claim, and the Fatimid rulers' adoption of the term *caliphs*, proved to be a devastating, permanent split in the ideal of a united caliphate.

- The Fatimids were a branch of Shia Islam called *Isma'ilism*—after an early Shia leader, Ismail. The Fatimids took their name from Muhammad's daughter, Fatima. In short, Isma'ilism holds that there are two ways to interpret the Quran. The first is the external, or exoteric form; that is, the words in the book, which speak for themselves. The second is the hidden, or esoteric, way in which every verse of the Quran is to be understood.

- Today, Isma'ilis make up a small fraction of the world's Shia population, although under the Fatimids they were far more numerous, and remained dominant for more than 200 years. There are also different schools of Isma'ilism functioning today, such as the Druze and Nizari.

**Rise of the Fatimids**

- The Fatimids established their dynasty in Tunisia, in 909. The Arabs, having invaded North Africa just 200 years earlier, were still a minority in the region, and were regarded as interlopers by many. At that time, the majority of North Africans still identified themselves as Berbers, not Arabs.

- In many instances, the native Berbers were unhappy with their Arab rulers in Baghdad. Tapping into local discontent in North Africa, the Fatimids conquered west to Morocco, and also held numerous Mediterranean islands, including Sicily, Malta, Corsica and Sardinia.

- From there, they turned east. It was in 969 that an army of the fourth Fatimid caliph, al-Mu'izz (r. 953–975) won the great prize of Egypt. Long before the rise of Islam, Egypt, particualarly the annually-flooding Nile, had been a vital source of wealth and food in the Middle East.

- After, taking Egypt, the Fatimids moved on to conquer the Levant and the western Arabian region of the Hijaz, all in swift succession. For the first time since the split between the two branches of Islam, there was a Shia authority ruling over the holy cities of Mecca and Medina.

**Al-Mu'izz**

- Desiring a new capital, the Fatimid caliph al-Mu'izz chose a spot beside the Nile, a few miles north of Fustat. Originally, a Babylonian astrologer was to calculate the most auspicious moment to start work, as dictated by the stars. But a raven landed on the rope attached to the signal bells, sounding the signal to start work, which in turn saw the workmen break ground and start digging.

- The astrologer took this as an ill omen. But Mu'izz, who was himself a competent astrologer, thought otherwise. At that moment, the planet Mars was at its highest point. So, taking a lead from Mars' Arabic nickname—Subduer or Victor of the Skies—al-Mu'izz ordered that the new city be called al-Qahira, the Victorious.

- For the first time in more than 1,000 years, Egypt was once more a sovereign state. And as an *Alid* state—that is, one with Ali as the exemplar—there now existed a powerful Shia realm after the faithful's more than two-and-a-half century struggle against Sunni domination. The changes to the existing religious, political, and social order were enormous, and Cairo was the very heart of this revolutionary moment in Islamic history.

- Domestic and overseas trade—combined with the flourishing manufacturing industries that grew up in Cairo—saw the Fatimids' capital grow to be very rich.

- Mu'izz also commissioned the invention of the fountain pen. It would be more than 500 years before the fountain pen was re-invented in Europe.

- Fatimid Egypt also grew rich beyond Cairo's urban center, providing the Nile behaved. This was thanks to the fertility of the land, both across the Delta and along length of the great river.

**Al-Aziz**

- Mu'izz's sons died before him, so it was his brother, al-Aziz (r. 975–996) who inherited the title, and became the fifth Fatimid caliph. His name means "the Almighty."

- It was al-Aziz, after Mu'izz himself, who did the most to secure the lasting legacy of the Fatimid capital. This brings us to another of our Cairo questions: Apart from being the largest city in the Middle East, why did Cairo become the greatest important city in the Islamic World?

- Al-Aziz followed his brother's enlightened view of living side-by-side with those of other faiths. He appointed a Christian as one of his main viziers, or advisors, as well as a Jewish governor for Syria-Palestine. He was also happily married—as far as we can tell—to a Russian Christian woman.

- Under such tolerant—or at least politically savvy—leadership, Cairo prospered. Streets were lit at night; five- or six-story buildings weren't unusual; crime was rare; and goods had fixed prices.

- Al-Aziz, like his brother before him, made no systematic attempt to impose Isma'ilism. Instead, Aziz did something far more constructive, and potentially smarter, to win acceptance for the Isma'ilis. In the very heart of his capital, he founded a university-mosque complex called al-Azhar, which was designed, in part, to teach Isma'ili scholars and missionaries.

**Al-Hakim**

- The sixth Fatimid caliph, al-Hakim (r. 996–1021)—who inherited the caliphate at the age of 11—soon showed himself an unworthy successor to his father, al-Aziz.

Al-Azhar Mosque

- Al-Hakim soon started reversing the traditional tolerance shown by earlier caliphs. Cairo became a seat of intolerance under al-Hakim, marked by a series of edicts that restricted the religious freedoms of all non-Isma'ili faiths.

- This intolerance was atypical. If we look at the records of all previous caliphs up to al-Hakim, only two others really stand out for their extreme discriminatory policies towards non-Muslims: the Umayyad caliph Umar II (r. 717–720), and the Abbasid caliph Mutawakkil (r. 847–861).

- In 1009, al-Hakim ordered the destruction of the Church of the Holy Sepulchre in Jerusalem. This deliberately provocative act is often cited as among the seeds of the Crusades that began later in the century. We begin to see why al-Hakim earned the sobriquet "Mad Caliph."

- In the last years of his reign, al-Hakim might even have come to see himself as a deity. While there's some dispute about this, it was a view circulated after his mysterious death in 1021, at the age of 36. One day, when walking in the Muqattam hills outside of Cairo, al-Hakim disappeared. Later, his donkey and blood-stained clothes were discovered, but the Mad Caliph was never seen again.

- As to his divine nature, this belief was taken up in some form by adherents of a new faith, the Druze, who hold fondly to the memory of al-Hakim.

- Soon after al-Hakim's death, peaceful relations were re-established between different faiths, thanks to his more rational successors. Non-Muslim pilgrims again travelled freely in the region, and the restoration work on the Church of the Holy Sepulchre began.

## Al-Mustansir and Consequences

- Al-Hakim's confrontational and peculiar behaviour earned the Fatimids more enemies than friends. Al-Hakim's son, al-Mustansir, ascended to the Fatimid throne when he was just six years old.

- Al-Mustansir's reign was marked principally by a serious decline in Fatimid fortunes. Soon enough, the Fatimids found their rule being cast off by former Berber subjects in North Africa, and their domains in the Levant and elsewhere invaded by Christian crusaders and Muslim, Turkic, and Kurdish tribes, among others.

- In quick succession, they lost possession of the Hijaz, Syria, and all of their North African territories beyond Egypt. The loss of so much land resulted also in the loss also of most of their tax revenue.

- In consequence, public works such as clearing canals and rebuilding flood defenses were neglected. Cairo's inhabitants felt the brunt of this neglect when the Nile refused to cooperate with the farming schedule. Years of irregular inundation led, with worrying Biblical parallels, to seven years of famine, which was swiftly followed by plague.

- Fatimid rule in Egypt ended in 1171, with the rise of a Kurdish general by the name of Saladin. Cairo, however, would live to breathe another day. Saladin would found his own Ayyubid dynastic line, and keep the Fatimid capital for his own.

- By re-incorporating Egypt into the Abbasid Caliphate, at least nominally, Saladin most importantly assured the future of the Fatimid capital, now reinvented as a Sunni as a center of learning.

- The end of the Fatimid shadow caliphate also spelled the beginning of the end of Shia Islam as a political force in North

Africa. Athough one can still find pockets of Shia in North Africa, these are tiny compared to the Fatimids' glory days.

- In the long term, the fissure the Fatimids created in the Islamic world has never been sealed. The Fatimids' challenge to Abbasid rule destroyed any semblance of central authority in the Muslim world, with all of the many unintended and unforeseeable consequences that resulted.

- Following this example, other regions also signaled unwillingness to be ruled from Baghdad. Across the Muslim world, a series of autonomous provinces sprang up that slowly took on the characteristics of de facto states.

- One of these was the exiled Umayyad leadership's Emirate of Cordoba in Spain. It was at this moment, and this declaration by the Umayyads, that saw the badly divided Muslim world lose its last real chance to consider a further conquest of Western Europe.

- Across once-secure Abbasid lands, powerful families established hereditary domains, independent of the Abbasids say-so. A further unintended result of the Fatimid challenge to Abbasid authority was the reaction of the Seljuk Turks, who responded by asserting their own right to be the true defenders of orthodox Sunni Islam.

- Finally, and most importantly from a European perspective, the cleavage that the Fatimid schism opened provided the crusaders with their opportunity to conquer Jerusalem. The capture of Jerusalem by a crusader army in 1099 is rightly seen as a direct result of Fatimid rule from their capital in Cairo.

## Suggested Reading

Bennison, *Cities in the Pre-Modern Islamic World*, chapter 6.

Hitti, *Makers of Arab History*, chapter 6.

———, *Capital Cities of Arab Islam*, chapter 5.

Lapidus, *A History of Islamic Societies*, chapter 15.

Marsot, *A History of Egypt*, chapter 1.

Rodenbeck, *Cairo*.

Walker, *Exploring an Islamic Empire*.

## Questions to Consider

1. How important was the discontent of North Africa's native, Berber population for the Fatimids' early success in the region?

2. As Ismai'li-Shia, did their non-mainstream form of Islam more or less guarantee the Fatimids' ultimate failure to win global authority over the Abbasid caliphate?

# Umayyad Exile in Cordoba—784–1031

Lecture 12

In this lecture, we're going to examine the flourishing of Cordoba, and see why this was a Middle East turning point in Muslim learning. We'll also learn how this was made possible by the generally peaceful co-existence of the three great Abrahamic religions—Judaism, Christianity, and Islam—over a period of two and a half centuries. It was a time when the brightest and best members of these three faiths not only understood the importance of working together for their mutual benefit, but in doing so stimulated the progress of scholarship in Muslim and non-Muslim Europe.

### Abd ar-Rahman

- At the time of the Arab-Berber invasion of North Africa in 711, the central authority in the Muslim world was the Umayyad caliphate, which ruled from its capital in Damascus. In 750, however, the Umayyads were overthrown by a family descended from Muhammad's uncle, Abbas, after whom the new Caliphate was named: the Abbasids.

- The Abbasids slaughtered almost the entire Umayyad ruling family, and then built a new capital in Baghdad. But a 19-year-old boy named Abd ar-Rahmam got away.

- After crossing the Strait of Gibraltar, and arriving in Andalusia, Abd ar-Rahman joined forces with some 500 Umayyad loyalists. With their help, and by exploiting local rivalries between Berbers and different Arab groups, Abd ar-Rahman was able to establish himself as the ruler of Cordoba in 756.

- He became first emir of Cordoba and head of the Umayyads in exile. Abd ar-Rahman's decision to limit himself to the title of *emir* (or prince) rather than *caliph* (or successor to Muhammad) was clever. There was no point in creating more enemies in the region than he already had, notably among those who had sworn allegiance to the Abbasid caliphs in Baghdad.

### Cordoba Thrives

- With the religiously tolerant Abd ar-Rahman as prince of Cordoba, the city's glory days were about to begin. It's often said that Abd ar-Rahman's tolerance for non-Arabs and non-Muslims was born purely from political expediency: He had few allies in Andalusia, or anywhere else. And with Muslims and Arabic-speakers on the Iberian Peninsula still a minority, he would need all the friends he could get.

- But it's unclear this was just a matter of pragmatism. For one thing, since his mother was a Berber, that fact alone would have made him sensitive to linguistic, ethnic, and religious diversity. Abd al-Rahman also had married a Christian, and while—according to Islamic law—any children should be raised as Muslims, the mother never converted, nor apparently did he ask her to.

- Apart from Abd ar-Rahman's capable leadership, other factors in Cordoba's favour were its well-watered, rich agricultural land—which lay close to the coastal plains—and its communications with other parts of the world.

- Not long after Cordoba's initial growth spurt, the city received a powerful economic boost when the Byzantine Empire lost naval control of the western Mediterranean. With the Christian Byzantine Empire no longer a threat to Iberian shores, Cordoba—as well as Seville and other cities of Andalusia—became free to develop greater trade networks, including with Christian states.

### The Blackbird

- Though the Umyyads-in-exile were still the enemies of the Abbasids in Baghdad, merchants and scholars from Baghdad did come to Cordoba. One of the most interesting and significant of these visitors from Baghdad was a man known as the Blackbird.

- Abu Hassan Ali ibn Nafi—originally from Persia— is also variously described as being an ethnic Kurd, Arab, Berber, or black African. He initially made his name as a musician, composer, singer, poet, and teacher in Baghdad, in the court of the Abbasid caliph al-Ma'mun.

- He is best known to us as *Ziryab,* which is Arabic for "blackbird." And though we're not absolutely sure, he might have gained his nickname because of the beauty of his singing voice. Ziryab was also a competent astronomer, as well as a keen meteorologist and cook.

- In around the year 820, Ziryab moved from Baghdad to Cordoba, where the local Umayyad rulers in exile eagerly welcomed him. Not only was Ziryab's move to Cordoba a snub to the Abbasids, but his presence in Iberia no doubt added to the prestige of this remote, and recently established, Islamic royal court.

- Ziryab introduced deodorant and toothpaste to Europe, as well as tablecloths (then made of leather), and, most stunningly, the three-course meal. Ziryab's ideal three courses: 1. soup, 2. meat or fish, then 3. a sweet course, dried fruits, or sorbet.

- He also popularized the use of glass instead of metal drinking vessels. In terms of fashion, he introduced the trend for a winter and summer wardrobe—for those who could afford it.

**The Great Mosque**

- Anyone who goes to Cordoba will agree that the Great Mosque was the unquestioned highlight of their visit to the city. Its history follows.

- The Germanic Visigoths built a Christian church on the site around the year 600 after they had defeated the Romans to take control of the Iberian Peninsula. In 784, the new Emir of Cordoba, Abd ar-Rahman I, ordered a mosque built on the same spot.

- But with extensions and improvements, the great mosque was not completed until the reign of al-Hakam II—the second Caliph of Cordoba—more than 200 years later.

- It was said that Abd ar-Rahman spent a third of his revenue on building works. When one looks at the sheer scale of the mosque complex, not to mention the ruins of his 270-acre palace complex some 10 miles outside of Cordoba, that seems entirely plausible.

- One of the most striking features of the mosque is the number of columns that form scores of aisles throughout the main hall. In the main arcade, there are 856 columns, variously built of granite, marble, onyx and other types of stone. Although the horseshoe arches above them would be familiar to anyone who'd visited the Umayyad mosque in Damascus, many embellishments and

decorative touches were added in Cordoba to create their own, distinctive, Moorish style.

- This architecture simultaneously allowed the Umayyads to look back to their far-away home in Damascus, and forward to their own re-invention in Cordoba. It seems a neat fit for the site of a Roman temple dedicated to Janus, the Roman god of beginnings and transitions.

## The Era of Three Caliphates

- During the reign of Abd ar-Rahman III, one of the most unusual situations in Islamic history occurred: the era of three caliphates.

- The Sunni-Shia split—in the aftermath of Muhammad's death in 632—meant that Shia Muslims didn't accept the leadership of the Umayyad or Abbasid caliphates, both of which were Sunni.

- Then in 909, the Shia Fatimids spread from their base in Tunisia, taking over North Africa from the Abbasids and their client states. In 929, with the Fatimids in North Africa threatening the Umayyads in Iberia, Abd ar-Rahman III declared himself caliph of the Umayyads in exile, ruling from Cordoba.

- Suddenly, the Muslim world was confronted by the unique situation of having three caliphs in place at the same time. Far from being a symbol of a united Islamic realm, the institution was becoming almost meaningless.

- The title didn't do Abd ar-Rahman any harm, and he reigned as caliph for more than 30 years. This period was marked by tolerance for all citizens of Cordoba, and by the continued increase of foreign scholars who moved to the city from around the Middle East and Europe.

**Scholarship Flourishes**

- Cordoba was a haven of original research. Scores of translators busied themselves with the great works of Ancient Greek texts, morphing them into Arabic, Latin, and Hebrew.

- The son of Abd al-Rahman III—and second caliph of Cordoba—was al-Hakam. He became central to the growth of Cordoba's great library, one of the most important repositories of knowledge on earth. The library had somewhere in the region of 400,000 different titles.

- Scholars and translators poured into Cordoba from across the Middle East, Persia, and Europe. By all accounts, Cordoba reached its brilliant zenith under al-Hakam II. According to one contemporary chronicler, there were 800 public schools in the city, as well as 3,000 mosques, and the same number of inns to accommodate visitors.

- The city also boasted 100,000 shops and 900 public baths. This at a time when church authorities condemned bathing as a dangerous, immoral, and heathen act to be avoided at all costs.

**Ethnic Diversity**

- Cordoba was an ethnically diverse place. Muslims of Arab descent made up about 10 percent of the population, a similar figure to North African Berbers and Jews alike.

- The majority native population—which was Christian or recently converted to Islam—found itself at the bottom of the social ladder, although typically still entitled to more legal protection as citizens than the smaller number of Muslims living in Christian-majority states elsewhere.

- No fewer than five languages existed in the city. Arabic, Latin, and Hebrew were employed on equal footing by Muslims, Christians and Jews respectively. Serious scholars would be expected to have a good command of all three. In addition, Andalusian Arabic and a Romance dialect like Latin—which would eventually become modern Spanish—were spoken to varying degrees by all three main faiths.

**Downfall**

- After al-Hakam II's death, power passed to his 10-year-old son, or, more accurately, into the hands of the child's unscrupulous vizier, who was also one of the caliphate's senior generals.

- Under the vizier, investment in scholarship was widely sidelined, and instead replaced with spending on mercenaries and a series of initially successful, expansionist wars. However, these wars created more enemies, and resurrected old resentment and rivalries within the caliphate.

- Certain Berbers turned against some Arabs. Some converts from Christianity backed their Muslim masters, while others did not. The Jewish population, likewise, found itself breaking into camps for, and against, whomever their local leadership was at that time.

- Urban centers found themselves being attacked by armed groups from the countryside, as law and order faltered. In this politically unstable period, arising from the military ambitions of those behind one young and inexperienced caliph after another, came the beginning of the end of the caliphate of Cordoba.

- Between al-Hakam II's death in 976, and the final end of the Caliphate of Cordoba 50 years later, in 1031, there would be another seven caliphs. None of them could match the talents of their most notable predecessors.

- The greatness of Cordoban scholarship didn't stop with the end of the Caliphate in 1031, however. Indeed, two of the city's greatest sons were born a century later. One was, the peerless Mediaeval Jewish philosopher, astronomer, and Torah scholar, Moses Maimonides; the other was the philosopher and polymath Ibn Rushd, known in the West as Averroes.

- On reflection, Cordoba's most important role was that of a bridge that brought together, in one place, the best available learning from Muslim, Christian, and Jewish Europe and the Middle East. In the process, it created a laboratory for further, even greater scholarship, which continued long after the caliphate faded away.

**Suggested Reading**

Bennison, *Cities in the Pre-Modern Islamic World*, chapter 5.

———, *The Great Caliphs*, chapter 2.

Gibbon, *Decline and Fall*, volume 5, chapter 52.

Hitti, *Capital Cities of Arab Islam*, chapter 6.

Hourani, *A History of the Arab Peoples*.

Kennedy, *Muslim Spain and Portugal*, chapters 2, 3, 4 and 5 .

Lapidus, *A History of Islamic Societies*.

**Questions to Consider**

1. Was a general policy of tolerance, and widespread freedom of religion, central to the success of Cordoba as a political centre and cultural hub?

2. Consider the cultural impacts and innovations of Ziryab. Can you think of similar characters that are responsible for introducing what would become such pervasive cultural norms as, for example, the three-course meal?

Lecture 13

# Al-Ghazali and Orthodoxy—1090

In terms of primacy, Muslims hold that not only is Muhammad the greatest of all prophets, but that there can't be another after him. With this point in mind, many Islamic scholars over the centuries have said that were it possible for the Islamic faith to accept, or produce, another prophet, it would be the man this lecture examines: Abu Hamid Muhammad al-Ghazali. This lecture consists of three parts: the life and times of al-Ghazali; al-Ghazali's writings, specifically a book, *The Incoherence of the Philosophers*; and the impact and continuing influence of al-Ghazali's work.

## The Life and Times of Al-Ghazali

- Al-Ghazali was born around 1058 in the Persian city of Tus, in Khurasan, now the most northeasterly province of Iran. Historically, it stretched into Afghanistan, and the modern central Asian states of Tajikistan, Turkmenistan, and Uzbekistan.

- His surname suggests that his family were spinners of wool. An early tradition states that his father died when he was young, so that al-Ghazali and his younger brother were raised by a local Sufi. If true, this could well explain the attachment both brothers had for this mystical, even esoteric, form of Islam.

- Al-Ghazali became known for his prodigious memory. One day, so the story goes, while still a teenager, he was returning home from a nearby town when he was attacked by bandits. They stole his notebooks and lectures. Bereft at this loss, al-Ghazali vowed to commit all his future learning to memory, as well as to paper.

- Early on, al-Ghazali began to study Islamic jurisprudence, in the nearby city and provincial capital of Nishapur. In 1085, when al-Ghazali was about 28 years of age, he left Nishapur for the city of Isfahan, also in Persia, or modern Iran. Isfahan was the capital of the still-expanding Seljuk Empire under the sultan Malik Shah.

- Ethnically a Turkic people, the Seljuks emerged at a time when the Abbasid caliphate seemed to be falling apart. The Abbasids relied for their survival on the Seljuks' military support. The Shia Fatimids in Cairo set themselves up as a rival religious authority.

- It was largely in response to the Fatimids that the Seljuks established a number of educational institutions throughout their realm. Collectively called the *Nizamiyyah*—after the Sultan's senior vizier, Nizam al-Mulk—the most important of these institutes was in Baghdad.

- Still based in Isfahan, al-Ghazali's erudition and abilities as a teacher had gained him notice from the senior vizier, Nizam al-Mulk. Impressed with his insight and knowledge of Islam, al-Mulk awarded al-Ghazali a string of titles, including "Brightness of the Faith" and "Greatest of the Religious Leaders."

- There was also promotion, and a move to Baghdad, as al-Ghazali was made senior professor of theology and philosophy of the Nizamiyyah. As the most prestigious school of Sunni theology at the time, it had been set up explicitly to tackle the rising threat from the Fatimids' Ismaili-Shia university in Cairo, known as al-Azhar.

**Al-Ghazali in Baghdad**

- When al-Ghazali arrived in Baghdad in 1091, the political aspects of his new post were just as important as the religious ones. He had to produce original research; deal with court intrigue and the sultan's vizier; and handle theological challenges. Last but not least, the Fatimids were suspected of hiring assassins to kill as many of the Seljuk and Abbasid leadership as possible, as well as their notable employees.

- If a hit list existed, al-Ghazali's name would have been on it. Within a year of al-Ghazali's arrival in Baghdad, the sultan Malik Shah and his vizier, Nizam al-Mulk, both had been murdered. Fingers were pointed at the Fatimids in Cairo.

- Following the murders of these two most powerful men in the realm, the Seljuk Empire started to fall into disarray. Al-Ghazali, while he might have feared for his life, didn't need to worry about his job, and he remained in Baghdad. There, he continued to lecture to packed auditoriums of 300 or more students, as well as write scores of sermons and longer works of Islamic jurisprudence and theology.

- Much of al-Ghazali's time was spent receiving visitors and responding to letters asking his advice and opinion on theological and legal matters. His responses offered a vigorous defense of Sunni orthodoxy.

**Al-Ghazali Wanders**

- In 1095, Pope Urban II launched the First Crusade with the goal of taking Jerusalem back from the Muslims. That same year, al-Ghazali had a crisis of confidence that some have seen as a mental breakdown. He quit his job and spent the next decade wandering the Muslim world.

- Outlining a new intellectual framework that René Descartes—the father of modern European philosophy—would follow more than 500 years later, al-Ghazali set out his mission as being to question everything he'd ever thought to be true.

- In spite of travelling in the humble garb of a Sufi—what we might think of as a monk—his fame meant that he was often recognized as he went from town to town. In his autobiography, *Deliverance from Error*, al-Ghazali wrote how he went first to Damascus and lived as a Sufi, replacing all comfort for a contemplative, solitary life.

- *Deliverance from Error* is a deeply personal work, which displays a great deal of humility and doubt. In it, Al-Ghazali relates how one day, upon entering a Mosque, he overheard a preacher praising his work. In response, al-Ghazali ran away before the devil could fill his heart with pride.

- He gave away all of his money and worldly possessions, and wandered on to Jerusalem. In that city, he gazed on the Dome of the Rock before moving on to Mecca and Medina. In all, al-Ghazali spent most of a decade wandering and wondering, before resurfacing in Nishapur, just a few miles from his hometown.

**Al-Ghazali's Writing**

- Apart from growing more sympathetic to the mystical form of Islam found in Sufism, al-Ghazali also spent this time writing. Al-Ghazali's published works are why he's still such an important figure. Particulalry impactful was *The Incoherence of the Philosophers*.

- In Islam, there's a tradition that each century, God sends a man to renew the faith. It seems that the Seljuk leadership persuaded al-Ghazali that he was this renewer—*mujuaddid* in Arabic—for Islam's fifth century. As such, anything al-Ghazali said, or wrote, now carried an authority virtually above any other on earth.

- With this in mind, it's easy to see why *The Incoherence of the Philosophers*—which Al-Ghazali published when he was about 33 years of age—became one of the most important books ever written. Ultimately, it would determine the course of Islamic theology.

- The "incoherence" at the heart of al-Ghazali's attack is that philosophy lacks the faith component that he saw as an essential element of religion. By philosophers, he specifically means Neoplatonists, influenced by Plato.

- The leading Muslim proponent of Neoplatonist theology was Ibn Sina, known in the West as Avicenna. Avicenna's life's work tried to reconcile rational philosophy with Islamic theology. His goal was to prove the existence of God through reason and logic alone. And it was this that al-Ghazali wrote against. Arranged in 20 chapters, each one is a refutation of the ideas of Avicenna and his followers.

- In all, al-Ghazali saw 17 of these 20 chapters, or ideas, as misguided but forgivable heresies. The remaining three, however, he said were so wrong as to be dangerous to the faith. As such, they were heresies.

    - The first of these heretical ideas, from al-Ghazali's standpoint, was the philosophers' view that the world is eternal. For al-Ghazali, this was completely unacceptable because it contradicts the Islamic belief that God created the world at some point in time, and before this it did not exist.

    - The second opinion that al-Ghazali condemned as irreligious is the philosophers' view that God doesn't know everything. Al-Ghazali condemned this view absolutely, because the idea of God's omniscience—of God as all knowing—is another central tenet of Islamic theology.

    - The third error that pushed the philosophers into heresy was their questioning of the bodily resurrection. For Islam and al-Ghazali, the bodily resurrection on Judgment Day is an unassailable article of faith.

- A prolific author, al-Ghazali wrote more than 70 works on Islamic theology, jurisprudence, mysticism and philosophy. He also wrote fluently in two languages: his mother tongue of Persian, and Arabic. In both languages, he sprinkled his texts with parables, not unlike the New Testament stories told by Jesus.

- Other works that remain essential parts of al-Ghazali's output include *Deliverance from Error,* and his detailed study of Islam called *The Revival of Religious Sciences.*

- Al-Ghazali's personal quest for answers is perhaps clearest in his autobiography. In that book, published just five years before his death in 1111, al-Ghazali betrays an approach to philosophy and religion that's been described as showing the courage to know, and the courage to doubt.

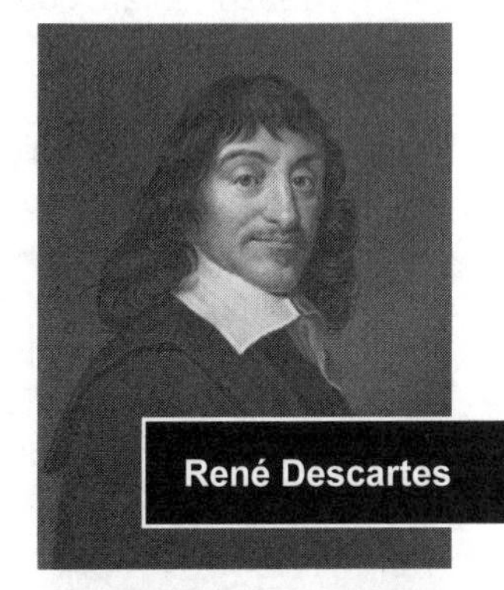

René Descartes

- In this respect, much philosophical thought of the European Enlightenment 500 years later echoed al-Ghazali. The 17th-century French philosopher Descartes closely followed al-Ghazali's approach in questioning everything. His writings, and those of the 17th-century French mathematician Blaise Pascal, both betray some distinctly Ghazalian threads.

Blaise Pascal

### The Influence of Al-Ghazali

- As a religious scholar and jurist, al-Ghazali was often responding to the big challenges of the day. In political terms, one of the biggest challenges was the rise of the Isma'ili-Shia Fatimids in North Africa.

- Internally, orthodox Sunni thinkers saw their faith as being under attack from the growing influence of Neoplatonism in Islamic theology.

- It is in this context that Avicenna was arguing for Neoplatonism and other forms of deductive reasoning, arguing that God had provided man with the power of reason, and that through reason man could come to know God and understand the divine purpose.

- On the other side, al-Ghazali maintained a more orthodox approach, saying that while reason was a gift from God, there were limits to what one could understand through reason alone. And if it were possible for mankind to come to any understanding of the divine, it would be through faith alone. If this sounds familiar, it's because the same arguments played out in Christendom during the 16th-century Reformation.

- Half a century after al-Ghazali died, the great Andalusian polymath Ibn Rushd—better known in the West as Averroes—tried to reclaim Aristotelian logic for Islam. But the young challenger failed to land a serious blow on the reputation of the older man.

- Al-Ghazali died in his bed at the age of 52 or 53. Under his head was a piece of paper on which he'd written a series of verses. They included the following lines:

    Do not believe that this corpse you see is me.
    I am a spirit and this is nothing but flesh.
    It was my abode and garment for a time. …
    I am a pearl that has left its shell deserted,
    It was my prison, where I spent my time in grief.
    I am a bird and this was my cage,
    From where I have flown forth and it is left as a token.
    Praise be to God, who has now set me free.

- As al-Ghazali suggests, it would be his words that really mattered, resonating as they do across the Muslim world and beyond—nearly 1,000 years after his death.

**Suggested Reading**

Al-Ghazali, *Al-Ghazali's Path to Sufism*.

———, *The Incoherence of the Philosophers*.

Canfield, *Turko-Persia in Historical Perspective*.

Crone, *God's Rule*, chapter 16.

Hitti, *Makers of Arab History*, chapter 8.

Lapidus, *A History of Islamic Societies*, chapter 12.

**Questions to Consider**

1. Consider al-Ghazali's condemnation of what he saw as the Neoplatonists' three heretical views of God and Islamic theology. What parallels do we find in the philosophical and theological traditions of the other Abrahamic, monotheistic religions, namely Judaism and Christianity?

2. In 1095, al-Ghazali left Baghdad, walking away from the most prestigious university post in the Islamic world at that time, exchanging fame and fortune for a decade of near solitary wandering and contemplation in the more mystical, Sufi tradition. Do you think al-Ghazali's decision was the result of exhaustion leading to a mental breakdown, as some scholars say; as a religious experience; or as some combination of the two?

Lecture 14

# Crusaders Capture Jerusalem—1099

The capture of Jerusalem, on July 15, 1099, marked the effective end of the First Crusade, which had the stated aim of recovering Jerusalem from Muslim occupiers. In this lecture, we're going to start by looking at the political situation in Europe and the Middle East when the First Crusade began, and some of the reasons for it. Then, we'll examine the First Crusade itself, from the call to arms to the final assault against Jerusalem. We'll conclude by assessing the immediate aftermath and long-term outcomes.

## Background on Jerusalem

- Jerusalem is one of the oldest urban centers on earth, with evidence of it first being settled more than 5,000 years ago. Israel's Central Bureau of Statistics pegged Jerusalem's recent population at about 800,000 people, of whom 62 percent were Jewish, 35 percent Muslim, and 2 percent Christian, with 1 percent choosing not to be identified by religion.

- Jerusalem has been destroyed at least twice, besieged on at least two dozen occasions, attacked more than 50 times, and been captured and recaptured 44 times—in recorded history alone.

- In religious terms, Jerusalem is of enormous importance to the three great Abrahamic religions: Judaism, Christianity, and Islam. When Muhammad experienced his first revelation in 610, it was in the direction of Jerusalem that he and the first Muslims prayed. This practice continued during the course of Islam's first 14 years.

- Having been alternately in Persian or Byzantine hands for centuries, Jerusalem was conquered by a Muslim army in 637 and ruled by various rival Muslim dynasties up until the time our story begins.

**Background on the First Crusade**

- Many of the Saxon, Hungarian, and Viking tribes that covered great swathes of Europe had been properly Christianized. But what had been a relatively stable heart of Europe—the Carolingian Empire, which reached its height under Charlemagne—was now falling apart.

- The warrior class that had recently been employed (and constrained by ties of kinship) was now unemployed, and at a loose end. The freelance fighting undertaken by this warrior class was responsible for a great deal of mayhem across the Holy Roman Empire.

- The Peace and Truce of God was a movement instituted by the Catholic Church at this time. It was an attempt to draw up battle lines, including the protection of non-combatants, church property, and setting limits on when fighting could or could not take place.

- In 1054, the Great Schism occurred. This was the moment when Christianity in Europe became divided between Roman Catholic Western Europe, on the one hand, and the Eastern Orthodox faith that covered the Eastern Roman Empire, the Byzantine Empire.

- Some historians have suggested that the desire of Rome to impose authority over the Eastern Orthodoxy was one reason for the First Crusade. However, there's no mention of this in Papal correspondence that survives from the period, so it's impossible to say for certain.

- Byzantium had Catholic Norman enemies to its west, in modern Italy; as well as the Muslim, Turkic, Seljuk Empire to its east, in Central Asia and modern Turkey. By 1095, the Byzantine Empire would find itself confined to the Balkans and north-western Anatolia in modern-Turkey, and seemingly set to lose more territory very soon.

**The Seljuks and the Fatimids**

- The Seljuk Turks—when they eventually came storming into the Middle East from their Central Asian homeland—were a new power to be reckoned with. They overran everything in their path, taking control of the Abbasid capital of Baghdad, in 1055, and invading the Byzantine Empire a decade later.

- As the Sunni Seljuk Turks swept into the region from the north—defeating their fellow Sunni Muslim Abbasids, and the Orthodox Byzantines—there was yet another regional power we have to take note of: the Ismaili-Shia Fatimids.

- Much of North Africa and Syria had been in the hands of the Shia Fatimids including ever since they'd declared a Shia caliphate in 909, and taken Jerusalem in 969. Now, fighting between Seljuks and Fatimids in the region became fierce, with the Seljuks eventually winning Jerusalem from the Fatimids in 1073.

- But Seljuk rule of the Holy City was not a happy time. Where once tolerance had prevailed, intolerance now reigned. Christian and Jewish pilgrims—and residents alike—were attacked, robbed, and killed.

- Kidnapping for ransom became commonplace, as did the wanton destruction of non-Muslim holy sites, to the horror of Jews, Christians, and non-Seljuk Muslims alike. Terrified refugees made their way to Europe, bringing with them tales of misery and mayhem. Calls were soon heard for something to be done about the hardships endured by Christians in the Holy Land.

- However, even as the Crusaders set off for Jerusalem in 1098, the Fatimids retook Jerusalem from the Seljuks. To highlight the political complexities, we can say that Crusader victories against Seljuk forces in Anatolia, or modern-day Turkey, delighted many Fatimid rulers.

- When the Crusaders pressed on into Syrian territory, however, the Fatimids' opinion shifted. While the Crusaders were besieging the ancient Greek city of Antioch they received Fatimid emissaries who suggested an alliance against the Seljuks and Abbasids. Temporary alliances between Franks and Saracens against other Muslims were commonplace during this period, as were unions between Crusaders and Muslim forces against fellow crusaders.

- So, far from being a black-and-white state of affairs, the political situation in Europe and the Middle East was a mass of complexity, with numerous competing interests at work.

**The Call to Arms**

- An appeal to Pope Urban II for help, made by the Byzantine emperor Alexios I, must have seemed tempting. Cynically, a weakened Byzantium might allow for territorial expansion by the Bishop of Rome, his allies, or proxies. Plus, European society had a restless and under-employed warrior class.

- On November 27, 1095—at the Council of Clermont, in south-central France—Pope Urban II made his fateful call to arms. While there are six accounts of what the Pope said, only one of these was written by an actual eye witness, Fulcher of Chartres. According to his account, while the Pope's speech urged men to go and fight in the Holy Land, he was also very concerned with the violent anarchy then afflicting Europe. Per Chartres, the Pope never mentioned Jerusalem by name.

- In August 1096, when the first wave of Crusader armies headed east, they numbered roughly 5,000 knights and as many as 30,000 foot soldiers. The vast majority were French or

Norman, although there were also German and southern Italian contingents.

- As they passed through modern-day Germany, bands of Crusaders attacked local Jewish populations, killing hundreds, perhaps thousands, in spite of attempts by local churchmen to stop them.

- As each force travelled towards their destination, they attracted more followers, mostly untrained and ill-prepared peasants. By some estimates, this peasant army, or mob, would number as many as 100,000, although few such crusaders ever reached Jerusalem.

- The princes and knights eventually met up in Constantinople, where they expected help, if not the leadership, of Alexios I. But the emperor showed no inclination to lead the knights anywhere, except across the Bosphorus, and out of his territory as quickly as possible.

- This is not as surprising as it might sound. Among the crusaders were any number of princes who'd previously invaded Byzantium and waged war against the emperor. He was, naturally, wary of their intentions now.

- As the European Christians inched closer to the Holy Land, the Fatimid Muslim governor made preparations to defend the city. For one thing, he expelled its Orthodox Christian population, believing they'd fight against him, once the crusaders approached. In the interim, the crusaders were delayed by an ultimately successful, eight-month siege of Antioch, 500 miles to the north. And so they rested for six months before marching on.

- They first laid eyes on Jerusalem on June 7, 1099. By all accounts, many of the Crusaders wept at the sight.

**The Assault on Jerusalem**

- The original force had been massively depleted by death in battle and disease, as well as by desertion. By the time they prepared to assault the city, the crusader army had been reduced to a force of about 12,000, including 1,500 mounted knights.

- One of the best eyewitness accounts of the short siege and fall of Jerusalem is the *Gesta Francorum*, or *Deeds of the Franks*, by an ordinary, anonymous soldier. There was never enough food or shelter, and once they reached Jerusalem, a shortage of water caused real problems. This is one important reason why the Crusaders attacked, after just a little over a month: Men and animals were literally dying of thirst.

- Added to this, the Fatimids were known to have sent a relief force from Cairo, while the Crusaders—thousands of miles from home, and alone in enemy territory— had no such chance of reinforcements.

- In order to attack Jerusalem's defensive walls, the Crusaders need to build siege towers. The *Gesta Francorum* talks about

The Siege and Destruction of Jerusalem

the construction of two, 50-foot siege towers—with wood brought from miles around—as well as from the cannibalization of two Genoese galleys recently arrived at Jaffa. The Crusade military leaders decided to launch a two-pronged attack against city walls.

- The carnage that befell the defenders and citizens of Jerusalem was awful. While mass killings were common practice, after cities were taken in mediaeval warfare, what took place in Jerusalem was beyond the commonplace. The city's Jews, having fought side-by-side with the Muslim defenders, were put to the sword just as readily.

**Aftermath of the Fall of Jerusalem**

- In simple housekeeping terms, the most pressing concern for the Crusaders—after installing themselves as Jerusalem's rulers—was to clean up the city. Thousands of corpses had to be disposed of quickly in order to prevent the spread of disease, let alone the stench that soon hung over the city.

- Leadership of the city—and the newly created Kingdom of Jerusalem—was handed to Godfrey of Bouillon. Godfrey, one of the leading lights of the Crusade and the final assault, refused to be called king.

- Between taking Jerusalem and his death the following year, Godfrey successfully defended his new realm against an attack by the Fatimids, as well another challenge from the Latin Patriarch of Jerusalem.

- As a turning point in the history of the Middle East, it's perhaps ironic that the greatest, long-term impact of the First Crusade was felt in the West. Ever since Pope Urban II uttered his rallying cry to reclaim Jerusalem, historians have been unable even to agree on how many Crusades there were, with some saying seven, others nine, in addition to numerous, smaller, unnumbered crusading events.

- And since they envisaged different aims besides re-taking Jerusalem, they shouldn't be lumped together, although in the popular imagination that's exactly what happens.

- Mediaeval Arab chroniclers saw the European invaders as cruel, ignorant savages, who represented an altogether inferior culture to their own. The great English scholar of the Crusades, Steven Runciman, tended to agree.

- In establishing Crusader kingdoms, however, Western European cities such as Genoa and Venice began to flourish, as trade with the Middle East was opened.

- The Kingdom of Jerusalem didn't survive in perpetuity. The dream of Christian rule over the holy city came to an end in 1187.

**Suggested Reading**

Gabrieli, *Arab Historians of the Crusades.*

Maalouf, *The Crusades Through Arab Eyes.*

Riley-Smith, *Oxford History of the Crusades.*

Runciman, *A History of the Crusades*, volume 1, book 5.

**Questions to Consider**

1. As a holy city to the three major Abrahamic religions—Judaism, Christianity, and Islam—Jerusalem has been one of the most contested and fought-over cities in history. Try to imagine the different claims made on the city as if you were a member of another faith, or none, and consider the arguments for and against such claims.

2. How far do you think the Crusades were driven by genuine religious fervour, and how much by other considerations, such as economic conditions in Europe or a yearning for travel, adventure, and possible material gain?

Lecture 15

# Muslims in the Court of Roger II—1130

The life and times of Roger II, king of Sicily, are rich and intricate. In this lecture, we'll divide Roger's story into three parts. The first part traces the path of how the Normans—led by Roger's father, also named Roger—came south from modern-day France to establish a kingdom in southern Italy: the Kingdom of Sicily. The second part stops to look at life in the kingdom, including art and architecture, the economy, and the legal system. The third part assesses Roger II's legacy.

The Coronation Mantle of Roger II

## Norman Rule

- How was it that the Normans came to rule southern Italy, including Sicily? Sicily had been a possession of the Byzantine Empire from the late 7th century forward. Muslim raiders periodically sailed from North Africa, and launched attacks on the island, eventually turning to conquest. The Muslim conquest of the island was a slow and steady affair, and it would take 75 years before Byzantine rule finally ended, in 902.

- Meanwhile, between the time the Muslims gained a foothold in 827 and for nearly the next 200 years of their rule, Sicily's population remained Christian.

- To the north, the Normans were running out of space within the confines of Frankish, or French, territory—in what we know of today as continental Europe. Consequently, their younger sons had to look elsewhere for domains of their own. Descended from the Vikings, and renowned as warriors, they migrated south to Italy and elsewhere, oftentimes taking employment as mercenaries.

- Indeed, upon settling in southern Italy, these Normans were happy to accept employment with the various rival powers that were vying for power in the region. Among the main factions were the Lombards, a Germanic tribe that held sway in what we'd call northern Italy today. The Lombards' main rivals in the south of the country were the Byzantines, who came from the Eastern Roman Empire, and its capital, Constantinople.

- The Norman mercenaries—fighting on either side only so long as it suited them—soon turned on their erstwhile employers. As they grew stronger, they began carving out territories of their own. Within about 50 years of their arrival in southern Italy, the Normans had overthrown a succession of weaker rulers. And that is where we encounter them, poised at the Strait of Messina, gazing towards Sicily.

- In recent decades, as Sicily had come under the rule of first one, and then another, Muslim dynasty from North Africa, there was no longer a single Muslim ruler. Instead, there were numerous, small, squabbling fiefdoms, who were far from united by their faith or anything else.

- But by then, the Christian church had split into two factions, as well—one in the west, and one in the east—to be known as the Roman Catholic and Eastern Orthodox faiths, respectively. Suddenly, Muslim-ruled Sicily, with its majority Byzantine Christian population, was a prize worth taking for the pope in Rome.

- With the blessing of the pope, Nicholas II, that the Normans invaded Sicily in 1061. This successful, and ultimately conclusive, invasion was led by Roger Bosso. He was a member of the famous Norman family, the Hautvilles, and kinsman to William the Conqueror.

- It wouldn't be until 1091 that the last of the Arab strongholds was defeated, and Sicily placed under united, Norman rule. Still, by the time of his death in 1101, Roger would be known as Count Roger of Sicily, and he would have married three times, fathering 12 daughters and four sons.

- Among his four sons, the eldest predeceased him while his second son contracted leprosy and, with no hope of inheriting, retired to a monastery. Roger's youngest two sons were the product of a third marriage. It was the last of these prospective male heirs—his namesake—who would become King Roger II of Sicily in 1130.

- By this time, the Norman Kingdom of Sicily covered territory that stretched far beyond a united island, to also include all of southern Italy, as well as the strategically vital island of Malta, and parts of the North African coast (namely modern day Tunisia, and bits of Algeria and Libya).

- All of this took place against the backdrop of the Crusades in the Middle East. Typically thought of as Christian holy wars, there were other controversial forms of Crusades. One of these involved the incumbent pope declaring a Crusade against another local European political opponent. The first person against whom this sort of crusade was declared was Roger II of Sicily by Pope Innocent II.

**Sicily under Roger II**

- In 1140, once Roger II quelled the various petty revolts that had destabilized Sicily and its surrounding area for generations, he promulgated a new legal code: the Assizes of Ariano, in 1140.

- Consisting of 40 clauses, the Assizes are a remarkably forward-looking set of laws that touched on almost every area of contemporary legal concern. They confirmed the king as the sole lawmaker in the kingdom, and that all Sicilians—Norman, Latin, Lombard, Greek, Jew, Muslim and Arab—were equal under the laws. Unusual for the day, these laws also took commoners' rights into consideration.

- The Assizes also established a powerful bureaucracy, and brought the existing feudal system firmly under Roger's control. They drew on various legal traditions in order to produce an equitable legal code that became widely recognized as one of the most advanced—and just—systems of its time. While the pre-existing Norman and French legal codes are obviously apparent in the Assizes, also present are legal theories from Byzantine—and even Muslim *sharia*—law.

- Elements of Islamic law found their way into other parts of Europe, because the Assizes of Ariano were eventually exported to other parts of the continent, notably to Norman France and Norman Britain.

- The most obvious area where previously established Muslim legal practice was adopted was in matters of trade, such as customs and tariffs. The need for trust and a common set of principles between merchants from different national, religious, and cultural backgrounds was obviously crucial for a kingdom such as Roger's.

Cappella Palatina

**The Economy**

- With peace at hand, and a new legal code in place, Roger sought to stimulate trade by introducing coins of a lower denomination. That allowed for more efficient and accurate transactions.

- Roger also stamped coins in Latin and Arabic alphabets and dates alike, immediately increasing their appeal among Muslim traders, and stimulating trade with the Muslim world. Roger was the only Western ruler minting gold coins at the time—one sure sign of a successful economic policy.

- While such innovations were deeply unpopular in the rest of Italy—where Roger's growing prosperity was seen as a threat—they proved to be good news for Sicily. Exports of products such as wheat, citrus, and cheese grew year on year, as did imports of luxury goods, and tax revenue.

- As the kingdom became more prosperous, Sicily also saw an increase in grand buildings, many of which were designed in a unique and innovative style, known by the rather clunking label Norman-Arab-Byzantine.

- The high water mark of the Norman-Arab-Byzantine style is undoubtedly the Cappella Palatina—or Palatine Chapel—which can be seen today, in Palermo, in all its glory. Commissioned by Roger II in 1132, the chapel is a fascinating marriage of Norman, Byzantium, and Muslim Middle Eastern influences all rolled into one.

***The Book of Roger***

- The most fascinating cultural exchanges that took place during Roger II's 24-year reign has to be a book whose Arabic title literally translates as, "The Book of Pleasant Journeys into Faraway Lands." Alas, the English title by which it's more commonly known loses all the poetry of the original, as we call it simply *The Book of Roger*.

- Commissioned by Roger II in 1138, it would take its author—Muhammad al-Idrisi—15 years to complete. But it, too, was well worth the effort. Born in the northern Moroccan coastal city of Ceuta, al-Idrisi was the foremost geographer of his day. Roger wanted a world atlas from al-Idrisi. Al-Idrisi was able to provide just that.

- One reason it took al-Idrisi 15 years to produce *The Book of Roger* was because rather than rely solely on his own experiences and knowledge of the world, he interviewed scores of travellers, merchants, pilgrims, and explorers. Al-Idrisi also sent out agents to ask questions of scholars in other parts of the world, doing everything possible to include only genuine knowledge.

- Written in Latin and Arabic—both languages in which Roger was fluent—the map follows the geographical system established by the ancient Greco-Egyptian geographer and author Ptolemy, first dividing the earth into seven distinct climate zones. Each of these seven zones is further divided into 10 smaller sections, with every one of them mapped in as much detail as possible.

- When assembled, the result is a single map of the known world at that time, including all of Europe and Eurasia, and the northern portions of Africa. The remarkable *Book of Roger* would remain the most accurate world map and gazetteer for the next 300 years.

**Roger II's Death**

- Just a few weeks after al-Idrisi submitted the *Book of Roger*, the king died at age 58. This death posed a sad moment for al-Idrisi, and marked the end of an era both for him and Sicily broadly.

- Roger II of Sicily wasn't the most powerful, or most famous, king who ever lived. But he represented a new face of European–Middle Eastern relations. And he presents us with a third view of the Crusades that looks beyond the simplistic narrative that tried to categorize these wars as some sort of existential—and eternal—fight between Christianity and Islam.

- Instead, Roger understood that the Crusades were a much more complex set of power struggles, which were more about power on earth—including Europe—than they were about theological differences.

- The tolerant and enlightened approach that Roger took to his subjects of all faiths continued under his successors. Thirty years after Roger's death, the Muslim historian and traveller from Andalusia, Ibn al-Athir, wrote how surprised he was at the warm welcome he received from the Christian Normans.

- When another Muslim chronicler from Andalusia, Ibn Jubair, visited Sicily in 1184, he, too, was astonished to find so many Christians able to speak Arabic. And Ibn Jubair made note that the kingdom's coins were struck with Western and *hijra* dates, and that many official documents were written in Arabic.

- Norman rule over Sicily ended in 1198, with the decline of Roger's line. The marriage of his last heir, Constance, saw the kingdom pass into the hands of a Germanic royal family. Alas, the tolerance that had marked Norman Sicily was not a feature of life that transferred to these new rulers. And the lot of the Muslim population declined accordingly.

- A generation later, in 1224, the Muslim population was expelled from Sicily. In spite of this, Arabic and Islamic influences persisted there until about 1300, when they were finally extinguished. As the Kingdom of Sicily lost its tolerant and pragmatic approach to governing its own people, so, too, it started to lose access to the markets of Muslim Spain and Portugal and North Africa. Sicily's heyday was behind it.

**Suggested Reading**

Hitti, *History of the Arabs*, chapter 42.

Houben, *Roger II of Sicily*.

Loud, *Roger II and the Creation of the Kingdom of Sicily*.

Norwich, *The Kingdom in the Sun, 1130–1194*.

Riley-Smith, *Oxford History of the Crusades*.

Runciman, *A History of the Crusades*, volume 2.

**Questions to Consider**

1. What character traits might be necessary to produce a ruler as wise and tolerant as Roger II, and how far do you think this perceived tolerance could survive a challenge to his political authority?

2. Employing the best scholars he could, regardless of their faith, clearly made the Kingdom of Sicily a richer and stronger state. With this example in mind, why do you think more rulers from this period in history failed to follow suit?

Lecture 16

# Saladin: Chivalry and Conquest—1187

In the West, Saladin may be the most famous Muslim in history. Saladin's life was a mixture of conqeusts and battle mixed with gestures of kindness. This lecture traces his early life and his initial rise to power. Then, it moves on to his dealings with two foes: Raynald of Chatillon, whom Saladin was not fond of, and Richard the Lionheart, whom Saladin treated a bit more kindly. The lecture particularly focuses on the Saladin's actions during the decisive Battle of Hattin and the more protracted Third Crusade.

**Saladin's Initial Rise**

- Saladin was a Kurd, not an Arab. He was born Yusuf ibn Ayyub—or Joseph, son of Job—in the town of Tikrit, in modern day Iraq, in the year 1138. Saladin was well educated. He knew much about Islam, and was fluent in Kurdish, Arabic, and probably Turkish. He also had a good grounding in Euclidean geometry, astronomy, and the genealogies of the great families in Arabic history (which would have included military history).

Saladin

- At the time when Saladin came into the world, there was nothing to prevent Kurds such as him—from an orthodox Sunni Muslim family—from rising to senior positions within the Seljuk Empire. A Seljuk-dominated Turko-Persian ruling court had recently swept to power across much of the region.

- The Abbasids in Baghdad held the title of caliphate, but they'd recently lost domains to rising powers such as the Seljuks.

- While the Seljuks ruled much of the Abbasid empire, Syria was administered on their behalf by the Zengid dynasty, of Oghuz Turk origin. At the same time, Egypt was ruled by the Ismai'ili-Shia Fatimids, from their capital, Cairo. The Seljuk-Fatimid rivalry was intense. The Seljuks were watchful for any weak point in Cairo's defences.

- When a recently overthrown Fatimid vizier arrived, seeking Seljuk help to regain his position, it was Saladin's uncle, Shirukh, who was selected to lead the military campaign. Shirukh insisted that the 26-year-old Saladin accompany him. From there, several twists occurred:

    - The overthrown Fatimid vizier, along with Saladin and Shirukh's Seljuk army, journeyed to Egypt to do battle with the vizier's local rival. Saladin had his first taste of battle. Their victory restored the Fatimid vizier to power.

    - Shirukh then refused to leave Egypt. The vizier, having relied on a foreign army to restore him to power, now found he could stay in power only at the behest of that same foreign force.

    - In response, the vizier signed an alliance with an army of European crusaders, hoping that they would defeat the Zengid forces of Saladin and his uncle. After a campaign that lasted several years, the Fatimid vizier was caught and executed.

    - Shirukh was installed as the country's new vizier, while the Fatimid caliph was allowed to remain in his position, under Zengid control. Later in the same year, however, Shirukh died.

- The Zengids now appointed another vizier, this one rejected by the Fatimid caliph. The Egyptian caliph appointed Saladin to the post of vizier, instead.

- Saladin sent for his father and the rest of his family to join him in Cairo, and appointed them to senior government positions, further consolidating his position at the heart of the Fatimid government. Then, in 1171, the Fatimid caliph died, and Saladin appointed himself local ruler, under the nominal authority of the Baghdad-based Abbasid caliphate.

- After 250 years of Isma'ili-Shia-Fatimid rule in Egypt, Saladin had restored Sunni orthodoxy to one of the region's wealthiest, and most important, countries. He'd also restored some degree of prestige to the Abbasid caliphate in Baghdad.

- Three years later, in 1174, the Abbasid caliph—Saladin's ally—died, likely by poisoning. Taking advantage of more confusion and the power struggles that resulted, Saladin now made the fateful decision to declare himself ruler of Egypt and Syria.

- Rather than living a life of excess, Saladin gave up wine, and gave away the accumulated wealth in the Fatimid treasury. Not only did this gesture win (or buy) him many allies, it also quite reasonably established his reputation for generosity.

**The Battle of Hattin**

- This lecture's turning point revolves around the Battle of Hattin, which occured in northern Palestine in July, 1187. Saladin—like the crusaders—was motivated by a combination of religious fervour and political ambition. The goal for each was always Jerusalem: the crusaders wanted to hold it, Saladin to take it.

- The actions of the crusader Raynald of Chatillon rank him as the villain of this story. Raynald's and Saladin's paths first crossed at the Battle of Montgisard in November 1177, in which Saladin marched on Jerusalem, was repulsed, and was lucky to escape with his life.

- Saladin agreed to a truce with Raynald's master, King Baldwin "the Leper." But Raynald broke the terms of that truce to pillage, torture, and murder Muslim pilgrims in the *Hijaz*, or western Arabia. Another truce was signed a few years later, but Raynald again showed his contempt for such agreements, and attacked another caravan of pilgrims.

- In 1187, Saladin has decided to deal the crusaders a fatal blow. His force of some 30,000 included more than 12,000 well-trained cavalry. In tactical terms, the crusader army—which numbered about 20,000—had no need to march out from its well-defended location. But Christians who urged caution were accused of cowardice. And so they all marched out into a desert plain, where water was scarce.

- The crusaders, after a day's march, found themselves caught between the Horns of Hattin—named for two hills that dominate the landscape—when they suddenly were surrounded by Saladin's forces.

- Wracked with thirst, the crusaders contended with Saladins' archers firing at them, and with smoke that poured into their ranks from fires lit by Saladin's troops. This made their thirst even worse. Exhausted and desperate, the crusaders launched a number of disorganized and ill-disciplined attacks, each one ending in slaughter.

- By day's end, only about 3,000 crusaders survived. About 200 of the elite Knights Templar and Knights Hospitallers were executed on Saladin's order.

- The remaining prisoners were taken to Damascus, where they would wait for ransoms to be paid. Among the prisoners taken were Guy of Lusignan, king of Jerusalem, and Raynald.

- Eventually, Saladin advanced on Raynald, and then beheaded him at Guy's feet. With Guy trembling before him, Saladin is reported to have said: "This man was killed solely because of his malfeasance and treachery."

- To Guy's obvious relief, he added: "It is not the wont of kings, to kill kings; but that man had transgressed all bounds, and therefore I treated him thus."

**After Hattin**

- After the crusaders' devastating defeat at the Battle of Hattin, Saladin's forces were also able to take (or re-take) a total of 52 towns and castles. The biggest prize of all fell on October 2, 1187, when the siege of Jerusalem ended, and the city was handed over to Saladin.

- In stark contrast to the Christian-led massacre of the city's Muslims and Jews that followed the crusaders' seizure of Jerusalem in 1099, Saladin did not slaughter the city's population. For one thing, the crusaders defending the city had threatened to destroy the sacred Dome of the Rock unless their safety was guaranteed. This persuaded Saladin to agree to terms whereby military defenders and the civilian population alike were ransomed.

- Jerusalem's Latin patriarch negotiated the ransom of about 18,000 prisoners. Of the remaining 14,000, Saladin granted his brother's request that 1,000 were to be given to him for his personal use. The brother then released them en masse, demonstrating a magnitude of compassion that was wholly absent among the crusaders in 1099. Saladin also listened to the pleas of those too poor to pay ransom, and released many of them too.

- One assessment of Saladin's actions is that they were humane but strategically unsound: In some instances, crusader knights regrouped. Saladin would later lose control of a number of coastal cities in the region, notably Acre, which gave the next wave of crusaders a foothold in the Middle East for the next century.

- The shock of Jerusalem's loss reverberated through Christian Europe. According to one Christian chronicler, Pope Urban III died of shock on hearing the news. His successor, Gregory VIII, called for another Crusade to retake it.

- One place where Saladin failed to consolidate the Muslims' victories was the port of Tyre, in modern Lebanon. This strategically vital seaside city became a major port of entry for many eager crusaders at the start of the Third Crusade, only a short time hence.

**Richard I**

- It would take two years for the next wave of crusaders to land in the Muslim heartland. Among their number was England's King Richard I, *Coeur de Lion*, or Richard the Lionheart. Soon after Richard arrived, he sent a message to Saladin, requesting a meeting. But Saladin responded that it wasn't customary for rival kings to meet in wartime until after a truce had been agreed to.

- The Muslim city of Acre, in modern Israel, fell to a crusader army after a siege that lasted almost two years, from August 1189 to July 1191. Richard and Saladin then entered into negotiations for the release of the nearly 3,000 Muslim prisoner the crusaders held.

- But Richard grew frustrated with the negotiations after about a month's time. The English king's response was to take the Muslim prisoners from Acre, including some women and children, to an elevation outside the city, where they could be seen by Saladin's army. He had them beheaded. In response, Saladin executed all of the Christian prisoners he was holding in Damascus.

King Richard I

- About a month later, in September 1191, Richard and Saladin met at the Battle of Arsuf, in modern Israel. Richard triumphed, largely due to his strong leadership. Richard was also at the heart of the fighting for part of the day, and even lost his horse during one attack by Saladin's troops. Seeing this, so the legend goes, Saladin sent two replacement steeds to Richard as a gift.

- Although Saladin lost the battle, he and his men lived to fight another day. As one year ended, and another began, the crusaders found themselves in control of much of the coast, but still unable to take Jerusalem.

- Richard fell sick during the winter, and, in another chivalrous gesture, Saladin sent his personal physician to tend to the ailing English king.

- Frustrated at his inability to take Jerusalem, Richard suggested that Saladin's brother marry his sister, Joan of England, who had accompanied him. He also proposed that Jerusalem should be their wedding gift, allowing both sides to hold the city jointly. This imaginitive plan didn't come to anything; Joan was furious at her brother's suggestion, and left for Europe on the next ship sailing.

- Richard had other problems to deal with: His brother John had launched a rebellion back home, and was claiming Richard's crown and titles. Richard was in a hurry to leave the Muslim word, and Saladin, now weakened militarily, was pleased to accommodate him.

- In June 1192, the Treaty of Ramla allowed Jerusalem to remain in Muslim hands as long as Christian pilgrims could visit. In addition, the crusader kingdoms would be restricted to the coastal areas.

- Richard sailed away to deal with his troublesome brother. Saladin returned to his beloved Damascus, where he died of a fever, shortly afterward. On his death, at age 56, Saladin's worldly wealth consisted of 40 pieces of silver and a single gold coin. Everything else he had given away to the poor and needy.

**Suggested Reading**

Gabrieli, *Arab Historians of the Crusades.*

Hitti, *Makers of Arab History*, chapter 7.

Ibn Shaddad, *The Rare and Excellent History of Saladin.*

Riley-Smith, *Oxford History of the Crusades*.

Rodenbeck, *Cairo*.

Runciman, *A History of the Crusades*, volume 2.

**Questions to Consider**

1. With hindsight, it seems the crusaders' days ruling over Jerusalem were doomed from the start. As a tiny, alien minority in a foreign land, with little or no outside support, how do you think the crusader knights imagined they could successfully rule over hostile local populations in the long term?

2. The Crusades still evoke a degree of romantic appeal, at least when seen through Western eyes. Bearing in mind the wanton destruction and murderous nature of events, is there anything to recommend this view of the Crusades?

3. Had these wars of conquest been against European Christian foes, and were stripped of their avowedly religious purpose, do you think they would still hold any romantic appeal?

# The Egyptian Mamluks—1250

Lecture 17

The tale of the Mamluks is one of how the Ayyubid dynasty was replaced by a unique, non-dynastic institution—where to rule you had to have been a slave first. During the course of this lecture, we will address who the Mamluks were, where they came from, and how they rose to power. We'll also look at the role of the legendary figure Sultana Shajar ad-Dur. And at the very end, we will revisit an event—the Battle of Ain Jalut—at which the Mamluks met a vast army that had never before been beaten in battle: the Mongols.

**Who the Mamluks Were**

- *Mamluk* is an Arabic word that means "one possessed," as in an item of property, or more simply, "a slave." While the Mamluks were certainly slaves, it's important to get away from thinking of them in conventional terms, as, for instance, black Africans who were shipped across the Atlantic in chains to the Americas. The Mamluks were white and enjoyed elevated standing in Egyptian society because of their extensive (and expensive) military training.

- Mamluks weren't found only in Egypt. At different times in history, Mamluks also established themselves as the ruling power in Iraq, Persia, and India.

- Although the Mamluks who rose to power in Egypt came from various places, they were usually Turkic. Non-Muslim Turkic tribes were an obvious recruiting ground for Arabs to buy the talented warriors whose horsemanship and fighting skills they so admired.

- Mamluks were sometimes taken prisoner by invading armies—for instance, when the Mongols swept across the region—or else traded as prisoners of war.

- Once an Arab Muslim purchased a Mamluk slave, the slave was expected to convert to Islam, as well. It should be noted that while sharia law always forbade the enslavement of free-born Muslims, a slave who converts to Islam doesn't automatically win the right to his or her freedom.

- The Mamluk class received a broad education, including religious instruction and Arabic. But combat training, including horsemanship and archery, came first.

### Fall of the Ayyubids

- Once Saladin died, rivalries among ruling-family members quickly weakened the Ayyubid dynasty from within. The last Ayyubid sultan to hold real power in both Damascus and Cairo was as-Salih Ayyub.

- In 1249, in the midst of a power struggle taking place in Syria, news reached as-Salih that a French army had invaded Egypt. With little choice, as-Salih returned to Egypt and the Ayyubid's capital of Cairo. However, as soon as he left Damascus, an uncle usurped the Syrian portions of the kingdom.

- Back in Cairo, as-Salih retreated behind the walls of the Citadel—the heavily fortified seat of power built by Saladin—as he feared he might be deposed by the very Mamluks he'd raised to be such a strong military force.

- As-Salih didn't even trust his son and heir, Turanshah, whom he sent away to modern-day Turkey. He significantly increased the size of his Mamluk army by purchasing thousands of new Kipchak-Turkic slaves.

- The transformation in the Mamluks' fortunes in Egypt came with the French invasion, under Louis IX, and the start of the Seventh Crusade. This foreign invasion would create the political uncertainty that provided the Mamluks with the opportunity to take power.

- While fighting against the French invaders, as-Salih was wounded in combat, and later died following a leg amputation and infection. This brings us to the story of Shajar ad-Durr—as-Salih's favourite wife, and the woman who would become the first Mamluk sultan. Of Armenian or Turkic origin, Shajar ad-Durr was by all accounts a beautiful woman, as well as pious and intelligent.

- Before he died, as-Salih had signed a large number of blank papers, allowing her to continue to issue decrees in his name, after his death. As a result, while the widowed Shajar ad-Durr shared the news of the sultan's death with his military commanders, she kept it from Turanshah, during which time she ruled in the young man's stead.

- But on Turanshah's return from Turkey in February 1250, Shajar ad-Durr was forced to tell him the truth, and Turanshah was duly installed as the new Ayyubid sultan in Egypt.

- After less than three months in power, he was assassinated by a senior Mamluk commander, Baibars, who had helped to beat the French invaders—and who remained loyal to Shajar ad-Durr.

- Shajar ad-Durr was made the sultana of Egypt on May 2, 1250. The Ayyubid line came to an end, and the Mamluks' 250 years in power began.

**Shajar ad-Durr's Rule**

- Shajar ad-Durr was clearly a shrewd political operator. Just winning over the senior Mamluk commanders—persuading them to be led by a woman in such a male-dominated world—was no mean feat. Shajar ad-Durr would rule under her own name for only three months, but it was an important period in Mamluk and Egyptian history.

- Alas for the Mamluks, the Abbasid sultan in Baghdad refused to accept the appointment of Shajar ad-Durr as permanent sultana.

As a compromise, in August 1250, Shajar ad-Durr agreed to marry the Mamluk commander-in-chief in Cairo, Aybak, making him sultan instead of her. This decision earned the Mamluks the blessing of the Abbasid caliph, even though the match was not one made for great happiness.

- A longstanding division between different branches of the Mamluks grew, a division that was more or less drawn along lines of the ethnic origins of the different Mamluk factions. Unfortunately, the husband and wife supported opposing factions, and each made quite clear they were unhappy with joint leadership.

- Fearing for her position, Shajar ad-Durr arranged for the Mamluk sultan, Aybak, to be murdered one night in his bath. Aybak's allies struck back quickly. According to the 15th-century historian al-Maqrizi, Shajar ad-Durr's servants confessed under torture to Aybak's murder, and they were executed.

- As for Shajar ad-Durr, she was stripped and beaten to death with wooden clogs—by maids who worked for Aybak's son. Her naked body was found outside the Citadel, taken away, and buried with dignity, thanks to her supporters. Her grave can still be visited today.

**Mamluk Maneuvers**

- As with the Ayyubids whom they'd replaced, the Mamluks were riven by these two main factions. One was centred in Cairo, and the other in Damascus.

- The Abbasid capital in Baghdad fell to the Mongol invaders in 1258, and the Mongols showed no sign of slowing down.

- Now, confronted with a face-to-face threat from the apparently unstoppable command of Hulagu Khan, the two rival Mamluk power bases recognized that in order to survive, they would have to stop fighting among themselves and unite.

- The sultan in Cairo at this time was a man named Qutuz. It was Qutuz who'd arranged for Shajar ad-Durr's murder. His main rival was the Mamluk general Baibars, who had been loyal to the sultana, and was now the emir in Damascus. Baibars and Qutuz had fought together against the French army of Louis IX before becoming powerful enemies.

- Under the Mamluks' unity pact, Baibars left Damascus to join the Sultan Qutuz in Cairo, where he was welcomed by his friend-turned-rival-turned-ally.

- The marauding Mongols fell upon Aleppo, Syria, in a week-long siege. And for resisting rather than surrendering, the city's population was massacred. Less than two weeks later, Damascus—devoid of its protector, Baibars—surrendered without a fight.

- At this stage Hulagu sent six messengers to Cairo, demanding that Qutuz surrender all of Egypt, or face a massacre. This was no idle threat. But by way of response, Qutuz had Hulagu's messengers sliced in two—at the waist—and mounted their severed heads on one of Cairo's main gates: Bab Zuweila (which is still standing).

- Qutuz then decided to take the fight to Hulagu. He formed a Mamluk army, with Baibars at his side, and marched into Syria.

- Unfortunately for the Mongols, the Mamluks had perfected horse archery, normally an advantage for the Mongols.

- Another disadvantage for the Mongols: The upcoming Battle of Ain Jalut would be the first occasion when hand cannons were used in battle. It was the Mamluks who used the guns against Mongol cavalry. They seem to have done their job, in part by terrifying the Mongol horses, and making them uncontrollable by their riders.

## The Battle of Ain Jalut

- The Battle of Ain Jalut was fought on September 3, 1260, in southeastern Galilee. The battle was certainly a turning point in the history of the Middle East. *Ain Jalut* means the "Spring of Goliath."

- In simple numerical terms, the two forces were evenly matched, both fielding between 10,000 and 20,000 troops, including cavalry. But Hulagu had gone back to the Mongol heartland for the election of the new khan, or ruler—he was running for the job. He took a significant part of his army with him.

- The Mamluks were on home ground, which meant that they knew the local terrain better than the Mongol invaders. Fighting at home might also have stiffened the resistance of the defenders.

- The Mamluks hid the bulk of their forces in the wooded hills and valley around Ain Jalut. During the first day, much of the fighting consisted of small units of Mamluk cavalry rushing at the Mongols before retreating. The Mamluks' goal was to draw the main body of the Mongol army into the lair of the concealed Mamluks. After hours of these hit-and-run attacks, the bothersome tactic worked, with the Mongol forces charging straight into the Mamluks' trap.

- Amid fierce fighting, some Mongol units beat a retreat, causing others to panic and run. In spite of a number of counterattacks by the Mongols, by the day's end the Mamluks were victorious. Those Mongol troops who weren't killed during the battle were mopped up as they tried to flee.

- The Battle of Ain Jalut was the first time that a Mongol force suffered such a devastating defeat. It was a fight from which they never recovered, and—apart from some very short-term gains elsewhere—marked the extent of their territorial advance in a Middle East now under full sway of the Mamluks.

### After the Battle

- Even as their combined army was on the road back to Cairo, Baibars murdered Qutuz and seized the sultanate for himself. He would rule for 17 years, during which period he secured many of the victories already won. Among other things, Baibars made sure that the Mamluks were never again seriously bothered by either the Mongols or the crusaders.

- In addition, Baibars eliminated the last remnants of the former Ayyubid dynasty in Syria, and united the fortunes of Syria and Egypt.

- On average, the reign of a Mamluk sultan was seven years. This led to periods of instability, and no doubt a great deal of worry among the sultans themselves. According to some historians, Baibars' main achievement was to preside for as long as he did—17 years.

- Eventually conquered by the Ottomans in 1517, the Mamluks would reassert their influence once more under the Ottomans, surviving and governing until Napoleon beat them in battle in 1798.

- The end of the Mamluks came about 13 years later, in 1811, when the remaining Mamluks were massacred by the new ruler of Egypt, Muhammad Ali, an Ottoman Albanian soldier-turned-viceroy. But from start to finish, the Mamluks held a central role in the military and political life of Egypt—and other parts of the Middle East—for almost 600 years.

### Suggested Reading

Hitti, *History of the Arabs*, chapters 47 and 48.

Hodgson, *The Venture of Islam*, volume 2, book 3.

Irwin, *The Middle East in the Middle Ages*.

Marsot, *A History of Egypt*, chapter 2.

Rodenbeck, *Cairo*.

**Questions to Consider**

1. The Mamluk system of rule by a slave class is virtually unique in history. Consider the factors that helped and hindered their distinctive government, including the often-bloody succession struggles.

2. The battle and Mongol defeat at Ain Jalut halted their westward progress in the Middle East. Do you think that Hulagu's absence from the battlefield was the sole reason for their defeat, or was it more that the Mamluks' military expertise that tipped the balance?

# Mongols Sack Baghdad—1258

Lecture 18

The Islamic Golden Age—from the 8th to the mid-13th century—was a period of great flourishing for human knowledge and progress. Baghdad was its focal point. A truly global repository of human knowledge, this Arab-Muslim imperial capital welcomed scholars from across the known world. As its wealth and fame grew, more and more scholars and engineers were drawn to the city, from all over the civilization. But in January 1258, a vast Mongol army reached the city's perimeter, and demanded that Caliph al-Mustasim—the nominal spiritual authority of the Islamic world—surrender.

## The Mongols

- The Mongols' name during this period in history was a byword for destruction. They were an ethnic group originating in north and central Asia. Typically pastoral, their nomadic lifestyle inevitably brought them into conflict with more settled populations. Probably the best example of how settled peoples tried to restrict their otherwise free movement is the Great Wall of China. The wall was essentially built to hold back incursions of these Mongolian neighbors to the north.

- Their priority, in terms of conquest, was for land for grazing and space rather than conquering cities. The Mongols' lack of interest in seizing cities enhanced their mobility. They often lived on a diet of mare's milk, or blood, if the mares were not lactating. Mongol custom meant that they never washed their clothes. This, along with a diet heavy in fat (both milk and meat), no doubt accounted for the Mongols' reputation as a very smelly, as well as scary, foe.

- Mongol warriors owned numerous mounts, allowing them to cover larger distances than more traditional cavalry found in the Near East and Europe. While they rode light into battle, the

Mongols used harnessed oxen to pull their heavier and more cumbersome possessions from place to place.

- An important facet of the Mongol way was their use of terror as a tactic. The banging of metal pots and the rattling of bells was their usual method of announcing the start of a battle. This created such a din that defenders of a city under siege would find it almost impossible to hear their officers' commands.

- Whenever they entered new territory, the Mongols would offer the local rulers an opportunity to surrender. This was a one-time offer. For those foolish enough not to surrender immediately, conquest and destruction without quarter would be their lot.

**The Khans**

- In 1206, just 52 years before the sack of Baghdad, the Mongol Empire was formed and led by the legendary Genghis Khan. *Khan* is originally a Mongolian word that means "military leader," "sovereign," or a "king." Being accepted as the Great Khan effectively elevated Genghis to the status of emperor.

- His grandsons now ruled the Mongolian Empire. In addition to Hulagu Khan, who led the attack against Baghdad, there was Kublai Khan, conqueror of China. Another, Mongke Khan, became the Great Khan and sent his brother Hulagu to Baghdad.

- Hulagu marched at the head of perhaps the largest Mongolian army ever assembled—consisting of as many as 150,000 troops—with Baghdad one of several goals for this military mission.

- First, Hulagu subdued southern Iran. Next, he was to destroy the infamous Assassins, a breakaway Nizari-Ismai'li-Shia sect that achieved infamy for political assassinations. After destroying the Assassins and their castle fortress at Alamut in northwestern Iran, Baghdad was the next stop on his list.

- The majority of Hulagu Khan's men were Mongolian warriors, but the force also contained Christians, including soldiers led by the king of Armenia; Frankish Crusaders from the Principality of Antioch; and Georgians. In addition, there were Muslim soldiers from various Turkic and Persian tribes, and 1,000 Chinese engineers—artillery specialists.

**The Abbasids**

- The Abbasids—the third Islamic caliphate to rule the Muslim Middle East since the death of Muhammad—had risen to power in 750, after overthrowing the Damascus-based Umayyads. The Abassids found themselves ruling over an enormous empire that covered the Arabian Peninsula, North Africa, the Levant, Syria, Iraq, Persia, and beyond to modern Afghanistan.

- A new Abbasid caliphate deserved a new capital, which they established in Baghdad in 762. They immediately built Baghdad into an imperial city worthy of their greatness.

- Within a couple of generations, Baghdad had attracted some of the world's greatest scholars. The city also boasted the House of Wisdom, which was what the best scholars and professors aspired to reach.

**Al-Mustasim**

- In the year 1242, al-Mustasim became the 37th caliph in the Abbasid line. Baghdad's and the Abbasids' glory days were now behind it. A weak-willed character, al-Mustasim was happier hanging out with musicians and drinking wine than he was ruling.

- The Abbasids already were in the habit of paying annual tribute to the Mongols. In 1251, the Abassids sent a delegation to pay homage on the coronation of Hulagu's brother, Mongke, when he became the Great Khan. But this was no longer considered enough.

- Now, Mongke insisted that al-Mustasim come in person to Karakorum, the 13th-century capital of the Mongol empire, to fully submit to Mongol rule. Al-Mustasim refused to do so, and so the final showdown between the Mongols and the Abbasids was set.

- Al-Mustasim is said to have slighted Shia Muslims by various acts and decrees. He should have known better, as his grand vizier, or senior advisor, was himself a Shia Muslim. This vizier is said to have sided with the Mongols, encouraging their takeover of the city.

- Baghdad was surrounded, and al-Mustasim realized too late that the Mongol army was far larger—and stronger—than he'd been told. Nor was the rest of the Muslim world about to rush to his rescue.

**The Siege**

- The siege of Baghdad began on January 29, 1258. The Mongols quickly built a palisade and ditch. They brought siege engines, such as covered battering rams, and catapults to attack the city's walls.

**The siege of Baghdad**

- At this stage, al-Mustasim made a last-ditch attempt to negotiate with Hulagu, and was rebuffed: a case of too little too late. Al-Mustasim surrendered Baghdad to Hulagu on February 10. Adding to the distress of those inside the city, Hulagu and his horde didn't make any attempt to enter the city for three days.

- Late in life, Hulagu would become a Buddhist. At this moment, however, the only sign of compassion he showed was towards Baghdad's Nestorian Christian community. Hulagu, upon entering Baghdad, told the Nestorians to lock themselves in their church, and ordered his army not to touch them.

- What was the reason for this act of kindness? Simply that Hulagu's mother and his favorite wife were both Nestorian Christians. With the Nestorians secure, Hulagu allowed his army an unfettered week of rape, pillage, and murder to celebrate their victory.

- About 3,000 of Baghdad's notables—including officials, members of the Abbasid family, and the caliph himself—pleaded for clemency. But all 3,000 were put to death, except for the caliph. He was held prisoner for a little while longer.

- Estimates of the death toll range from 90,000 at the lowest end to 1 million at the other. Apart from being a conveniently round number, the population of Baghdad was around a million, and we know for a fact that not everyone was killed.

- Whatever the actual number, it included the army that had dared to resist Hulagu's advance, and the civilians, who had no choice either way. Men, women, and children were put to the sword or clubbed to death.

- Al-Mustasim was forced to watch these murders and the plundering of his treasury and palaces. As for how the caliph met his end, one account, as reported by several chroniclers, goes like this:

- Hulagu had been warned by his astronomers that royal blood shouldn't be spilled onto the earth. If it were, the earth would reject it and earthquakes and natural destruction would follow.

- One might not think Hulagu an especially cautious man. However, in this case he plotted the safer course. Hulagu had the caliph rolled in carpets, which would catch any blood spilled, and had him trampled to death by his cavalry.

- Apart from the human casualties, there was the destruction of the 500-year-old city itself. Fires were set so that the fragrant scent of sandalwood and other aromatics drifted up to 30 miles away.

- After a week, Hulagu ordered his camp out of the city. He moved upwind, away from the stench of rotting corpses. Hulagu left Baghdad a broken and depopulated city. It would be more than a decade before anyone from Baghdad performed the *hajj* pilgrimage to Mecca.

- In attacking Baghdad, Hulagu also destroyed the network of canals than irrigated the arable land thereabouts. Famine and plague followed the Mongol horde to Baghdad.

- The destruction of Baghdad saw the center of Islamic life move westwards, towards the eastern Mediterranean, or Levant, and beyond to Egypt.

**After the Siege**

- In March 1260, the independent Ayyubid dynasty in Damascus fell to the Mongols. Then, Hulagu made plans to leave the Middle East in a great hurry. His brother Mongke, the Great Khan, had just died and Hulagu—as a strong contender to inherit the title—rushed back to the heart of the Mongolian empire.

- Before returning home, Hulagu sent envoys to Cairo demanding that the Mamluk sultan Qutuz immediately surrender. Qutuz decided this was the moment to go head-to-head with the invading tribesmen. Qutuz responded by beheading Hulagu's messengers, and mounting the severed heads on stakes at Bab Zuweila, one of Cairo's main gates.
- He then assembled his army and rode east to meet the Mongols. In September 1260, the westward push of the Mongol horde came to a juddering halt. At the Battle of Ain Jalut in southeastern Galilee, the Mamluks defeated the Mongols, and halted what looked to be the Mongols' ineluctable conquests.
- For the first time since Genghis Khan began his wars of conquest half a century earlier, the Mongols had suffered a major battlefield defeat, which they would never reverse.
- Elsewhere, Hulagu's conquests in Persia would form the basis of the Safavid dynasty in Persia, which emerged in 1501. The Mongol conquests also opened southern Persia to new influences from Europe and China. Now under Mongol control, Persian scholars also largely abandoned Arabic as the language of learning—although not of Islam—reverting to their native Persian tongue.
- The Muslim Middle East never again enjoyed the same level of prestige or importance as a civilization as it did before the Mongol destruction of Baghdad. Among the many political consequences of the sack of Baghdad, the shift in Islamic political power and influence away from Baghdad—via Damascus to Cairo—was probably the most significant. For the Abbasids, their empire was finished in all but name.

- Baghdad was left more or less in ruins for a couple of generations, after its sack at the hands of the Mongols. And just as it was recovering, it was sacked again in 1401, by the Turko-Mongol conqueror Timur, known in the West as Tamerlaine.

- Baghdad would, of course, eventually be rebuilt. And in the aftermath of the First World War, it became in 1921 the capital of the newly minted, semi-independent nation state of Iraq. Once again it emerged as an important, and iconic, regional center of the Muslim Middle East. But to this very day, it never has recaptured the cultural and intellectual prominence that it had during the days of the caliphs.

**Suggested Reading**

Hitti, *Capital Cities of Arab Islam*, chapter 4.

Hodgson, *The Venture of Islam*, volume 2, book 3.

Hourani, *A History of the Arab Peoples*, chapters 8 and 9.

Lewis, *Islam in History*, chapter 18.

Runciman, *A History of the Crusades*, volume 3.

**Questions to Consider**

1. The sack of Baghdad is usually cited as marking the end of the Islamic Golden Age. If the destruction of one city, however glorious, wasn't enough to change the course of Middle Eastern history, what other factors might account for the steep decline in original scholarship coming out of the region?

2. While it would be an oversimplification to say the Mongols' nomadic lifestyle meant they would inevitably come into conflict with settled populations, did the Mongol pastoralists fail to see any value in sedentary civilizations?

# Ottoman Empire Rises—1299

Lecture 19

In 1258, in a small town of northern Anatolia, a son was born to a minor Turkish prince. That child, Osman, would inherit his father's title, position, and responsibilities as head of his tribe at the age of 23. Before he was 30, Osman would have a dream that changed not just his family's fortunes but also the history of the Middle East. His dream was nothing less than the creation of the Ottoman Empire. And its founding would be a turning point that would resonate for centuries, beginning 600 years of Ottoman rule.

## Background

- The origins of the Ottoman Empire are among the most studied, and arguably least understood, research areas in the history of Middle Eastern politics and empire. But what we can say with certainty is that there were some external, and some internal, reasons why the Ottomans were able to establish their dynasty.

- External reasons include the decline of the Byzantine Empire to the west and the rise of the Mongols the east. In the very year that Osman was born, the Mongols laid waste to Baghdad, the capital of the Abbasid caliphs.

- The speed with which the Mongol empire spread was disruptive on a scale unlike the emergence of any empire before or since. Apart from the millions killed, many more—entire ethnic groups, in some cases—were displaced. Moving out of their ancestral homelands, searching for safety and new lands, they, of course, came into contact with other people already living there. This was the case in Anatolia.

- Also known as Asia Minor, Anatolia is a peninsular landmass that's roughly contiguous with modern Turkey, and some adjoining areas. Throughout the 13th century, existing Turkic powers in Anatolia were destroyed, or severely weakened, while others were displaced.

## The Seljuks

- According to one tradition, Osman came to Anatolia with 400 horsemen, intent on fighting the Byzantines on behalf of the Anatolia-based Seljuk Sultanate of Rum. (*Rum* in this case means Rome, or lands once held by Rome. The Sultanate of Rum had been carved out of former Eastern Roman, or Byzantine, territory.)

- The Seljuk Turks originated from an area around the Aral Sea in Central Asia. Like many Turkic tribes, the Seljuks were nomadic, and they drifted into Anatolia, establishing an empire there in the middle of the 11th century.

- But by the 1240s, the Seljuks were fighting a series of losing battles against the emerging power of the Mongol empire. Their vassals and sometime allies in Anatolia took advantage of the disruption caused by the Mongol threat by breaking free of Seljuk control.

- By 1294, when the Mongol leader Kublai Khan died, the Mongols had split into four realms. A different descendant of Genghis Khan ruled each one of these. And Anatolia consisted of dozens of small, independent or semi-independent principalities. Those were *beyliks* in Turkish, after the Turkish word for prince: *bey*.

## Osman's Dream

- After inheriting his father's title—bey—Osman was staying one night with a family friend: the prominent Muslim religious authority, Sheikh Edebali.

- Osman's pleas to let him marry the sheikh's daughter had been rebuffed by the older man. But this night, after falling asleep, we're told that Osman had the following dream. As this is the

Osman

central foundational myth of the Ottoman Empire, it's worth hearing in some detail.

- In his dream, Osman saw himself and Sheikh Edebali next to each other. Suddenly, a full moon emerged from the sheikh's chest, rose into the sky, and then descended into Osman's own chest.

- This was followed by the appearance of an enormous, beautiful tree. Under the tree, four mountain ranges arose: the Caucasus in Eurasia, the Atlas in North Africa, the Taurus in Anatolia, and the Balkans in Europe.

- Then, four rivers sprouted from the base of the tree: the Tigris, Euphrates, Danube, and Nile. After this, Osman envisioned plentiful harvests, and traders coming in ships from all corners of the earth.

- Next, the leaves on the tree turned into swords, which were blown by a mighty wind until they all pointed toward Constantinople. This great city, lying between two seas and two continents, looked to Osman like a diamond set between two sapphires and two emeralds. It formed the most precious stone in a ring that would be a global empire.

- Just as Osman was about to put the ring on his finger, he woke up. Osman asked the sheikh what his dream meant, to which the religious elder replied, "God Almighty has bestowed sovereignty upon you and your generation. My daughter will be your wife, and the whole world will be under the protection of your children."

**Osman Declares Independence**

- As the ruler of a beylik, Osman Bey was under the authority of the Seljuk Sultanate of Rum. But having once dominated central and eastern Anatolia, the sultanate was now militarily and politically weak. On July 27, 1299, Osman declared his independence. Osman was fortunate on two counts: one, that the Mongols were so strong, and two, that the Byzantine Empire was so weak.

- Many Muslim-Turkic tribes pushed west across Anatolia. The farmers among them needed land on which to settle, including pastures for their livestock. In turn, the warrior class was looking for a renewed sense of personal pride and honour. The Ottoman Empire could offer both. These *ghazis*—or religious warriors—would jump at the chance to prove themselves in battle.

- Anatolia's border with the Byzantine Empire abutted Osman's principality. So, the young, energetic founder of this new empire declared a holy war against the declining Christian power next door.

- By calling Byzantium a religious objective, he could appeal to warriors who might otherwise not have fought for him. The *ghazi* warriors—believing they were fighting for the defense, or expansion, of Islam—showed themselves to be very effective.

- Many Byzantine settlements, alarmed by the rise of this Muslim Turkish warrior king on their borders, were abandoned without a fight. Local populations moved west, first to the Anatolian coast, and then to Europe. As a result, Osman quickly won the support of many of his Anatolian neighbours.

- Through a series of pacts and treaties, those Turkic tribes that agreed to be folded into the nascent Ottoman Empire were promised a fair share of ever increasing booty.

- Osman was the first Turkish ruler to mint coins in his own name, which in Islamic practice of the day was a privilege reserved for kings. He was a keen promoter of marriages between members of his tribe and other local powers, which was another effective means of increasing the size and power of his domains. In his 25-year reign—from independence in 1299 until his death in 1324—Osman enjoyed a number of military gains against the Byzantine Empire in Anatolia.

**Sunni Islam**

- One central unifier during the Ottoman Empire's 600-year span of common identity and success was the adherence to Sunni Islam. Osman on his deathbed advised his son and heir, Orhan, to "be careful about religious matters" in part because "religious precepts build a strong state."

- Starting with Osman, the earliest Ottoman sultans made numerous appeals in the name of the Islamic faith. A look at the available evidence shows that such pleas were designed purely to get much-needed military support, rather than Islam being the central force behind their campaigns.

- In 1517, the Ottoman sultan Selim I—also known as Selim the Grim—conquered Islam's two holiest cities, Mecca and Medina. And he almost immediately declared himself caliph (Muhammad's successor). In this way, Selim and all subsequent Ottoman sultans were putting themselves at the head of the Sunni Muslim faithful.

- Ottoman leadership had sought political legitimacy in other ways. They were keen sponsors of Islamic institution, such as charities, schools, and mosques. They also introduced, and promoted, more formal control over a Sunni judicial system across their realm.

- This was important in weeding out heresies—mainly the potential threat from Shia political challengers—and also in establishing firm control over all Ottoman subjects. As for language: Even though Ottoman Turkish was used for Ottoman court documents, Arabic retained a central place as the language of Islam.

**After Osman**

- When Osman died at the age of 66 in 1324, his son Orhan succeeded him. Orhan's first major achievement was to complete the siege and conquest of the city of Bursa, in northwestern Anatolia. Orhan marked Bursa's capture by making it the Ottoman Empire's first official capital.

- By 1345, the Ottomans had conquered other important cities in Anatolia, including Nicaea, second city of the Byzantine Empire after Constantinople. At this stage, the Byzantine Empire had given up trying to retake lost territories in Anatolia.

- Sidestepping Constantinople, Orhan shifted his imperial aims to Europe via Gallipoli. From there, he and thousands more *ghazi* warriors pushed west into the Balkans, eventually leaving the Byzantine capital surrounded by a rump state in eastern Thrace, which today marks the European bits of Turkey.

- Ottoman conquests in the Balkans would lead to centuries of Muslim rule in Eastern Europe. Rather than viewing these centuries as a period of constant tension and conflict, many historians refer to it as the Ottoman Peace—the *Pax Ottomana*.

- Under Orhan, a professional standing army of both infantry and cavalry was established. Orhan also introduced the institution of the janissaries. The word *janissary* is Turkish for "new soldier." Such units consisted of male Christian youths taken as slaves from lands the Ottomans conquered. They were converted to Islam and militarily trained. In time, they rose to the highest ranks of Ottoman administration.

- Orhan seems to have been a natural-born administrator. He also benefited from the disarray affecting not just eastern Anatolia but other parts of the Muslim world. This wasn't just political disorder either, but the outbreak of the Black Death pandemic, which reached the Middle East and Europe at almost the same time, in 1347. Administrators, merchants, scholars, and artisans all made their way to his domains, and he put their skills to good use.

**Rule of the Ottomans**

- During the reign of Orhan's son, Murad, still more of the Balkans were brought more firmly under Ottoman control. Murad brought the princes of northern Serbian and Bulgaria into submission, and also forced the Byzantine Emperor John V Palaiologos to pay him tribute. Murad then divided the Ottoman Empire into two provinces: Anatolia and the Balkans. This made the job of ruling easier, as did his choice of capital city.

- In the 1360s, troops loyal to Murad took the Byzantine city of Adrianople, which was renamed Edirne and became the Ottoman Empire's new administrative and political center. Its location, just 150 miles west of Constantinople, placed it firmly in Europe—sending a signal the Ottoman Empire wouldn't just be lurking in Anatolia.

- One of Murad's successors, the Ottoman Sultan Mehmed II—or Mehmed the Conqueror—defeated Constantinople in 1453, bringing about the final collapse of the Byzantine Empire. Mehmed II then moved the Ottoman's capital to the former Byzantine center, where he consolidated power.

- The founding of Osman's empire, in 1299, had marked the start of 600 years of rule in the Greater Middle East by non-Arabic former nomads. The later expansion of the empire—beyond Anatolia and Eastern Europe, across the wider Middle East, and North Africa—saw the Ottomans become a transcontinental superpower.

**Suggested Reading**

Finkel, *Osman's Dream*.

Goodwin, *Lords of the Horizons*.

Hodgson, *The Venture of Islam*, volume 2.

Hourani, *A History of the Arab Peoples*, chapter 13.

Lapidus, *A History of Islamic Societies*, chapter 14.

**Questions to Consider**

1. How far did the Mongol conquest of Central Asia lead to the rise of the Ottoman Empire? And to what extent was the rise of the Ottoman Empire dependent on Osman's vision and ambition?

2. What are some of the factors that saw the Ottomans becoming the longest reigning of any Middle East empire since the dawn of Islam?

# Mansa Musa, Richest Man—1324

Lecture 20

A few years ago, *Forbes* magazine ran a feature on the richest people of all time. According to *Forbes*, the richest man who ever lived was an African Muslim by the name of Mansa Musa. *Forbes* put Mansa Musa's net worth in the region at $400 billion. By comparison, Bill Gates's fortune was about one-third of that. Musa wasn't just rich: There was a time when his name and legend had enough power to drive the European Age of Discovery in Muslim North and West Africa. This lecture describes Mansa Musa, his vast wealth, and his legacy.

**Mansa Musa's Empire**

- Mansa Musa's wealth depended on his position as ruler of the Mali Empire. This was a regional trading hub that grew rich and powerful because it was blessed with an abundance of two invaluable commodities: salt and gold.

- The Mali Empire emerged as a regional power about 100 years before Mansa Musa's reign. This empire wasn't contiguous with the modern state of Mali, although it did cover much of the same territory, as well parts of other modern countries, including Mauritania, Senegal, Niger, Guinea, and the Ivory Coast.

- In the early 1300s, the empire covered roughly half a million square miles, making it one of the largest territorial expanses under central authority anywhere in the world. The most important parts of the empire were isolated places in the heart of the Sahara.

- Mali's rich veins of salt and gold were carefully protected, although the remoteness of each made any surprise attack by outsiders virtually impossible. Within the empire, all gold was the personal property of the *mansa*, or emperor, and anyone caught stealing it could expect a quick execution.

- In addition to the salt and gold trade, Mansa Musa also enjoyed another significant source of income in the form of taxation. These taxes were taken from merchants' caravans that passed through his kingdom. Apart from its natural resources, the empire contained numerous oasis towns that were the southern termini of the busy trans-Saharan trade routes.

- Mansa Musa was the 10th man in his family to hold the title of emperor. According to one history, Mansa Musa's grandfather made him his deputy, in advance of the older man setting off with his own navy to explore the farthest reaches of the Atlantic Ocean. The appointment of a deputy would always be done in advance of a potentially dangerous endeavor.

- Whether any members of this expedition reached the New World, nobody knows. What we do know is that just one ship returned to Africa. The survivors reported that they had lost the others vessels as they sailed west. So, Mansa Musa became king.

- It's unclear when Mansa Musa's people converted to Islam, although it's most likely it was around the same time that the Empire of Mali started to emerge—that is about 100 years before Mansa Musa came to power.

**Mansa Musa's Pilgrimage**

- After a few years in power, Mansa Musa, as a Muslim himself, decided to make the long, arduous journey to Mecca, to perform the *hajj* pilgrimage.

- Mansa Musa's journey from his West African empire across North Africa to the Arabian Peninsula—and back again—was an incredibly challenging undertaking because of its length and grueling nature. In addition, for a ruler there always existed the very real peril of being overthrown while absent from the kingdom.

- The Sahara is the world's largest hot desert. The entire United States—including Alaska and Hawaii—would fit within the Sahara's borders.

The Sahara

- From the time it came into being in its current state, about 6,000 years ago, the desert has never stopped people from moving across it. To the contrary, it has proven to be a river of sand, people, and precious commodities.

- Mansa Musa's caravan would have followed well-established trade routes, undertaken with guides who possessed local knowledge of where the next oasis would be. Nevertheless, the journey presented human and geographical challenges, including the threats of sandstorms or bandits. But Mansa Musa's caravan was so large that it's unlikely anyone but a fool would've confronted it.

- The distance from Timbuktu to Cairo is 2,347 miles. From Cairo it's a further 800 miles to Mecca. And then there was the journey home again. In all, Mansa Musa's caravan had a round trip of just under 6,500 miles, and the whole journey took about two years. It's a clear sign of Mansa Musa's power and confidence that he felt he could be away from home for so long.

**The Caravan and Gold**

- Once we take into consideration Musa's personal bodyguard and the need for a larger armed force to protect the traveling column—including his servants, cooks, guides, the porters, and those responsible for taking care of the horses and camels—we start to get a sense his caravan must have consisted of thousands of people.

- One report says the caravan's total number was 60,000 people, including 12,000 slaves, each of whom carried a four-pound gold bar, among other things. Eighty camels were also present to carry gold: 300 pounds per animal, so we're told. If accurate, this would equal 24 tons.

- Musa provided all necessities for the procession. He's said to have given away gold to the poor along his route, as well as handing out elaborate gifts to local rulers—no doubt securing promises of friendship and safe passage wherever he went.

- His caravan would have covered no more than 10 or 15 miles per day. This tallies with accounts that say it took more than six months to reach Cairo.

- When he reached Cairo, in July 1324, Mansa Musa camped in the desert near the great Pyramids of Giza, on the outskirts of modern Cairo. From his camp, he sent a message to the Egypt's Mamluk sultan along with a gift of 50,000 dinars in gold. Predictably, the Sultan was delighted with the introduction and lent Mansa Musa his summer palace for a three-month stay.

- The best account of his time in Egypt is by the historian Shihab al-Umari, who was in Cairo 12 years after Mansa Musa's visit. Al-Umari recounts Mansa Musa flooding the city with gold.

- Overnight, however, the price of goods and services became hyper-inflated—and the price of gold crashed, by some accounts losing more than a quarter of its value. Imagine the effect of this on local merchants and families, who saw their hard-earned incomes melt away.

- In an attempt to rectify this, Mansa Musa borrowed as much gold as he could from Cairo's moneylenders—at unfavorably high rates of interest—when he and his entourage passed back through Egypt on the homeward journey. In spite of this gesture, contemporary chroniclers say that Mansa Musa's spending single-handedly ruined the local economy for 20 years.

- Mansa Musa's spending wasn't just in handouts. He also founded, and endowed, scores of mosques and *madrasas*, or schools. During his pilgrimage, it's recorded that Mansa Musa ordered a mosque built wherever the caravan happened to find itself on every single Friday—the holy day for Muslims.

- In this way, he was able to spread the means for education, worship, and employment across his kingdom—and beyond. This is the main reason why Mansa Musa's *hajj* pilgrimage can be thought of as a turning point in Middle Eastern history.

**Mansa Musa and Race**

- The sight of Mansa Musa, a black African ruler, challenged the predominant racial views of the period.

- In spite of Muhammad's oft-repeated message that all people are equal in God's eyes, there was a powerful strain of race-driven bias at that time. Such an idea led many Arabs to view black Africans as naturally inferior to themselves.

- This prejudice came about in part from the fact that Muhammad, the prophet, was an Arab, a trump card for many in such debates.

- Of course, such a narrow outlook wasn't limited to Arabs or Muslims. The same thought was commonplace in Britain. As George Bernard Shaw famously quipped, "The ordinary Britisher imagines that God is an Englishman."

- With this in mind, imagine how the appearance of this wealthy, powerful, and pious African Muslim emperor challenged the prevailing view. The local elites he met must have been especially struck by the contrast between their relative wealth and position when compared to Mansa Musa's incomparable wealth and absolute power.

**Mansa Musa's Return**

- Upon leaving Mecca—and then Cairo—Mansa Musa persuaded a number of scholars, architects, and artisans to come and work for him. Having taken in the sights in Cairo and elsewhere, Mansa Musa saw endless possibilities for building his empire's urban centers.

- As soon as he got home, Mansa Musa set his new employees to the task of construction on a scale the Mali Empire had never before seen. Libraries, schools, universities, mosques and palaces sprang up.

- Tuareg nomads founded Timbuktu in the 11th century, and now it would become the most famous city in Mansa Musa's empire. The oasis, just a few miles from the Niger River and possessing spring water, grew into a city and medieval center of learning.

- Timbuktu's university, which Mansa Musa established in 1327, was without equal in the Islamic world for much of the 15th and 16th centuries. Its fame attracted aspiring scholars and established men of learning alike.

- Beyond his kingdom, Mansa Musa's pilgrimage meant his name and that of his empire spread far and wide, both across the Middle East and in Europe. Within seven years of his pilgrimage, Mansa Musa's name was appearing on European maps, though the location of his empire was often misplaced.

**Decline and Legacy**

- When the great Arab historian Ibn Khaldun wrote his magnum opus, the *Muqaddimah*, in 1377—just 50 years after Mansa Musa's pilgrimage to Mecca—the Mali Empire had already started its slow decline. Eventually, the Songhai Empire based in West Africa, with its capital at Gao on the Niger River, would emerge from and outgrow the fading Mali Empire in the late 14th, 15th, and 16th centuries.

- In 1591, a Moroccan army attacked and conquered the Mali Empire, which barely existed as such by that time. The invading troops were sadly disappointed when they discovered that the streets of Timbuktu were not paved with gold.

- The gold trade that once spread far beyond the Sahara had by now dwindled, and with it the great university complex. Timbuktu was a shadow of its former self—a dusty desert town and a memory.

- In spite of this, the legend of Timbuktu remained the elusive goal of many Saharan explorers. The French Geographical Society offered prize money of 10,000 francs to the first person to reach Timbuktu and return with information about the city. The prize was eventually claimed in the 1820s by the French explorer René Caillié. Caillié reported there was nothing exciting or golden about the once-legendary city.

- Today, by contrast—aided by modern technology that extracts the precious metal where once it was thought to be lost—gold is Mali's third largest export, and the country is Africa's third largest gold producer.

**Suggested Reading**

Bovill, *The Golden Trade of the Moors*, chapter 9.

De Villiers and Hirtle, *Timbuktu*.

Gearon, *The Sahara*, chapter 4.

Hopkins, *Corpus of Early Arabic Sources for West African History*.

Ibn Khaldun, *The Muqaddimah*.

Lapidus, *A History of Islamic Societies*, chapter 20.

Shillington, ed., *Encyclopedia of African History*.

**Questions to Consider**

1. Consider some of the possible motivations behind Mansa Musa's decision to perform the *hajj* pilgrimage to Mecca in 1324. These might include, but not be limited to, a sense of religious obligation, a desire to increase regional diplomatic contacts, the development of trade with other territories, and a longing to display the prestige of an otherwise remote empire to one's co-religionists who are living closer to the Middle East's centers of power and influence.

**2.** Bearing in mind the 19$^{th}$-century consequences that followed the legend of Timbuktu's gold, including the "Scramble for Africa," how different might things have been in the Victorian era and beyond if Mansa Musa's name been unknown, and gold's appeal so strong?

Lecture 21

# Ibn Khaldun's Masterpiece—1377

The historian Ibn Khaldun was a unique and brilliant individual, and his *Muqaddimah* is one of the most original books of scholarship ever written. In the *Muqaddimah* we see the birth of three new fields of scholarly pursuit: economics, sociology, and historiography (the philosophy of history). This alone justifies the publication of the *Muqaddimah* as a turning point in the history of the Middle East, not to mention scholarship the world over. This lecture traces Ibn Khaldun's early life, his writing of the *Muqaddimah*, and the impact it had.

## Ibn Khaldun's Beginnings

- Ibn Khaldun was born in Tunis in 1332, 70 years after the destruction of Baghdad. The Abbasid caliphate of old existed in name only, having been re-invented by the Mamluks and ruled from Cairo, since 1261. During his 75 years, Ibn Khaldun lived in Tunisia, Spain, Morocco, Algeria, and Egypt. And he worked in various royal courts as a diplomat, counsellor, and eventually a senior judge.

- Ibn Khaldun liked to claim he could trace his family tree back more than 600 years to southern Arabia, in the area of Yemen today. His family—which arrived in Andalusia in the early eighth century, soon after the Arab-Berber conquest of the region—had risen to positions of prominence in various royal courts in and around Seville.

- The fall of Seville to King Ferdinand II of Castille, in 1248, saw the family forced to leave Andalusia for North Africa, settling in Tunis. And if all this political upheaval weren't destabilising enough, another disaster struck when Ibn Khaldun was 16: the Black Death, or bubonic plague, which spread to and devastated North Africa, including Tunis.

- In his autobiography, Ibn Khaldun relates how the disease killed his mother and his father, numerous other family members, and all his teachers.

- Perhaps driven by the upheaval in his environment, and the knowledge of his family's former better fortunes, Ibn Khaldun grew up to be an intensely ambitious man. He seemed to realize early on that North Africa was a relative backwater in the Islamic World, with much of the learning of the Islamic Golden Age having passed the region by.

- And if North Africa were a backwater, then Tunis was an even remoter, sleepier spot. Ibn Khaldun would have to go elsewhere.

**Ibn Khaldun Sets Out**

- In 1352, four years after the Black Death turned his life upside down, Ibn Khaldun set off for the city of Fes, the capital of the Moroccan Marinid dynasty. He was schooled in the standard subjects of an educated Muslim at that time, including theology, Islamic law, mathematics, philosophy, logic, and the formal study of Arabic grammar and poetry. Ibn Khaldun would have been confident of obtaining some form of employment in the royal court in Fes, which he did.

- Eventually, Ibn Khaldun travelled to Granada. He was on a diplomatic mission to meet with the king of Castile, Peter the Cruel. That monarch not only offered Ibn Khaldun a job in his court, but also promised to restore to him his family's ancestral lands and property—lost when they'd fled from Seville to Tunis.

- Ibn Khaldun politely declined, seeing better political opportunities back in North Africa, to which he now moved. In 1359, at the age of 27, he became a judge, practicing the Maliki school of jurisprudence (which remains the most prevalent Sunni Islamic tradition North Africa).

- The last important post Ibn Khaldun held for the purposes of our story—before settling down to write the *Muqaddimah*—was as a tax collector, living among the desert-dwelling, nomadic Bedouin of modern Algeria. Engaged in the rather sensitive mission of collecting taxes from the Bedouin, Ibn Khaldun's diplomatic skills and personal charm must have worked their magic, because the Bedouin took to him, and he was fond of them, in turn.

**The *Muqaddimah***

- As the guest of a Bedouin chief in western Algeria, Ibn Khaldun wrote the *Muqaddimah* over a four-year period in the late 1370s. The *Muqaddimah*'s material is arranged in six sections. They deal respectively with:

    1. The different kinds of human society, and their geographical distribution

    2. Nomadic societies, tribes, and "savage peoples," as he terms them

    3. States of spiritual and temporal powers, and different political ranks

    4. Sedentary societies, the growth of cities and provinces

    5. Crafts, or the different means of earning a living, and economic activity in society as a whole

    6. Learning, or knowledge of the world, and how people acquire this

- In short, Ibn Khaldun's ambition, or scope, is a universal history of the world. Instead of a simple list of events, Ibn Khaldun offers an analysis of why things happened, and what lessons we might learn from them.

Statue of Ibn Khaldun in Tunis

- Ibn Khaldun begins the *Muqaddimah* by discussing just where so many historians before him have gone wrong. Among what he highlights as critical errors are: partisanship, favoring one opinion or faith over another; hubris, or overconfidence in one's sources; a failure to understand what the author intended; and ignorance of the laws governing the transformation of human society.

- Unlike historians before him, Ibn Khaldun tried to understand the laws that govern the transformation of human societies, including environmental factors, human failings, and social cohesion (or the lack thereof). He put forward ground-breaking theories that were fundamental for the discipline of historiography (which refers to the study of history, and to the methodology of gathering data for the study of history).

### Asabiyya

- One word is central to everything Ibn Khaldun writes about. It is *asabiyya,* an Arabic term that originally referred to unity based on kinship, or tribalism. It can be imagined as a spirit of unity, or single purpose, that exists within a group of people. Ibn Khaldun argues that a degree of *asabiyya* is essential for any ruler who wants to found a dynasty. Without it, a putative ruler will fail before he begins.

- Ibn Khaldun offers an additional, interesting thought: *Asabiyya* contains within itself the seeds of its own destruction, typically taking three to five generations. Here, the Bedouin tie in. These people were massively important for Ibn Khaldun. Not only had the hardy desert dwellers taken Ibn Khaldun in, but in the Bedouin he also saw the best example of *asabiyya*, born, he said, out of the harshness of life in the desert.

- It's impossible to live in a harsh environment without the support of others, which is why the nomads' sense of working for the common good was so highly developed. However, once nomads settled in towns and cities, and their lives became easier, their sense of *asabiyya* lessened. In the absence of environmental demands for common cause, this sense of solidarity is slowly replaced by the pursuit of luxury items and soft living.

- Kings move into palaces. They become alien figures to the people who ensured their earlier successes. Ibn Khaldun believed that by the fifth generation, a dynasty would lose its social cohesion, and become easy prey for another, external group—with stronger *asabiyya*—to come in and take over.

### Economics

- Ibn Khaldun's thoughts about economics and economic growth were closely related to those on the rise and fall of dynasties. He saw population growth as a function of wealth, while also tying his theory of *asabiyya* to economics in more complex societies. In this view, as population in a society increases, there will arise the need for more complex divisions of labor, which will promote greater economic growth.

- Ibn Khaldun also observed that growth and development stimulate supply and demand, and that supply and demand determine the price of things. He wrote on areas as diverse as human capital development, technology, and the negative impact of degrading one's environment. These were revolutionary ideas in their day, and are not without merit more than 600 years later.

- Unsurprisingly, for a man who once had the job of collecting taxes from the desert-dwelling Bedouin, Ibn Khaldun held some pretty strong ideas about taxation. He saw it as necessary in a functioning state.

- Ibn Khaldun worried that higher tax rates destroy the incentive to work, whereas lower rates were more likely to mean that people would happily pay what they owed. Further, if taxes were too high, this could lead to the destruction of the dynasty, as people simply stopped paying their obligations.

- Fully grasping the implications of the need to find the right level of taxation for incentive and productivity, Ibn Khaldun's solution was for a ruler, or government, to follow a policy of wise and productive public expenditure. If only that were easy to define.

**Ibn Khaldun and Timur**

- In 1401, the Turco-Mongolian conqueror Tamurlaine laid siege to Damascus. Better known in the West as "Timur the Lame," he was a notoriously violent warlord, among the last of Central Asia's great nomadic conquerors. His overarching goal was the restoration of the earlier great Mongol empire of Genghis Khan.

- Ibn Khaldun, then 70 years old, was sent from Cairo to meet with Timur as a negotiator. There were fewer than 100 qualified defenders remaining in the city when Ibn Khaldun was lowered from the walls to rendevous with Tumor.

- Ibn Khaldun wrote, "As I entered the audience tent, [Timur] was reclining on his elbow while platters of food passed before him." After some flattery from Ibn Khaldun, the two men engaged in a wide-ranging discussion.

- Timur asked Ibn Khaldun to write a description of North Africa, and Ibn Khaldun in turn lectured Timur on his theory of history and *asabiyya*. The two men spoke for hours before Timur is called away, believing Damascus to have surrendered.

- As it turned out, Damascus hadn't surrendered, and Ibn Khaldun would remain with the Mongols for another 35 days, and enjoy several more conversations with Timur. Even more importantly, Ibn Khaldun secured safe passage home to Cairo for him and his colleagues.

### The *Muqaddimah*'s Legacy

- Anticipating Machiavelli by a century, Ibn Khaldun posed the question of whether it is better for a ruler to be loved or feared.

- Machiavelli—writing about the political situation in 15th-century Florence—said that if one had to pick between two preferred outcomes, it was better to be feared. By contrast, Ibn Khaldun said that if forced to choose, it was better for a ruler to be loved, as the negative impacts of being feared outweigh the benefits.

- Predating Darwinian theories of evolution by 600 years, Ibn Khaldun also argued that humans were the most evolved form of animal life because they had the power of reason.

- The 20th-century British historian Arnold Toynbee called the *Muqaddimah*, "a philosophy of history which is undoubtedly the greatest work of its kind that has ever been created by any mind in time or place."

- The philosopher and anthropologist Ernest Gellner thought Ibn Khaldun's definition of a government as "an institution which prevents injustice other than such as it commits itself" the best in the history of political theory.

- While the *Muqaddimah* was meant to be an introduction to a larger history of the world, even if we choose to see it as an unfinished work, it is no less amazing for what it accomplishes.

**Suggested Reading**

Brett and Fentress, *The Berbers*, chapter 4.

Hitti, *Makers of Arab History*, chapter 13.

Hourani, *A History of the Arab Peoples*, chapters 12 and 13.

Issawi, *An Arab Philosophy of History*.

Ibn Khaldun, *The Muqaddimah*.

**Questions to Consider**

1. Ibn Khaldun's *Muqaddimah* is rightly hailed, in Western and non-Western intellectual circles, as one of the greatest books ever written. With this in mind, suggest reasons why Ibn Khaldun's name and reputation are not more widely known in the West.

2. Ibn Khaldun argues that *asabiyya* (social cohesion) is essential for the rise and continuing health of all societies. In the contemporary Western setting, there is a great deal of emphasis on the primacy of individual rights. Is Ibn Khaldun wrong, or have societies changed fundamentally since the $14^{th}$ century?

Lecture
22

# Ottomans Seize Constantinople—1453

In European history, the Roman Empire enjoys an understandably preeminent position in the popular imagination. The most obvious reason for this is its enduring span of military and political power and its legacy in Western culture and society. But in this lecture, we're going to look at the story from the other side. We're going to concentrate on the Ottomans, and how they managed to take the incredibly important city of Constantinople in 1453. The lecture also looks at the fall of Constantinople in historical context.

## Reasons for the Attack

- Strategically located on the Bosphorus, a waterway that ultimately connects the Black Sea to the Mediterranean, Constantinople boasts a deep-water harbor, making it ideal for shipping. The city also sits astride the invisible border between Europe and Asia, so it was of vital importance for global trade in the 15th century and earlier.

- The Ottomans weren't the first to attack Constantinople. Over the centuries, dozens of attempts were made to take Constantinople. The Ottomans were only the latest in a succession of would-be conquerors.

- But it's easy to see why they were keen for this objective. At the time of their assault, the Ottoman capital was the city of Edirne, at the edge of Europe, and 140 miles west of Constantinople. The Ottomans had amassed significant European territories, and all of Anatolia—that is, the peninsular territory that comprises much of modern-day Turkey.

- If they could turn back for a moment to conquer Constantinople, they'd no longer have this source of annoyance and trouble to their rear. Its possession would allow them to push even further forward into Europe.

- Another reason why the young Ottoman sultan, Mehmed II, wanted the city was because Constantinople had long offered refuge for challengers to the Ottoman leadership. This was a policy that continued under the incumbent, and last, Byzantine emperor, Constantine XI.

- A final reason why the Ottomans so eagerly sought Constantinople was because it was renowned as a place of great wealth.

**Constantinople in 1453**

- By this time, the Roman Empire had essentially been reduced to a few square miles of land around Constantinople, and on the Peloponnesian Peninsula in southern Greece. Turkic tribes also had been attacking Byzantium's holdings in nearby Anatolia since the 11th century. One of these tribes became known as the Ottomans.

- The fact that Constantinople had withstood many invasions in the past is an important point to bear in mind. Time and again, Constantinople's defenders' success was due to an impressive system of double defensive walls and a moat.

- For those unwilling to make a frontal assault by land, they'd face equally formidable defenses on the waterfront, whether approaching from the Sea of Marmara or the Golden Horn.

**The Forces**

- Constantine XI's army numbered 4,773 Greeks, plus 3,000 non-Greek foreigners, including some Turkish troops, and even one Scotsman—a mining engineer named John Grant.

- By way of contrast, the Ottoman sultan had a much larger, more fully functioning empire at this stage. While we can't be certain, estimates for Mehmed's army suggest as many as 60,000 Ottomans against the fewer than 8,000 Byzantine defenders.

- In addition to these fighting men, Mehmed's army was supported by thousands of laborers, ordnance specialists, and mining engineers.

**Weapons and Tactics**

- Sieges usually favored defenders. It was essential for those under attack to have access to clean water and food. In this respect, Constantinople was well served, meaning the difference in size of the two armies was not a guarantee of Ottoman victory.

- The Byzantine defenders were initially fairly confident that they could see off the attacking forces, as the city had dozens of times before. However, a technological advance had radically altered the balance of power: cannons.

- The assault on Constantinople in 1453 wasn't the first time cannons were used in battle. That occurred more than a century

The walls of Constaninople, restored in modern day.

earlier. But improved technology allowed for the casting of much larger armaments, which could fire larger objects over longer distances.

- A Hungarian master cannon maker named Urban had first offered his services to the Byzantine emperor. But Constantine XI said he couldn't afford Urban's asking price. And so the Hungarian turned instead to the Ottomans.

- Urban promised Mehmed he could build an incredibly powerful cannon. The Ottomans hired him. Just three months later, Urban's super gun was ready.

- The cannon Urban produced was state of the art for its day. There are reliable descriptions of this cannon firing projectiles more than a mile—a distance that surprised, and seriously worried, the defenders of Constantinople. Though it fired slowly, taking three hours to reload, it was a terrifying weapon that eventually ensured victory for the Ottoman attackers.

### The Call for Help

- Behind Constantinople's defensive walls, Constantine XI had an inkling that this time was, indeed, different—that Constantinople was in trouble. He sent envoys to Rome, as well as to the heads of important European kingdoms, principalities, and city-states.

- Due to the centuries of disputes between the churches of Rome and Constantinople, help was sadly lacking. The Roman Catholic pope's determination to see the two churches reunited under his authority was an important sticking point.

- While Constantine XI ultimately agreed to this demand, he lacked absolute authority. Orthodox authorities—along with priests and laity—refused to accept the decision. The emperor was ultimately unable to deliver.

- The largest foreign army to come to Constantine's aid was a 700-strong force from Genoa. Giovanni Giustiniani, an accomplished and respected soldier, led it. He and his troops were given the command of the city walls.

- As for other city-states that remained on the sidelines, many of them—including Venice and Pisa—had established booming trade with the Ottoman Empire.

**Sea Battle**

- Mehmed understood that to take Constantinople he had to surround the city from the sea *and* the landward side. As such, he amassed a blockading fleet of about 140 ships.

- Constantine ordered a heavy chain stretched across the entrance to the harbor. This would prevent attacking ships sailing into the harbor.

- In the third week of the seven-week siege, his navy seemingly locked out by this forbidding chain, Mehmed II simply ordered the fleet picked up and carried overland.

- The Ottomans hastily built a road of greased logs, pulled and pushed their ships overland, then dropped the vessels back into the water behind the chain. Mehmed was now able to attack the city from both the land and the water.

**Land Battle and Final Assault**

- As the sultan's forces launched attack after attack against the walls, the walls held up to their reputation, and failed to yield. Hundreds of Ottoman warriors were killed, or wounded, in each wave of assault.

- As the weeks dragged on, however, Urban's massive cannon took a growing toll, physically as well as psychologically. The noise of the gun was terrifying. So, too, must have been the defenders' realization that no reinforcements were on the way.

- Mehmed, after seven weeks of being locked outside of the city's walls, held a meeting of his council. Opinion was divided about whether to abandon the siege, or launch one more, perhaps final, attack. Those in favor of attacking carried the argument, and so began three days of preparations.

- The Ottomans didn't employ stealth. Instead, it was common for them to make noise to spread fear. They brought to bear a large numbers of drums and trumpets—as well as the booming of the super gun, and many smaller cannons—in a thunderous campaign to lower the morale of the besieged.

- Shortly after midnight, the Ottomans' final assault began. Wave after wave of the sultan's troops threw themselves against the city's northwest walls, which had been repeatedly struck by the super cannon. This section was now the weakest point in Byzantine defenses.

- Byzantine defenders initially repelled breaches in the city's outer walls. But in a last throw of the dice, Constantine ordered the bulk of his troops to stand and fight—in the space between the outer and inner walls—with the gates to the city locked behind them.

- At this stage, Genoese commander Giovanni Giustiniani was seriously wounded. Giustiniani's injuries rendered him unable to fight. Constantine agreed to open the gates to allow his ally back into the city. As the Ottoman attackers saw the disabled Genoese commander entering, they, too, rushed for the gates. Panic ensued in the defenders' ranks.

- More and more Ottoman troops forced their way through breaches in the walls. The defenders fell back, fighting as they were able, while others jumped from the walls to their deaths, rather than be taken prisoner.

- According to one eyewitness, Constantine himself threw off his purple imperial robe and charged—sword in hand—into the ranks of his Ottoman foes. The emperor's body was never found.

- The Ottomans had broken any serious resistance by midday. Constantinople was theirs. Reaching the massive Hagia Sophia cathedral—which was packed with civilians—the Muslim invaders broke down the doors. They divided the terrified citizens into groups, according to how much ransom they might get.

- In the rest of the city, the Sultan Mehmed II permitted his troops three days of pillaging, during which time anything they could take away was theirs for the keeping. When Mehmed himself entered Constantinople, however, the scale of the destruction and slaughter is said to have horrified him.

- The very next day, the sultan ordered the Hagia Sophia converted into a mosque, which explains its minarets—the tall, slender towers integral to a mosque, from which the Muslim faithful are called to prayer. In contrast, Mehmed left untouched most smaller churches.

Hagia Sophia

**Constantinople's Fall in Context**

- The sultan's conquest of Constantinople—and the subsequent establishment of his capital there—instituted a political system that would remain in place until 1922.

- The Ottomans now possessed a capital at the junction of two continents, across which they could continue to spread their domain, free from the worry about having an enemy to the rear. This conquest allowed the Ottomans to consolidate, and increase, their European domains.

- To some historians, the fall of Constantinople marks the end of the ancient world. The Roman Empire, after a long, slow decline—first in the West and now in the East—had finally come to an end. Byzantium was no more. And a 1,500-year chapter in human history was over.

- Because historical periods don't come with definite, universally agreed margins, many historians also describe the fall of Constantinople as the end of the medieval period, or the Middle Ages. By this perfectly acceptable reckoning, the Middle Ages started in the 5th century, with the fall of the Roman Empire in the West, and lasted the roughly 1,000 years until the Ottoman victory of 1453.

- This accounting offers a neat segue into the next period of European history: the Renaissance. With Byzantium consigned to history, numerous Greeks and other intellectuals fled, settling instead in Italy. This concentration spurred the rebirth of classical art and culture.

- While its seizure secured the Ottoman Empire's power and influence for several centuries at this transcontinental crossing point between Europe and Asia, it also forced unfriendly European powers to look for new trade routes to the Far East.

- Just a few years later, in 1492, the Catholic Monarchs of modern-day Spain—Ferdinand and Isabella—financed a westward voyage for new trade routes. They entrusted this important mission of exploration to one Christopher Columbus.

## Suggested Reading


Finkel, *Osman's Dream*.

Freely, *Istanbul*.

Goodwin, *Lords of the Horizons*.

Lapidus, *A History of Islamic Societies*, chapter 14.

Runciman, *The Fall of Constantinople 1453*.


## Questions to Consider

1. Does the fall of Constantinople represent just another chapter in an intractable battle between the Christian West and Muslim Middle East, or do the religious elements behind the Ottoman and Byzantine Empires hide the fact that this was nothing more than a straightforward imperial power struggle, upon which a religious narrative is used as justification?

2. Was the Ottoman's conversion of the Hagia Sophia a tribute or an insult to once-mighty Byzantium?

# Fall of Granada—1492

Lecture 23

The fall of Granada to Catholic conquerors marked the moment when, after nearly 800 years, Muslim rule on the Iberian Peninsula came to an end. What had been a unique Hispano-Muslim culture would become something very different, as the modern states of Spain and Portugal took shape. This lecture examines the background leading up to Granada's fall. It also describes the failed efforts of the last sultan of Granada, Muhammad XII, also known as Boabdil, to fend off the attackers. The lecture closes by identifying a surprising eyewitness to these events.

### Iberia and the Reconquista

- The initial Muslim invasion of the Iberian Peninsula took place in the year 711. A soldier force of about 1,700, mainly indigenous North African Berbers, landed near Gibraltar, and made quick battlefield gains against divided Christian Vandal rulers. Within a decade, these North African armies—growing to perhaps 50,000 people strong—crossed crossed the Pyrenees into modern-day France.

- However, as swiftly as the conquest of the Iberian Peninsula undoubtedly was, so, too, was the start of the fight back, on the part of the recently dispossessed local rulers. The *Reconquista* ("re-conquest") is traditionally pegged as beginning in 718 or 722—about a decade or less after the initial invasion.

- The whole uneven process took close to 800 years, ending with the fall of Granada. By the year 1249, Granada was the sole remaining Muslim kingdom in Iberia, and would remain so until its final defeat by Ferdinand and Isabella, 250 years later.

- A reason the Reconquista took as long as it did was that Christian rulers were not always trying to conquer Muslim-ruled lands. There were two main reasons for this.

- At first, numerous smaller kingdoms predominated on the peninsula, and any increase in the power of one would see the relative decline in influence of another. Thus, it was often in the best interests of putative rivals to keep the peace with one another.

- After 1031, and the fall of the caliphate of Cordoba—the greatest of all Muslim Spanish kingdoms—the bottom third of the Iberian Peninsula broke up into a series of petty Muslim kingdoms. The Christian kings might have had the military capability to conquer Granada and the other Muslim kingdom southern Spain at that time, but it was more profitable to accept financial tribute from them.

- By the 13th century, this was no longer the case. As the various Christian kings made territorial gains, they were quick to establish Christian peasants and minor nobility in these same lands—a process known as *repopulation*—in large part to defend their new borders in the event of any Muslim pushback.

- The Reconquista got going again in earnest in 1482, partly because of the repopulation efforts, and partly because of shifts in balances of power. One of the major shifts had occurred in what we think of today as Spain: In 1469, Ferdinand II of Aragon married Isabella I of Castile. They became known as the Catholic Monarchs.

- Isabella was 18 and Ferdinand was 17. It was perhaps the most important political union in Spanish history, joining their respective kingdoms and effectively creating modern Spain.

- After the marriage, the couple began the final conquest of Muslim Iberia. They were determined to create a wholly Catholic realm. And so, the Granada War began in 1482.

Ferdinand and Isabella

## Conflict in Granada

- By the second half of the 15th century, Granada's economy was in tatters. High taxation made a bad situation worse. In spite of the virtual collapse of the local economy by the time of the Granada War, citizens were still required to pay higher rates of tax in order to support the kingdom's large army.

- Disruption to trade caused by internal divisions didn't help matters. Nor did the fall to Ferdinand's forces in 1487 of the port city of Malaga. It was a serious loss.

- One of Ferdinand's and Isabella's main domestic concerns was to establish their authority over numerous, independent Christian nobles and their private armies. Corralling these otherwise independent armed forces allowed them to foster a degree of unity.

- One important tactical advantage the Catholic monarchs had over the Muslim defenders was better artillery. Before this war, defenders—behind high castle walls—might have had a defensive advantage. The sultan, Boabdil, certainly thought he did, until the advanced firepower that had developed elsewhere in Europe was brought to bear against him.

### Catholic Influence

- Among the most high-profile supporters of the Granada War was Pope Sixtus IV. As for Sixtus's support for the Reconquista, he fell in line only after a degree of pressure from Ferdinand. Ferdinand said that if Sixtus didn't send troops to help his campaign against Granada, then Ferdinand would withhold military support for the pope's own military efforts in and around the Papal States.

- As a result, until his death in 1484, Sixtus implemented a crusading tax to help bolster Ferdinand's and Isabella's war chest. In 1478, again under pressure from Ferdinand, Sixtus issued the papal bull that introduced the now-infamous Spanish Inquisition.

- From 1487, Boabdil was pressed by local Muslim rivals within Granada—as well as by the rising Christian tide outside the kingdom—and was able to maintain a tenuous hold on power only as a vassal of the Ferdinand and Isabella.

- In April 1491, with no further need to keep Boabdil as even a vassal, Ferdinand and Isabella's forces surrounded Granada. An eight-month siege followed, during which time Boabdil wrote a series of increasingly desperate letters to fellow Muslim rulers in North Africa and beyond. None offered him the military aid he desperately needed.

- Even had Boadbil's pleas reached more sympathetic ears, by this time he no longer controlled any of Granada's southern coastline. And so there was nowhere for this desired foreign assistance to land.

- Without external support, and with the situation inside Granada and the Alhambra becoming increasingly uncomfortable, Boabdil agreed to terms with Ferdinand and Isabella. On November 25, 1491, the Treaty of Granada was signed, which gave Boabdil and his subjects just two months to leave. Despondent at losing Granada, Boabdil spent the next 40 years in exile in Morocco.

- From the perspective of Muslims who had conquered and claimed this land as their own for the past several hundred years, there was also great sadness at giving up such gains forever. On the other victorious side, Christian monarchs from across Europe sent messages of congratulations to King Ferdinand and Queen Isabella.

**Aftermath**

- Before the Granada War, the best available estimates had put the number of Muslims in the Kingdom of Castile at around half a million. By the war's end, when a new spirit of intolerance took hold, some 100,000 were dead or enslaved, 200,000 had fled, and about 200,000 remained.

- On March 31, 1492, less than three months after taking the city and empire of Granada, the Catholic Monarchs issued the shameful Alhambra Decree, ordering the conversion or expulsion of all Jews, as well, from the kingdoms of Castile and Aragon.

- While the Jewish population was allowed to leave with its possessions, this did not include gold, silver, jewels, or other valuable items. If any Jews failed to either convert to Catholicism or leave before the end of that July, a state decree warned that they would face death without trial.

- Any non-Jew found offering shelter or protection to Jews after the deadline would have their belongings seized as well, and lose any hereditary privileges. Later that same year, Ferdinand issued a letter inviting these same Jews back, contingent on them converting Christianity. Few accepted.

- Not until 1968, and the guidance offered during the course of the Roman Catholic Church's Second Vatican Council, was the Alhambra Decree formally revoked.

- As for the 15th-century Spanish Jews, most settled across the breadth of North Africa. Jewish exiles also settled in large numbers in the Ottoman Empire.

- In 1501, an edict similar to the Alhambra Decree was issued to deal with the Muslim populations in Castile and Aragon. These native Spanish Muslims were offered a third, not terribly attractive, alternative of enslavement.

- In 1526, an edict forcing Muslims to convert, go into to exile, or volunteer to be enslaved was rolled out across the whole country. Alas, forced conversion did little to promote integration, and instead created a subset of second-class citizens in society.

- Those Muslims who had volunteered or been forcibly converted became known as Moriscos—or Moorish—after the word used to describe all Muslims from Morocco, Algeria, and Tunisia, the Iberian Peninsula, and other parts of Mediterranean Europe, such as Sicily and Malta.

- The so-called Moriscos failed to win genuine acceptance, or protection, in the freshly minted Catholic kingdom of Spain. Questions quickly arose about just how devoutly Christian were those subjects who'd been forced to convert.

- Recent converts to Christianity—suspected of secretly retaining their former faiths—suffered violent persecution. Unsurprisingly, they sometimes responded with violence. Such outbreaks included the destruction of property and looting.

- The violence fed suspicions in the Christian sector of society that these former Jews and Muslims were fifth columnists—that is, a rear guard within the country, working against its enemies—in the recently united Catholic kingdom. Naturally, this led to a cycle of more persecution and resentment.

- In 2014, Spain's parliament passed a law allowing a "right to return" to the descendants of all Jews expelled as a result of the Alhambra Decree of 1492. The question is sometimes asked as to when—or if—Spain will extend a similar offer of the right to return to the descendants of the country's expelled Muslim subjects.

**An Eyewitness**

- One eyewitness to the surrender of Granada wrote:

  > "After your Highnesses ended the war of the Moors who reigned in Europe, and finished the war of the great city of Granada, where this present year 1492 on the 2nd January I saw the royal banners of Your Highnesses planted by force of arms on the towers of the Alhambra."

- This particular eyewitness had a special reason for being excited by these events. His name was Christopher Columbus. By January 1492, Columbus had already spent seven years trying, without success, to get funding for his exploratory dreams.

- Columbus was convinced that he could sail west to reach Japan, China, and India. Such a route could be a lucrative replacement for the old, overland silk route to the Far East, which was shut down to most Europeans after the Ottomans won control of Constantinople.

- Ferdinand's and Isabella's experts had rejected Columbus's petition for this daring ocean expedition. But the Catholic Monarchs paid him a stipend for two years, to stop him from lobbying their European rivals. This also gave them time to reconsider his plan.

- After the fall of Granada in 1492, Ferdinand and Isabella were faced by the large debt the conflict had created. They decided to gamble on the lucrative upside of Columbus's idea. World history was about to change forever.

- The Canary Islands, sitting in the Atlantic, off the coast of Morocco, would be the starting point for Columbus's westward exploration. He estimated it was less than 2,500 miles further to Japan. The actual distance is closer to 7,500 miles. We know how that story turns out.

## Suggested Reading

Hitti, *History of the Arabs*, chapter 39.

Hourani, *A History of the Arab Peoples*, chapter 12.

Irwin, *The Alhambra*.

Kennedy, *Muslim Spain and Portugal*, chapter 11.

## Questions to Consider

1. How important was the marriage of Ferdinand and Isabella to the unification of what we now call Spain, and the final defeat of the Muslim Kingdom of Granada?

2. To what extent did the forced conversion and or expulsion of the local Jewish and Muslim populations have a negative impact on the culture and economy of Spain under Ferdinand and Isabella?

3. What do you think about the 21st-century decision to offer a right of return to the descendents of expelled Jews, but not Muslims?

## Safavid Dynasty of Persia—1501

Lecture 24

In this lecture, we're going to consider three broad areas that will explain why the Safavid empire and its founder, Ismail, were so radically different and important. First, we'll examine the birth of the empire and the personality of Ismail, a warrior and poet. Second, we'll take a closer look at Ismail's vision for his new empire, which involved replacing centuries of Sunni Islamic traditions with his own Shia Islamic faith. Finally, we will consider Ismail's development of new military structures, and the adoption of the latest military technologies.

### Ismail

- Ismail was born in 1487 in the city of Ardabil, in northwest Iran, about 40 miles from the Caspian Sea. His ethnic origins are disputed, although some combination of Kurdish, Persian, Azeri, Georgian, and Greek seems probable.

- When Ismail was one year old, his father died in battle. His eldest brother was likewise killed when Ismail was seven, at which point he was forced to go into hiding.

- With the death of his male elders, Ismail inherited the leadership of the mystical Sufi sect, known as the Safaviyya. Originally a Sunni Sufi order, the Safaviyya was founded in northwest Persia in the 13th century.

- Ismail claimed he was a direct descendant of Muhammad's son-in-law, Ali. This was important because in the Shia tradition, it's Ali and his descendants who were the rightful heirs of Islamic orthodoxy and power.

- It appears that Ismail also claimed to be the *Mahdi*, or "the rightly guided one." The Mahdi is considered to be the redeemer of Islam, whose appearance will presage judgement day. While identifying yourself as the Mahdi invests the claimant with messianic gravitas among the faithful, any failure on his part will lead to a similarly powerful reversal of fortune.

- At the age of 12, Ismail came out of hiding. Supported by his devoted followers from the Safiviyya order, he set about uniting the six largest Turkic-speaking tribes in the area.

- In July 1501, the 14-year-old Ismail was enthroned as the king—or shah—of Azerbaijan, after a decisive military victory fought in his name. The boy king established his capital in the Azerbaijani city of Tabriz, a vital hub on the crossroads of several important trade routes

- The next year, after further battlefield successes, Ismail was crowned the shahshanah (king of kings) of Iran. In less than a decade, he conquered the whole of modern Iran. Ismail's empire grew quickly to also encompass Armenia, the majority of Georgia, Kuwait, Iraq, and Afghanistan, as well as parts of Turkey and Syria. The Safavid dynasty, which would rule for 250 years, was born.

- Not only did Ismail make Shia Islam the state religion, he also established the role of the shah as someone who was viewed as the divinely appointed head of state, and the head of the Shia faithful in Persia.

- The Safavid Empire shows us the roots of the modern state of Iran: its borders, its language, its religious ideology, and its worldview.

## Empire Building

- Ismail's genius as an empire builder was in combining the particular skills of two groups of peoples—the nomadic Turkic warrior class, known as the *qizilbash*, and the settled Persian bureaucrats. The word *qizilbash* is Ottoman Turkish, and literally

A qizilbash soldier

means "red headed," after the distinctive red headgear worn by these Shia Safavid soldiers.

- Together, the men of the sword and the men of the pen—as the two groups became known—provided Ismail with military power and security. They also gave him a functioning bureaucracy.

- It seems that Ismail's own personality was a combination of the two: sword and pen.

  - One of the most memorable and grotesque stories from the battlefield sees Ismail beheading an opponent, and having the slain enemy's skull encrusted with jewels and made into his favorite drinking vessel.

    - Ismail grew up bilingual, speaking Azerbaijani—a Turkic language—and Persian. He was an accomplished poet in both languages.

- The new Safavid empire functioned as a meritocracy, with promotions going to those who could prove their worth. The meritorious approach to governing was no doubt carried over from a system that was typical of nomadic tribes, where success depended on rule by the best, not the best connected.

- Ismail emphasized the central importance of Persian-ness in the Safavid state. Ismail's plan involved overturning centuries of majority Sunni Islamic tradition. In its place, he would forcefully impose his own Messianic vision of Shia Islam, with him at its center.

- When Iran and Islam are mentioned in the same breath today, it's often in reference to the country with the world's largest Shia population. That is because of the Safavids' 250 years in power, and a policy of forced conversion of Sunni Muslims during the reign of Shah Ismail I.

- Probably the most important reason behind Ismail's decision to convert Persia to his own Twelver branch of Shiism was to set his empire apart from the main Sunni powers: the Ottoman Empire to the west, and the Uzbeks to the north and northeast.

- In deliberately highlighting his empire's Persian and Shia identity—that is, its non-Sunni and non-Turkic nature—Ismail was able to foster a higher degree of loyalty from his subjects. Ismail also removed any threat of a Sunni fifth column, or domestic opposition.

- There are a number of distinct forms, or schools, within the Shia tradition. Before Ismail's time, two of the more prominent of these were the Ismaili and Zaydi schools. Shah Ismail's own Twelver school was a minor player.

- Today, thanks to Ismail and his Safavid dynasty, Twelver Shiism is the largest, and most prominent, of all Shia schools. It accounts for 90 percent or more of all Shia in Iran, and roughly 80 percent of the global Shia population.

- Under Ismail, the persecution of the Sunni majority could be severe and even deadly, especially in conquered territories beyond the Persian heartland—for example, in Azerbaijan and Iraq. However, many scholars today would argue that these periods of violence were actually the exception rather than the rule, especially in Persia itself.

- But his policy of forcibly converting Persia's Sunni majority was a reality, and he used any means possible to make sure his campaign was a successful one. Among the more obvious tactics were making Shia Islam the official state religion.

- Ismail also reintroduced the practice of religious leaders—the Arabic word is *sadr*—who were responsible for supervising what was said in mosques and taught in schools. These *sadr* were also responsible for dissemination of Twelver doctrine.

- Ismail ordered the conversion of all mosques from Sunni to Shiism, as well as the destruction of Sunni shrines; the desecration of Sunni graves; and the reading of official curses against the first three caliphs at Friday prayers. This last step reflects the Shia belief that the fourth caliph, Ali—Muhammad's son-in-law—was the first legitimate caliph or successor, and that the first three were interlopers.

- Yet it also appears that Ismail could be satisfied with only a nominal conversion from Sunni to Shia Islam. The important thing was a public pronouncement that you were on the same side as the shah. Ismail also invited all Shia to come and settle in Persia. Shia clerics were especially welcome, and granted land and pensions for settling in Persia.

## The Battle of Chaldiran

- Qizilbash support for Ismail verged on the idol worship. But these well-armed, professional soldiers were also well aware of their role as kingmakers. Ismail, having relied on the qizilbash to put him on the throne, now felt the need to impose checks on their power, hopefully without antagonizing them too much in the process. In this last respect, he failed.

- Amid his early attempts to curtail their power, Ismail appointed a series of five Persian advisers, or overseers, to command these troops. The qizilbash murdered three of them.

- The qizilbash's reputation and power were finally dented by defeat at the Battle of Chaldiran in 1514, at the hands of the Safavids' arch-enemies: the Ottoman Empire. Unfortunately for Ismail, the Battle of Chaldiran also destroyed Ismail's aura of divine sanction, and gave his devoted followers pause for thought as to just how infallible he was.

- Before the battle, the Ottomans had long been uneasy about the Safavids' recruitment of Turkic men for their army. After all, the Ottomans, too, were a Turkic people, and they saw the rising power of the Shia Safavid Empire as a direct challenge to the regional hegemony they hoped to establish across the Middle East.

- Most sources agree that Ottoman forces outnumbered the Safavid qizilbash troops by a margin of two-to-one or three-to-one at Chaldiran. In spite of this, the disadvantaged Safavids fought well, and might have carried the day if not for the Ottomans' use of artillery.

- Cannon and other artillery blasted through the ranks of his elite but defenseless cavalry. Ismail himself was wounded and lucky to escape with his life. Although he remained ruler in name, Ismail—only 26 years old at the time—retired from public life, and is said to have descended into alcoholism and self-pity.

## After Ismail

- For the last 10 years of his reign, Ismail left the running of the empire to his chief advisor, under whom traditional divisions resurfaced between various tribes.

- When Ismail died, his son and heir was left to tackle a long civil war, before he finally was able to restore order under his own command. Ismail's son ultimately introduced a new military force—a royal guard—that swore loyalty to the person of the shah, as opposed to the state. Known as the *ghulams*, they were a useful counter-weight to the qizilbash.

- The Safavids, after their defeat at Chaldiran, invested in the same military hardware that had handed the Ottomans victory. In time, three Muslim empires—the Ottomans, the Safavids, and the Mughals (who ruled much of India)—would all make effective use of, cannons and artillery to complement traditional infantry and cavalry forces. They became known as the "gunpowder empires."

## Importance of the Safavids

- Unlike many competing empires—such as the Ottomans to the west and the Mughals in India—the Safavid Empire remained more or less the same size for generations, after expanding rapidly in its early days.

- The Safavids weren't the largest or longest-lasting empire in Islamic history. In spite of this, the Safavids—for having established the modern boundaries of Persia, as well as the bureaucratic framework for the modern nation of Iran, and the imposition of Shia Islam as the state religion—represent an important turning point in the histories of Persia and the Middle East.

- Once the borders of the Ottoman and Safavid empires became more or less established, outbreaks of war between the two became the exception rather than the norm. Even after the

Safavid dynasty's ultimate demise in 1736, Persia remained an important economic hinge between the markets of the East and the West.

- The capital moved, in 1598, to Isfahan. The relocation to Isfahan was ordered by Shah Abbas, the fifth Safavid shah. He engaged in a building program to transform the city, with many examples of his work still extant today. So grand did the new capital become that generations of inhabitants and others across the region came to know Isfahan by its nickname, "Half the World."

**Suggested Reading**

Gelvin, *The Modern Middle East*, chapter 2.

Hodgson, *The Venture of Islam*, volume 3, book 5.

Lapidus, *A History of Islamic Societies*, chapter 13.

Lewis, *The Middle East*, chapter 7.

Streusland, *Islamic Gunpowder Empires*, chapter 4.

**Questions to Consider**

1. How important was it for Shah Ismail's success that he converted Persia from Sunni to Shia Islam, and how important is this in the modern state of Iran?

2. Consider the role and importance of a professional army in the development of the Safavids' empire, and the importance of the ghulams, the former Christian slave force, within the imperial army.

# Selim the Grim—1512

Lecture
25

The Ottoman sultan Mehmed II's grandson, Selim I, became sultan himself. He is known to posterity as Selim the Grim. From the time of ascending to the Ottoman throne in 1512 until his death in 1520, Selim tripled the size of his empire, and neutralized any significant opposition in the Middle East. The Ottomans went from being one empire among several, to the new, undisputed caliphate of the Muslim world. And Selim himself officially became the first Ottoman caliph. This lecture traces Selim's rise to power, his reputation for violence, and his overall legacy.

Selim

### Selim's Origins

- Bayezid, Selim the Grim's father, had been the eighth Ottoman sultan. By all accounts he was a pious and scholarly individual, unlike his own father, Mehmed II.

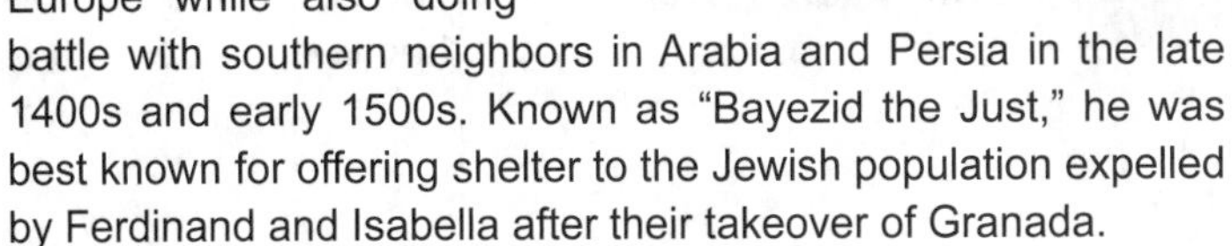

- Bayezid consolidated the Ottoman's hold in central Europe while also doing battle with southern neighbors in Arabia and Persia in the late 1400s and early 1500s. Known as "Bayezid the Just," he was best known for offering shelter to the Jewish population expelled by Ferdinand and Isabella after their takeover of Granada.

- When Bayezid, late in life, decided he'd had enough of the cares of high office, he announced plans to retire and turn power over to his eldest son Ahmed. A younger son, Selim, bristled.

- Selim raised an army of his own, and went on the offensive. Selim defeated his father's army, whose lackluster performance in battle mirrored the older man's fatigue and decline. Selim forced his father to adbicate and expelled him to a remote corner of the empire, where Bayezid died—apparently of natural causes—shortly thereafter.

- As spilling royal blood was considered going too far, Selim had Ahmed and another brother—as well as five nephews—dispatched in the time-honoured fashion of ritual strangulation, with silk cords. Selim had removed the possibility of any future challenge to his authority—at least from within his own family.

- "The Grim" is not a title that easily inspires affection, nor warmth. So just how grim was Selim? In Ottoman Turkish, the word applied to Selim is *Yavuz*, which is variously and best translated as "strong, stern, or implacable." Alas for Selim, in English it's *grim* he's stuck with.

- One memorable story has Selim's most senior vizier asking in jest, "Sire, I would hope that if you were going to have me killed, you might be kind enough to give me a little advance warning so that I could put my affairs in order."

    - Selim replied, "I have been thinking of having you killed, but I haven't yet found a suitable replacement."

    - During Selim's rule the following Ottoman curse was created and popularized: "May you become a vizier in the Sultan's court."

## Early Moves

- The empire Selim inherited in 1512 was not the transcontinental superpower it would become. In spite of the fact that the Ottoman Empire had been founded in 1299, it remained very much a regional, rather than global, power. Its major land holdings were limited to Anatolia and portions of Eastern Europe. Under Selim, all this would change, as he engaged in a highly successful expansionist policy.

- The first serious challenge to Selim's plans came about thanks to another rising power of the time: Persia's new Safavid empire. The Safavids knew from the beginning that the Ottomans were a threat to their own imperial ambitions. They went on the offensive against this older, better established regional power.

- In the first 10 years of their reign, the Safavids engaged in a policy of the forced conversion of all Sunni Muslim Persians to the form of Shia Islam known as the Twelver school. With this conversion process well under way, the Safavids found it easier to isolate any possible Sunni Muslim challengers to their power.

- At the same time, instead of confronting the Ottomans head on—a military task that the Safavids weren't ready for—they supported a pro-Shia, anti-Ottoman uprising in Anatolia, the Asian portion of modern Turkey. (This uprising was ultimately unsuccessful.)

- When Selim came to the throne in 1512, he quickly took action to counter this challenge in his empire's east with a suitably firm military response at the Battle of Chaldiran—just northeast of Lake Van, in eastern Anatolia. Gunpowder, and the artillery and musketry it powered, tipped this battle in favor of the Ottomans.

- This defeat ended Shia uprisings in the Ottoman Empire. For the Ottomans, their victory at Chaldiran couldn't have been more important. Crucially, it meant they'd secured eastern Anatolia on a permanent basis. In addition, northern Iraq was now under their control. And, at least temporarily, so too was northwest Persia—snatched from the bruised and beaten Safavids.

## Safavids Survive

- After entering the Safavid capital of Tabriz in northwest Iran, unopposed, Selim's forces began fearing a counterattack. Far from home, they mutinied, and demanded that the sultan withdraw from Persia. Selim did indeed withdraw. But had Selim prevailed over his men, and pressed on, there's a good chance that he could have defeated the Safavids permanently.

- While Selim might have regretted his inability to pursue the Safavids deeper into Persian territory, perhaps dealing them a fatal blow, he was also a practical man. The Safavids were never going to become his best friends, but an uneasy peace was easier to live with than a continuing, unpopular war far from his center of power.

- Proving this point, after Selim's death, his son would pursue three campaigns against the Safavids, none of which ended in a decisive victory for either side. The Ottomans and the Safavids ultimately signed a peace treaty in 1554.

- Under this treaty, the opposing empires agreed to stop leading raids into each other's territory, and agreed where their respective territorial boundaries lay. The Ottomans returned Tabriz to the Safavids, while the Safavids conceded Baghdad and lower Mesopotamia, including the mouths of the Tigris and Euphrates rivers, and all-important access to the Persian Gulf. (These borders are not dissimilar to the modern frontier between Iran and Iraq.)

## Religious Dealings

- Selim offered significant legal protections to the Jewish and Christian populations that lived in his domains. But he showed ruthlessness toward fellow Muslims who, in his opinion, strayed from the straight path.

- Selim saw the Safavids' mystical form of Sufi-Shiism as heretical. He is alleged to have offered the infamous observation that "the killing of one Shia has the same other-worldly value as killing 70 Christians."

- Such disregard for human life was, in part, a response to the Shia Safavid challenge. However, it might also have had a more fundamental aim. Since the early 15th century, Ottoman sultans had been taking the title of caliph for themselves, although without anyone else in the Muslim world accepting these claims.

- As a non-Arabic, Turkish dynasty, Ottoman claims to the caliphate were hard to press home, not least because—at this stage—they didn't have significant territorial holdings in the Middle East proper. With the Safavid threat neutralized, however, this was about to change. Selim set his sights on the Mamluk empire, with its capital in Cairo.

**Selim Becomes Caliph**

- Selim now marched south through Syria and the Levant, which includes modern Israel, Palestine, and the surrounding area. A single Ottoman victory—at the Battle of Marj Dabiq, in August 1516—was enough to secure the whole of Syria for the Turkish invaders. From there, the Ottomans continued moving south, through the Levant, arriving in Egypt in January 1517.

- The Egyptain Mamluks had risen to power as a result of their military prowess. The Mamluks prided themselves with fighting in a traditional—what they considered honorable—fashion. They were expert mounted archers.

- Thirty years earlier, the Ottomans and the Egyptians had waged a previous war that ended in stalemate. But, by the start of the 16th century, the Mamluks had lost their edge as a martial power. Their archers were no match for Ottoman artillery and musketry. As a result, Ottoman advances were now both swift and decisive.

- Selim led his troops into Cairo, beat the Mamluks, and occupied the center of their power. The Mamluk sultan, Tuman Bay, was captured and killed. His body was body strung up from one of the city's main gates as the victorious Ottoman army sacked Cairo. While it might not have been the powerhouse it had once been, Cairo was still a prize of great wealth.

- The Ottomans were now in charge of the city that had been home to the caliphs for more than 250 years—since just after the Mongol sack of Baghdad in 1258. As word of Selim's victory over Egypt spread, most of the Mamluks' regional governors who hadn't already been conquered immediately capitulated, bringing regional Mamluk rule to an end.

- For symbolic and propaganda value alone, the Mamluks' most important loss occurred when the emir of Mecca surrendered Islam's two holy cities—Mecca and Medina—to Ottoman control. More important than the land was the long-coveted title nobody could now deny the Ottoman sultan: caliph. Selim the Grim was now the first Ottoman caliph, and successor to Islam's main prophet, Muhammad.

- In a little over a year, Selim had led his army in the conquest of Syria and the Levant, Egypt, and the western edge of the Arabian Peninsula—the Hijaz, birthplace of Islam. Selim invested in building up a significant Ottoman fleet to reinforce his control over the western Arabian littoral and the whole of the Red Sea.

**Selim's Legacy**

- In 1520, after eight years in power, Selim announced his intention to take his conquering juggernaut west into Europe. Selim had a somewhat weakened Hungary in his sights.

- But suddenly, at the age of 55, he was dead. According to a contemporary chronicler, his mortality was the result of an infected boil. The symptoms described suggest that Selim succumbed to a form of anthrax, which he likely contracted from a horse. Hungary had been saved—for now—by a horse's whisker, or perhaps by a boil.

- With a violent temper and a great vision, Selim the Grim transformed what had been an Anatolian- and Balkan-based empire into an altogether grander Ottoman Empire, with new territories in Africa and Arabia. But more than that, he'd inherited the mantle of caliph, becoming the inheritor of the great Muslim empires that had come before him.

**Suggested Reading**

*Cambridge History of Turkey*, volume 2.

Finkel, *Osman's Dream*.

Freely, *Istanbul*.

Goodwin, *Lords of the Horizons*.

Hodgson, *The Venture of Islam*, volume 3, book 5.

Lewis, *The Middle East*, chapter 7.

Streusland, *Islamic Gunpowder Empires*, chapter 3.

**Questions to Consider**

1. How important was it for the non-Arab, Turkic Ottomans to capture the cities of Mecca and Medina, and so claim the title caliphate, and with it religious authority over the region's Sunni Muslim populations?

2. Even without ordering the murder of his own brothers and nephews—a common practice in the Ottoman Empire, to avoid wars of succession—how grim was Selim?

Lecture 26

# Suleiman the Magnificent—1520

Between the founding of the Ottoman Empire in 1299 and its abolition in 1924, there were 36 Ottoman sultans. Of these, Suleiman the Magnificent ruled the longest, and is undoubtedly the best known and most celebrated of them all. Suleiman became one of the most important rulers anywhere on earth. Even today, almost 500 years after he came to power, Suleiman's vision continues to provide the model of what we think of when our thoughts turn to the Ottoman Empire.

## Overview of Suleiman

- Suleiman was the 10th Ottoman sultan since the dynasty was established in 1299. He inherited an already substantial realm thanks to the conquests of his father, Selim the Grim.

- Suleiman expanded his father's territories. He consolidated and formalized rule over the billion-acre Ottoman Empire, which spanned three continents: Asia, Europe, and Africa.

- Two qualities, in particular, qualify the reign of Suleiman the Magnificent as worthy of being considered a turning point in the history of the Middle East.

    - The first is his reign's sheer length. Having come to power at the age of 25, he ruled for 46 years, until his death in 1566 at the age of 71.

    - The second factor is the energy and the vision he brought with him. It would guarantee the Ottoman Empire's continuing vitality for centuries, even as it was later ruled by a series of inferior sultans and their venal viziers.

## Early Life

- Suleiman was Selim the Grim's only son. He was born in 1494, in the Black Sea city of Trabazon, in what today is northeastern Turkey. At the age of seven, he was sent to the Ottoman capital of Constantinople. There, he received a standard education for an imperial heir, studying military history and tactics, science, literature, Arabic, and Islamic theology.

- When his father died in 1520, Suleiman inherited the Ottoman sultanate without the fratricidal plots that had challenged his father and grandfather

- As for his name: *Suleiman* is the Turkish and Arabic rendering of Solomon, the Old Testament king and one of King David's sons. Solomon's name is a byword for wisdom and good governance. With Solomon honored as a prophet in the Islamic tradition, it was a name that could only enhance Suleiman's reputation.

## Suleiman and Roxelana

- The romance of Suleiman and Roxelana is a love story that has inspired poets, artists and composers for centuries. We know very little about the early life of Roxelana, except that she was a Christian slave girl.

- What is clear is that Roxelana entered the Sultan's harem as one of an unknown number of concubines. She became Suleiman's favourite consort. Eventually, she bore numerous children for him, including, most importantly, sons.

- In a startling break with Ottoman tradition, the sultan married Roxelana. He granted the former Christian slave girl her freedom. For the first time in Ottoman history, a concubine had become a sultan's legal wife. Moreover, she was given the title Haseki Sultan, or "favorite wife." (Roxelana might have been Suleiman's favorite wife, but she wasn't his only one.)

- In order for the Ottoman dynasty to last and prosper, it was essential that there always be the smoothest possible transition of power from one sultan to the next. This led to all sorts of palace intrigues, infighting, lies, and power struggles. The harem was one of the worst places for this, as mothers of sons did everything in their power to ensure that one of their boys would inherit the coveted sultanate.

- Roxelana was as desperate as anyone else to see her son, Selim, inherit the sultanate. During this age, boys who didn't inherit tended to be ritually strangled. In this way, there was no chance of them, or their supporters, posing a challenge to the throne at some future date.

- Roxelana persuaded Suleiman that his eldest son of another wife was plotting against him, and so the father ordered the execution of his own child, his firstborn son Mustapha.

- With her own son, Selim, as heir apparent, Roxelana's position in the palace was secured. In a further upending of the old order, Roxelana—after she passed childbearing age—wasn't dispatched to the provinces, but instead remained at Suleiman's side.

- Roxelana would become arguably the most influential female political figure in more than 600 years of Ottoman history.

Roxelana

She was certainly the first *sultana*—or sultan's wife—to advise her husband on an official footing.

## Conquests

- Suleiman's father, Selim the Grim, had in less than a decade had tripled the size of the Ottoman Empire. Suleiman's own conquests were not on the same scale, but they were no less important.

- Suleiman started his reign by pushing further into Europe. In 1521—a year after he came to power—Suleiman captured the city of Belgrade, and the southern and central portion of the Kingdom of Hungary.

- Later, his historic 1526 victory at the Battle of Mohacs secured Ottoman rule in much of Hungary and other parts of Central Europe for centuries. Further westward progress was halted, however, after he twice failed to take Vienna in 1529 and 1532.

- Suleiman would go on to capture Baghdad from the Persian Safavids in 1535. This not only secured the whole of Mesopotamia, but also provided the Ottomans with direct access to the Gulf. Seizing Baghdad also meant that this Turkish superpower now controlled every former caliphal capital: Medina, Damascus, Baghdad, and Cairo.

- Supported by his expanding navy, Suleiman then extended Ottoman power along the coast of North Africa, from Egypt to Algeria. Elsewhere in the Mediterranean, Suleiman lent his navy to help an ally in need: the king of France.

- France and the Ottomans shared a common antipathy towards Hungary. And so, led by Suleiman's legendary Admiral Barbarosa, Ottoman forces helped the French capture Nice, Corsica, and other Mediterranean prizes. The Franco-Ottoman alliance lasted until well after the deaths of the French king and

Suleiman alike. In fact, it remained in force for another two-and-a-half centuries.

### Suleiman's Society

- A big factor in Suleiman's success was the development of a single bureaucratic system across the length and breadth of the Ottoman Empire, from North Africa to the Black Sea, and from Hungary to Baghdad.

- This bureaucracy allowed the two main languages of state—Arabic and Ottoman Turkish—to exist alongside each other, with officials able to function in both. Arabic, the language of the Quran, was always present for religious matters, while anyone who wanted to work in the temporal world of government had to use Turkish.

- While the Ottomans didn't worry much about ethnicity, they were interested in their subjects' distinct confessional identities. The Ottomans, naturally, put their own faith at the top of the different religious groups. They also had—under Muslim sharia law—a responsibility to protect all "People of the Book," that is, Jews and Christians in their realm.

- It also made sense in purely pragmatic terms for the Ottomans to rule over happy, rather than unhappy, subjects. Suleiman's challenge was therefore to put into place a single, unified legislative code that protected all subjects, regardless of religion.

- Drawing up such a legal code was hard enough. But Suleiman's task was further complicated by two factors. First, any laws he drafted couldn't contradict sharia law. Second, in trying to put a single legal code into practice, he was confronted by nine distinct preexisting legal systems, one by each of his predecessors.

- Therefore, Suleiman collected all existing judgments and cut out any duplicates. After removing this legal dead wood, he also removed laws that were contradictory.

- When he'd finished the *Qanuni Osmani*, or Ottoman Code, it provided the basis of an imperial law that would last for more than 300 years, until the mid-19th century. It's highly unlikely that the Ottoman Empire would have lasted as long as it did without this code.

### Suleiman's Architecture

- Suleiman's creation of a distinct architectural style, like his success in establishing a strong bureaucracy and systematic legal code, came about because of two factors: his personal vision, and his length of tenure.

- Suleiman employed the most talented architect alive in his day: Mimar Sinan. Sinan was an early proponent of designing earthquake-proof structures. This was especially useful in the Ottoman heartland of Anatolia, an area that's still prone to earthquakes.

- When he was approaching age 50, Sinan found his true calling. That's when he attracted the patronage of the sultan, and was appointed chief royal architect. During his lifetime, he oversaw the completion of some 300 major building projects, including mosques, schools, bathhouses, and bazaars.

- Two prominent examples of what Sinan built while working for Suleiman were the Suleimaniye Mosque in Istanbul and the Selimiye Mosque in Edirne, the Ottoman's former capital.

    - The Suleimaniye Mosque was built between 1550–1558, and remains the largest purpose-built mosque in Istanbul today. In constructing the Suleimaniye, Sinan echoed the majesty of the earlier, Byzantine domes of the Hagia Sophia, while also applying numerous elements of Islamic architecture. The most obvious of these are the spire-like minarets, from which the five-times-a-day call to prayer was traditionally made.

- Sinan considered the Selimiye Mosque his greatest single project. Built between 1569–1575, it's rightly hailed as a high point in Islamic architecture. That's because while Sinan deliberately borrowed certain Byzantine architectural styles in designing the Suleimaniye Mosque, the Selimiye is a more consciously Ottoman structure.

- With its massive dome and four lofty minarets, the Selimiye mosque is actually just one part of a wider complex. It's the centerpiece of a community of buildings that includes a hospital, schools, steam baths, shops, and a cemetery.

- Even after his death in 1588, Sinan's legacy lived on in the many young apprentices he trained. Sinan's protégés would go on to build some of the most iconic buildings in the Muslim world, including the Taj Mahal in Mughal India.

- Sinan also had a hand in memorializing Suleiman and Roxelana. In the garden behind the Suleimaniye Mosque, Sinan built tombs for each of them. Sinan himself is buried just a short distance away, in a tomb that he also designed for himself.

**Suggested Reading**

*Cambridge History of Turkey*, volume 2.

Finkel, *Osman's Dream*.

Freely, *Istanbul*.

Goodwin, *Lords of the Horizons*.

Hodgson, *The Venture of Islam*, volume 3, book 5.

**Questions to Consider**

1. Do you think Roxelana was a manipulative and conniving woman who wanted nothing but power, or was she a devoted and loving wife, whose alleged plotting against harem rivals was nothing less than a fight for survival?

2. Would the Ottoman Empire have survived for 350 years after Suleiman's death if he hadn't instituted his wide-ranging program of administrative and legal reforms?

Lecture 27

# Second Siege of Vienna—1683

This lecture looks at the events surrounding the 1683 Siege of Vienna and the subsequent battle. The lecture focuses on three angles: the state of Hapsburg-Ottoman relations before 1683; the siege and battle in and around Vienna; and the aftermath and impact of the battle. Closing the lecture is an examination of three oft-repeated views of the events: that the Habsburg victories stopped the Ottomans from overrunning Europe; that this was the beginning of the Ottoman Empire's end; and that the battle of Vienna marked just one more chapter in a clash of civilizations between Christendom and Islam.

**Relations Before the Conflict**

- Between the Habsburg—or Austrian—Empire and the Ottomans, there existed a mutual antipathy that lasted for more than 250 years. The antagonism was especially acute because of their close proximity, and their shared, albeit shifting, borders.

- The Ottoman Empire, born in 1299, spread into the Balkans in its first century of existence. After the Ottoman Turks' conquest of the Eastern Roman Empire capital of Constantinople in 1453, this new Muslim powerhouse was in a position to pursue more extensive inroads into Europe. The House of Habsburg—which occupied the throne of the Holy Roman Empire from 1438 to 1740—rightly saw the Ottomans as a threat. The tension between them arose from questions of power, conquest, and prestige rather than of religion.

- The 1683 attack on Vienna was not Ottomans' first attempt. A little more than 150 years earlier, in 1529, an Ottoman army led by Suleiman the Magnificent had also tried and failed to conquer Vienna.

- Vienna was an attractive economic prize. Starting from roughly the early 1200s, the power that held Vienna, on the Danube River, could control trade routes throughout the middle and south of Europe.

- Leading up to the 1683 attack, there was certainly talk about a battle between Christendom and Islam, although not generally on the Ottoman side. The promise of plunder appears to have been incentive enough on the Turkish side, without the need to sell it as a religious war.

- In Central and Western Europe, by contrast, most talk did revolve around the coming collision of empires as a religious clash. The most important reason for this was an attempt, on the part of the Habsburgs, to get financial and military support.

**Mehmed IV and Kara Mustafa Pasha**

- Mehmed IV had ascended to the throne at just six years old. He relied on his mother to protect him. She in turn relied on the grand vizier to rule and keep her son alive.

- Mehmed IV himself was more interested in outdoor pursuits like hunting than in reigning. From this point on, a sultan's grand vizier typically held more executive power than the sultan himself.

- On March 31, 1683, a formal declaration of war arrived at Vienna. It came from Sultan Mehmed IV via his grand vizier and the commander of his army, Kara Mustafa Pasha. The next day, Kara Mustafa Pasha's march commenced.

**Ottoman Forces**

- When they'd tried to take Vienna 150 years earlier, Ottoman forces didn't arrive until late September, just as the autumn started turning wet and cold. This greatly hampered their efforts. But in 1683, Ottoman forces reached Vienna on July 14. They

they were a sizable force numbering about 150,000 men, although by no means were all of these soldiers.

- The bulk of the Ottoman army consisted of non-combatants. These were support personnel: everyone who made such an expedition possible, from cooks to stable boys.

- The Ottomans, being used to siege warfare from their many military campaigns that had greatly expanded this Muslim empire, had with them about 130 field guns, as opposed to heavy cannons.

- Previously, the Ottomans had assaulted Vienna with heavy cannons, which quickly got bogged down in the rain and mud. Another reason why they now brought lighter field guns was that the plan wasn't to blast the city into submission but rather to persuade the defenders to surrender within a couple of days, in the face of their overwhelming numbers.

- A city destroyed by artillery is not much of a prize. In addition, if a population surrendered rather than being taken in battle, the conquering troops were not entitled to the standard payment of plunder. This made such victories more profitable for the commander and concurrently less profitable—if also less dangerous—for ordinary soldiers.

**The Siege**

- The Habsburg emperor Leopold I fled as soon as he heard of the Ottomans' approach. He was accompanied by as many as 60,000 Viennese. At the same time as Leopold was running away from Vienna, tens of thousands of local peasants flooded into the city for protection behind its walls. Inside the gates, the defending army numbered no more than 15,000 men, about a tenth of the number of the Ottomans outside.

- The Ottomans also cut off virtually all supplies entering Vienna, so rationing was introduced. The Viennese soon ran out of

Leopold I

most standard foodstuffs. They resorted to eating cats and rats. Deprived of sufficient food and clean water, it's reckoned that about half of the total garrison of 24,000 died.

- The officer in charge of the defense ordered that any soldier found sleeping at his post was to be shot on site. This probably did little for morale, but it may have kept the defenders on guard.

- Outside, Ottoman morale fell as expectations of a fast victory dissipated. While not yet reduced to eating rats, the Ottomans' supplies were also being depleted, and, with winter approaching, they needed victory sooner rather than later. Over the course of the two-month siege, some 20,000 Ottomans died.

- Leopold I, although he'd abandoned Vienna to its fate, nevertheless sent out appeals for help. Various European allies committed to send troops to aid the Habsburgs. Among them, Bavaria, Saxony, Franconia, and other German principalities did send troops to the Hapsburgs' aid, along with 18,000 Polish cavalry under the direct command of their king, John III Sobieski.

- Sobieski had already clashed with Ottomans on a number of occasions, and the Turks were rightly fearful of him. He led the defense. Meanwhile, the refusal of King Louis XIV of France to also assist was duly noted by Leopold, as was France's highly controversial, longstanding alliance with the Ottoman Empire.

- On the other side, the Ottomans were reinforced by troops from Moldavia, Transylvania, and elsewhere. A 40,000-man force from the Khanate of Crimea did not arrive in time for the battle. As it was, they were still some days' march away on the fateful morning of September 11, 1683, when fighting commenced. Nevertheless, the Ottomans launched an aggressive attack.

**The Battle**

- Kara Mustafa Pasha ordered his men forward at 4:00 am, in the predawn darkness, determined to inflict mayhem on the defenders before they could be properly deployed. German and Holy Roman troops fought back without giving ground.

- Similar clashes continued throughout the day, but by early afternoon it was clear that the Ottomans, in spite of securing a section of the city walls, were not as well organized or as motivated as was the defending army led by Sobieski.

- As the battle turned, the Ottoman commander Mustafa is said to have ordered the execution of 30,000 prisoners. Whether this was driven by panic, anger, or hatred, history doesn't record, but it added to the charnel-house atmosphere.

- The Ottomans' elite janissary units were still attacking when Sobieski issued orders that would commit his heavy cavalry, the famous Winged Hussars, to a final flanking counterattack. By about 4:00 pm, Kara Mustafa Pasha had an inkling of the eventual outcome, and he retreated.

- Numerous Ottoman units, whether or not seeing their commander retreat, made a similar decision to turn and run. At 6:00 pm, with Sobieski personally leading the charge, a combined force of 18,000 horsemen raced full tilt at the Ottoman lines. A rout ensued, and retreating Ottoman forces were pursued and cut down for days after.

- About 40,000 Turks and their allies were killed during the battle and the pursuit that followed. But the Battle of Vienna was essentially over by nightfall.

**The Aftermath**

- Emperor Leopold's brother-in-law, Charles V, Duke of Lorraine, continued to take the fight to the Ottomans, retaking Belgrade and much of Serbia three years later. By 1687, Habsburg control had been established over southern Hungary and portions of Transylvania.

- A Habsburg triumph was not the outcome France's Louis XIV wanted. But he took advantage of Leopold I's preoccupation with the Ottoman threat in Central Europe and incorporated Habsburg Alsace into his own kingdom.

- Although France would remain Europe's most powerful kingdom for a time, the Habsburg victory assured the Austrians of political supremacy in Central Europe, an advantage that would remain place until the First World War.

- As for Kara Mustafa Pasha, once he'd been defeated, there was never any real doubt about his ultimate fate. Mehmed IV ordered his ritual execution in Belgrade in the manner reserved for high officials in the Ottoman Empire: strangulation by silk cord. The last words of the Ottomans' defeated commander were to his executioner, telling him to make sure the knot was properly tied.

## Three Opinions

- Worthy of examination are three commonly voiced opinions about the Siege of Vienna and subsequent battle.

- The first of these ideas is that the victory of the Habsburg alliance saved Europe from being conquered by the Ottoman Turks. While this was a frequent claim made at the time, the evidence shows that even if the Ottomans had taken Vienna, it's not likely they'd have been able to push much further west.

    - Vienna marked the logistical extreme of the Ottomans' military reach. The fact that the Ottomans failed to take the city supports the veracity of this claim.

    - The Ottomans' failure to take Vienna didn't much mark the end of Ottoman-Habsburg rivalry so much as the start of a long conflict known as the Great Turkish War, in which the two imperial powers would clash in Central and Eastern Europe for the next 15 years. In 1699 the two sides finally negotiated the Treaty of Karlowitz, in modern Serbia.

- A second opinion often put forward about the Ottomans' defeat at Vienna is that it marks the beginning of the end of the Ottoman Empire. This is possible, but if it was the beginning of the end, the end was a long time coming—another 241 years, to be precise. The Ottoman Empire remained a formidable imperial force long after the events of September 1683.

- The third opinion is that the 1683 conflict at Vienna was another chapter in the so-called clash of civilizations between Christians and Muslims.

    - The desperate defenders of the Hapsburg Empire were trying to sell the siege of Vienna as a battle for Christendom. But that certainly wasn't how the Ottomans saw it. The Ottomans were after a much more temporal prize: the expansion of their influence from conquest and trade.

    - While the Habsburgs and the Ottomans certainly did come from two distinct religious backgrounds, they were fighting for the retention, or extension, of their respective imperial power.

**Suggested Reading**

*Cambridge History of Turkey*, volume 2.

Finkel, *Osman's Dream*.

Goodwin, *Lords of the Horizons*.

Hodgson, *The Venture of Islam*, volume 3, book 5.

Stoye, *The Siege of Vienna*.

**Questions to Consider**

1. Is the longer-lasting legacy of the failed Siege of Vienna the creation of the croissant and the start of European café society, or is it the beginning of the centuries-long decline of the Ottoman Empire?

2. In 1683, the Ottoman Empire was the dominant force in what we think of as Eastern Europe. With this in mind, how do our view of and attitude toward the Siege of Vienna shift if we instead talk about Western Asia?

Lecture 28

# The Saud-Wahhab Pact—1744

Almost exactly halfway through the 18th century, there occurred a revolutionary moment that fused politics and religion in the Middle East—and which would turn out to be among the most significant tidal changes in history. With the power of hindsight, it's possible to see why this moment was largely ignored at the time. Yet 200 years later, this transformation of almost entirely local concern became a subject of global importance. This lecture looks at that moment—the Saud-Wahhab pact—and its fallout.

## Background

- This lecture's turning point occurred in a remote spot in the Arabian Desert, in a small oasis town called Diriyah. This lightly populated settlement would become the capital of the first Saudi state. Diriyah is today a suburb of the modern-day Saudi capital of Riyadh.

- In 1744, Muhammad ibn Saud, the son of a local desert ruler, married the daughter of a religious reformer, Muhammad ibn 'Abd al-Wahhab. 'Abd al-Wahhab is a forerunner to one of the most conservative branches of the Sunni Muslim faith, which today predominates in Saudi Arabia.

- This marriage cemented an unusual alliance between two families that led to the creation of the first Saudi state, which initially lasted until 1818. An army of the Ottoman Empire ultimately destroyed that first Saudi nation, in 1818, for challenging its authority. A second Saudi state would arise a few years later, and last for most of the 19th century.

- In the early 20th century, a third Saudi state came into being, which we know of today as the Kingdom of Saudi Arabia. In each instance, the political authority of these Saudi states originates in the blood ties forged between Muhammad ibn Saud and Muhammad ibn 'Abd al-Wahhab in Diriyah, in 1744.

- At the time the Saudi state founders Muhammad ibn Saud and Muhammad al-Wahhab came together, Diriyah had been home to the Saud family for about 200 years. The Arabian Peninsula—in spite of being the birthplace of Islam—was then a political backwater.

**Muhammad ibn Saud**

- Muhammad ibn Saud, born in about 1710, was the emir—or prince—of Diriyah, a title he inherited upon the death of his father. He was an ambitious young man who was looking an opportunity to expand his influence and income. And so it was, according to one account, that he heard about the religiously zealous Muhammad Ibn 'Abd al-Wahhab, and invited him to come and settle in Diriyah.

- Originally from a nearby oasis, even smaller than Diriyah, Ibn 'Abd al-Wahhab began his religious studies at an early age, not least because his father came from a line of scholars. He considered himself a religious reformer. But what was it about Islam that he wanted to reform?

- Central to Islamic faith—at the very heart of the religion—is the concept of the oneness of God, a doctrine called *tawhid* in Arabic. The belief in God as a single, united, indivisible entity, is a characteristic trait of monotheism shared also by Jews and Christians. If the oneness of God is central to your faith, then believing in, or worshipping, numerous gods—which is a trait of polytheism—is obviously a serious offense. It was in this central tenet of Islam that 'Abd al-Wahhab decided that his fellow Muslims had strayed.

- When 'Abd al-Wahhab began wandering around Arabia accusing people of polytheism, and otherwise having strayed from the true path of Islam, it didn't make him very popular. They all denied his charges.

- 'Abd al-Wahhab based his accusations on the traditional practices of the people, visiting the tombs of the dead, venerating the memory of saints or holy men, and similar rites. Veneration is not worship, the defenders would say. But 'Abd al-Wahhab thought differently.

- He likewise condemned all Shia Muslims and Sufis, who are primarily Sunni and adopt a more mystical approach to their faith and practices than the likes of al-Wahhab. In this regard, his message was unwavering and uncompromising. He was unforgiving toward those he considered guilty of polytheism.

- Central to our story, both Saud and Wahhab were from the Sunni branch of Islam (the meritocratic view of who should be Muhammad's successor), which sets them at odds with adherents of Shia Islam (the family-based view). And while there is a minority Shia population today in Saudi Arabia's Eastern Province, the largest concentration of Shia Muslims is in Persia, or modern Iran.

- In Sunni Islam, there are four main schools of sharia law. Of these, al-Wahhab belonged to the Hanbali school. This was, and remains, the smallest and most religiously conservative of the four. Like the other three, the Hanbali school relies heavily on the Quran and the *hadith*, or sayings of the prophet of Islam, Muhammad, for its religious judgements.

- In addition, the Hanbali puts a great deal of importance on the first three generations of Muslims, that is to say those on Muhammad and his immediate heirs. Collectively, these founding generations of Islam are called *salaf*—meaning predecessors—and one who follows their example is, thus, a Salafi.

- Very often, if one hears the terms *Salafi* and *Wahhabi* used in the West, they are referred to interchangeably, which is not strictly accurate. Those we might think of as Wahhabis, i.e. followers of Wahhab, take great exception to the term because they do not consider themselves as following him.

- As their opponents often use *Wahhabi* and *Wahhabism* as terms of opprobrium, those who follow the example of Wahhab are more likely to refer to themselves as Salafis. However, the term Wahhabi is in such widespread use that those who follow the example and teachings of al-Wahhab find they are rather stuck with it.

- The important point to note here is that many other Muslims also claim to follow the example of the earliest generations of Muslims—the salaf. Thus, all Wahhabis are Salafis, but not all Salafis are Wahhabis.

**The Saud-Wahhab Pact**

- Muhammad ibn Saud eventually invited 'Adb al-Wahhab to live in the Diriyah oasis, under his protection. And Wahhab was in need of protection by now. His damning accusations had important consequences.

- Having decided that visiting tombs and other such practices were un-Islamic, 'Abd al-Wahhab also concluded that apostate Muslims weren't entitled to legal protection, and that they could be—even should be—killed for their heresy.

- 'Abd al-Wahhab was now seen as a dangerous man preaching a dangerous message. So why did Muhammad ibn Saud offer him protection? In 'Abd al-Wahhab, he saw not just a preacher with passion, but one whose self-belief could perhaps be harnessed to help ibn Saud achieve his dreams of greater temporal power.

- Saud, the emir of a small desert oasis, committed himself to accepting—and never expelling—this radical religious reformer.

In and of itself, this was a bold, if not potentially dangerous decision, as remote as Diriyah was. 'Abd al-Wahhab granted Saud his political authority, but he also insisted that Saud secure for Wahhab his particular religious agenda.

- The two men sealed this with a wedding between their families' heirs. Muhammad ibn Saud's son was married to Muhammad 'Abd al-Wahhab's daughter. Since that day in 1744, intermarriage between the Saud and Wahhab families has continued apace.

- Nearly 300 years later, the al-Saud family remains in control of all formal political and military power in the kingdom. Working hand in glove, adherents to 'Abd al-Wahhab's tradition—many of them descended from his family—maintain control of the kingdom's religious and educational affairs.

**After the Pact**

- What made the pact between 'Abd al-Wahhab and ibn Saud distinct was that it was, in the words of Islamic scholar Ira Lapidus, "the first political expression of the reformist tendency." Typically, the *reformist tendency* sought to rid Islam of anything that wasn't present at the time of Muhammad. Therefore, it considers any beliefs or practices not present in Islam in the early 7th century as an innovation and, as such, to be gotten rid of.

- Among the first joint Saud-Wahhab actions was to attack neighboring oases, conquering them in both the military and religious senses. After beating these neighbours, al-Saud would take over the business of local government, while Wahhab's followers would impose their view of Islam on the people: destroying tombs and other now-forbidden sites of religious commemoration or veneration.

- This was an uncompromising and bloody campaign. It might have had claims of religious righteousness at its heart, but it was also undeniably a war of conquest, where success built upon success. The Saud-Wahhab machine attracted many willing followers. And where towns resisted, the people could expect no quarter.

- Destruction and killings took place from one side of the peninsula to the other. Shia Muslims suffered especially harsh treatment, and were killed in unknown numbers.

**Clash with the Ottoman Empire**

- Any religious ideology that is so aspirational is almost certain, sooner or later, to run afoul of political authorities. In the case of the spreading Saudi-Wahhabi movement, the countervailing authority was the Ottoman Empire.

- Among those whom Wahhab condemned as apostates and unbelievers were the Ottoman authorities themselves. This was a particular affront as since 1517, the Ottoman sultan had claimed—and been widely accepted—as the caliph, or successor to Muhammad.

- A clash between the two parties was almost certainly inevitable. And that point came in 1803, when the Saudi-Wahhabi military-religious machine took Mecca and Medina from the Ottomans. The first century of Ottoman rule over Mecca and Medina—from 1517 to the early decades of 17th century—had been a period of peace and great prosperity, and they wanted the cities back.

- To re-conquer the holy cities, the Ottomans called on—or demanded—the support of one of their vassals: Muhammad Ali. An Albanian, Ottoman army officer, Muhammad Ali had taken control of Egypt amid the power vacuum created by Napoleon's invasion, in 1798, and subsequent withdrawal in 1801.

- In 1807, Muhammad Ali sent his son, Ibrahim, at the head of an army to deal with the Saud-Wahhab rebels, who had all but conquered Arabia. The clash was harder than he'd imagined.

Fighting from town to town—and oasis to oasis—the Ottoman troops weren't the best trained or prepared. It would take the Ottomans seven years, but eventually they made it to Diriyah, the capital.

- Even then, the Wahhabi-inspired fighters held out for five months. When they were eventually forced to surrender, the religious leaders of the rebellion were sent to Constantinople, and executed. The political leaders fared better, and were spared, although now without any power.

- And so, the first Saud-Wahhab state was quashed, more than 70 years after Muhammad ibn Saud and Muhammad Ibn 'Abd al-Wahhab forged their compact.

- Perhaps the most significant legacy of this story is the lasting impact of that religious revivalist, Muhammad Ibn 'Abd al-Wahhab. The wider spread of Wahhabism, that is beyond the Arabian Peninsula, only began in the second half of the $20^{th}$ century, and was made possible entirely through the explosion of oil wealth in Saudi Arabia.

- Since the 1980s, the result has been that a radical (but once-fringe) reformist movement has spent freely on the global propagation of its less-than-tolerant ideology. Even so, only about 23 percent of the population in Saudi Arabia today identify themselves as Wahhabi (compared to 45 percent or more of the population next door in the United Arab Emirates and Qatar).

**Suggested Reading**

Al-Rasheed, *A History of Saudi Arabia*, chapters 1 and 2.

Crawford, *Ibn 'Abd al-Wahhab*.

Hourani, *A History of the Arab Peoples*, chapter 15.

Sardar, *Mecca*.

Yergin, *The Prize*.

**Questions to Consider**

1. Ibn Khaldun once wrote, "[Blindly] following ancient customs and traditions doesn't mean that the dead are alive, but that the living are dead." Consider this in relation to Abd al-Wahhab's reformist program.

2. To what extent did the remoteness of the oasis of Diriyah—which lay far beyond Ottoman control— not only shape the world view of Muhammad bin Saud, but allow him to act with impunity in central Arabia?

Lecture 29

# Napoleon Invades Egypt—1798

On the morning of July 1, 1798, 400 ships sailed into the Egyptian port of Alexandria. Unchallenged by local forces, this French fleet quickly offloaded its cargo of soldiers: 36,000 French troops, including 3,000 cavalry, 2,000 artillerymen, and thousands of support staff. The massive invasion force was led by a 28-year-old general: Napoleon Bonaparte. In the invasion and conquest of Egypt, Napoleon was embarking on the most ambitious challenge of an already dramatic life. Victory would secure his fame, whereas defeat could easily wipe his name from the pages of history.

## Napoleon's Ambition

- For Napoleon—a man who believed in personal destiny—invading Egypt would allow him to literally walk in the footsteps of Alexander the Great, and perhaps even surpass the fame of his hero. He outlined his proposal for the invasion of Egypt in a letter to the Directory, which was then ruling France.

- Napoleon outlined three closely related arguments in his letter.

    - The first reason was that the invasion would disrupt British interests in the Eastern Mediterranean and beyond.

    - Napoleon's second reason was that an invasion of Egypt would promote French commercial interests and aid imperial expansion.

    - The third and final reason Napoleon offered in support of the planned invasion was the entirely reasonable calculation that France was simply not strong enough to mount a direct attack against Britain.

- Apart from Napoleon's three-point rationale for an invasion of Egypt, the Directory had a fourth, secret, reason. Napoleon had become a national hero in France, and, therefore, a threat to it. Rumours abounded that Napoleon was planning to seize power.

- To prevent a possible coup, the Directory gave its blessing to the invasion, which, after all, was going to take place a very long way from Paris, and could easily end in failure.

- When Napoleon eventually returned to Paris from Egypt, he did mount a coup. He fulfilled the Directory's worst fears in 1799. For now, however, on May 19, 1798, he set sail from Toulon, with a fleet of 400 ships.

## Egypt's Status

- Egypt had been part of the Ottoman Empire since 1517, but it was no longer under the control of Selim III, the sultan in Constantinople. Instead it was ruled by the local warriors known as Mamluks. They paid only nominal fealty to a distant sultan.

- Famous for their bravery and skill at arms, the Mamluks' inherently militaristic nature meant that they lived in a near-permanent state of murderous infighting. This seriously undermined their ability to rule, as one Mamluk ruler after another was murdered by rivals.

- The constant infighting had led to a sharp rise in taxes, most of which were borne by merchants. As a result, trade had declined and profits had fallen. As if that wasn't bad enough, Egypt was struck by the bubonic plague. French traders appealed to anyone they could for help, writing both to the Directory in Paris and to Selim III in Constantinople.

- Napoleon hoped, somewhat forlornly, that after decades of chaos and insecurity, the Egyptians would welcome him as their liberator. Now, while French traders in Egypt saw Napoleon's arrival as the answer to their prayers, the locals were less impressed.

## Napoleon Lands

- Napoleon and his 36,000 troops landed unopposed in Alexandria on the July 1, 1798. A British fleet had recently been spotted in the vicinity, and Napoleon knew time was not on his side: Britain was unlikely to stand idly by.

- Napoleon set off with 25,000 men on a forced march across the desert in the heat of the Egyptian summer. Ten days into the march, they had their first encounter with a small Mamluk force.

The French easily prevailed, both because they had superior weapons, and because of their use of modern tactics, as yet unknown to the Mamluks.

- One of the most important tactics was the use of the square. This formation sees foot soldiers arranged along the four sides of a square, two or three ranks deep. With their backs to the square's empty interior—and their faces looking out—the infantry have a 360-degree firing arc.

- A highly effective formation, an infantry square makes individual foot soldiers part of a solid wall, against which charging cavalry are virtually useless.

**The Battle of the Pyramids**

- The first *major* engagement between the two sides took place a week later, in a suburb of Cairo, on July 21. What would become known as the Battle of the Pyramids actually took place about nine miles away from them.

- The Battle of the Pyramids was the first major clash between one modern and one essentially medieval-style army. Although numerically inferior, Napoleon's army was actually far superior to that of the Mamluks. The more than 20,000 Egypitian infantrymen prepared for combat consisted mostly of ill-trained peasants, pressed into service.

- The only Mamluk force of real quality was their cavalry. To confront them, Napoleon again arranged his infantry into large, defensive squares, providing protection for the foot soldiers, the cavalry, and the army's baggage. This formation also protected the artillery.

- The artillery proved devastating to the Mamluks when they charged. The battle quickly became a rout, as the ill-equipped, ill-trained Egyptian infantry fled from the battle-hardened French.

- Running for their lives, the Egyptians went straight into the Nile, where thousands of them drowned. The long-anticipated confrontation between the best armies that Europe and the Middle East had to offer was over in less than hour. Total French fatalities numbered 300, while estimates of the Mamluk dead were as high as 6,000. That night, French troops entered Cairo unopposed.

**The Battle of the Nile**

- The second major battle of Napoleon's Egyptian adventure took place at sea, two weeks later. But whereas the Battle of the Pyramids was a cause for French celebration, the Battle of the Nile marked a low point in French fortunes.

- The French were caught at anchor in the Bay of Aboukir, east of Alexandria, by the Royal Navy. That force was led by the legendary Admiral Horatio Nelson.

- On the bay's eastern extremity, there is a town that sits at the mouth of the Nile, which is from where the battle takes its name. Known locally as Rashid, or "The Guide," the town is better known in the West as Rosetta.

- At the time, hundreds of French supply ships had already been sent away, so the two sides were evenly matched. They faced one another with 13 warships on each side, plus a few, smaller frigates. The French—thinking that their rear was protected on the landward side by the coast—assumed they could be attacked only on one side and, consequently, that they held a secure position.

- But the French hadn't reckoned with Nelson, who slipped half of his fleet behind them. When the battle began, the French were bombarded from both sides. Although it is recorded as lasting three days, much of the damage was done in the first few hours. By August 3, when the surviving French surrendered, British dead numbered just over 200, while French fatalities were more than 3,500, with a similar number taken prisoner.

### The French in Cairo

- In spite of this devastating defeat, the French secured their position on land in Egypt without serious trouble. Keen to court local opinion, Napoleon set about a propaganda campaign, making use of the printing presses he had brought with him.

- But translation was a problem. Napoleon relied heavily on Maltese scholars for Arabic translations of his propaganda. Unfortunately, these Maltese understood a form of Arabic only distantly related to the Egyptian dialect, which greatly reduced any possible positive impact of Napoleon's carefully scripted proclamations.

- After establishing a French-style Directory in Cairo, Napoleon decided that Egypt was not where he wanted to stay. In letters to friends back home, he said he would soon be returning. While he complained about the poverty and lack of glory in Egypt, there was another reason he was keen to get back. News had reached him that his wife, Josephine, was having an affair.

- Announcing that he was going on a tour of the Nile Delta, Napoleon sailed from Egypt in August 1799. Informing only his closest confidants, he handed power to a trusted ally, General Kleber. After six weeks at sea, Napoleon landed in France, and made straight for Paris. In November 1799—within a month of his return—he seized power, declaring himself First Consul.

### French Scholarship

- Napoleon's departure from Egypt didn't mean the end of the French occupation. That lasted for another two years, during which time they embarked on one of the most fascinating works of scholarship ever seen. Napoleon had journeyed to Egypt accompanied by 167 scientists and scholars—artists, naturalists, cartographers, and engineers—who were commissioned to make a complete record of everything they saw.

- They travelled the length and breadth of Egypt, producing one of the largest, most comprehensive works of scholarship of any age. Published between 1809 and 1829, the *Description of Egypt* would run to 23 volumes: 10 of text, 12 of prints, and 1of maps. The *Description of Egypt* was the midwife to a new field of scholarship known as Egyptology.

- Another cornerstone of Egyptology also resulted from the expedition—if by accident. While building up the defenses in the town of Rashid, a young engineering officer named Pierre-François Bouchard spotted a black stone with inscriptions on one side. Measuring 45 by 28 inches, it soon became known as the Rosetta Stone.

- Inscribed in 196 B.C., the stone bears a decree in three languages: ancient Egyptian hieroglyphics, Demotic—the Egyptian language that followed hieroglyphics—and ancient Greek. Having the same text in three languages proved to be the elusive key that allowed scholars to translate Egyptian hieroglyphics.

- Unfortunately for the French, the Rosetta Stone and most of the more than 5,000 other antiquities they uncovered were handed over to the British, who only then gave the French safe passage to leave Egypt, in 1801.

**Two Questions**

- Let's consider two questions: One, was Napoleon's invasion of Egypt successful? Two, what were the main consequences of the invasion?

- The first question, whether or not the invasion was successful, is fairly easy to answer. The three aims of the invasion were to disrupt Britain's military and trade dominance in the eastern Mediterranean and India; to secure Egypt for French military and commercial purposes; and to avoid a head-on attack against British forces.

- In each instance, the French expedition must be considered a failure. While the French had achieved a swift initial victory over the Mamluks, just three years later what was left of its isolated force was desperate to get home. Thousands had died, either in battle or from disease. And to add insult to injury, they had to sue for peace with Britain in order to get safe passage.

- As for the second question, about the consequences of the invasion: These are what really make this a turning point in the history of the Middle East. Although the Ottoman Empire was already weakening at the time, Napoleon's arrival increased the pace of disruption and change across the empire.

- Starting on the fringes, ambitious men rose up, challenging the existing power structures. The Ottoman Empire was clearly falling apart. The once-feared empire was now known as "the Sick Man of Europe."

- In Egypt, the French invasion radically weakened the Mamluks' power, while the French withdrawal created a power vacuum. The man who ended the Mamluks' more than 600 years of intermittent rule was Muhammad Ali, an Albanian Ottoman, who used his native Albanian army to challenge the Mamluks head on.

**Suggested Reading**

Al-Jabarti, *Napoleon In Egypt*.

Cole, *Napoleon's Egypt*.

Hodgson, *The Venture of Islam*, volume 3, book 6.

Institute of Egypt, *Description de l'Egypte*.

Marsot, *A History of Egypt*, chapter 3.

Rodenbeck, *Cairo*.

Strathern, *Napoleon in Egypt*.

**Questions to Consider**

1. To what extent do you think Napoleon's invasion of Egypt was driven by the wish to increase the size of the French empire, or to prevent the British from expanding their own territories? Explain the apparent contradiction in the French Republic's declaration of "Liberty, Equality, and Fraternity" with the invasion and conquest of foreign lands.

2. Consider the Euro-centric view of Napoleon's invasion of Egypt as the start of the so-called modern era in the Middle East. Given that such a designation might be guilty of reducing the locals to passive onlookers in their own destiny, how accurate, useful, or problematic is such an opinion?

# Murder at the Citadel—1811

Lecture
30

Muhammad Ali's 1811 slaughter of hundreds of Mamluks was a turning point in the history of Egypt, and of the wider Middle East. Until now, the Ottomans had succeeded at maintaining their grip, albeit remotely, over this land on the Nile—which was among the sultan's most valuable pieces of real estate. After the slaughter, however, it became clear that Muhammad Ali's aims were much greater than ruling in the name of a distant emperor. He wanted Egypt for himself. This lecture tells the story of how he achieved this goal, and began the long process of modernizing Egypt.

## The Slaughter

- On March 1, 1811, the Egyptian viceroy Muhammad Ali threw a party in Cairo at the Citadel, the seat of power since the 10th century. Invitations had gone out to about 470 men from Cairo's ruling class, the Mamluks.

- Six years earlier, Muhammad Ali was appointed to his post—being viceroy made him the effective head of state. His own boss was the Ottoman sultan, who ruled from distant Constantinople.

- Early on, Muhammad Ali had faced stiff opposition from many of the Mamluks, whose forebears ruled the country before the Ottomans conquered them in the early 16th century.

- Recently, both sides made concessions and friendly overtures, following years of armed clashes. By the spring of 1811 it looked like a peace agreement between the Mamluks and Muhammad Ali might be possible.

- It was at this moment that Muhammad Ali invited the Mamluks to the Citadel. Almost without warning, the great doors of the

Citadel slammed shut, and every last Mamluk present was murdered where he stood.

- In an instant, Muhammad Ali had eliminated all internal opposition, and secured his rule. Now we are going to see how this event sits at the center of an even bigger story.

**Egypt's Status in the Middle East**

- Let's begin by considering Egypt, and the country's place within the Ottoman Empire, just before Muhammad Ali ordered the slaughter of the Mamluks. The Mamluks ruled the country for more than 250 years before the Ottoman sultan—Selim the Grim—led the Turkish empire's conquest of Egypt in 1517. By the time of the Ottoman invasion, they'd already lost much of their vigor.

- In the early 19th century, Cairo, 800 miles from Constantinople as the crow flies, was never the easiest of territories for the Ottoman sultans to control. This lack of strong central control, coupled with the Mamluks' innate martial skills and major landholdings, allowed them to remain a force in the country, albeit unofficially.

- Napoleon invaded Egypt in 1798, radically weakening the power of the Ottomans and the Mamluks alike. Three years later, the British defeated—and expelled—the French from Egypt. But when the British themselves withdrew in 1803, the power vacuum they left behind was almost more damaging than the original French invasion had been.

- In the midst of all this political turmoil, the Ottoman sultan had to try and reassert his power over Egypt as one of his more important territories. It was among the very richest agriculturally, and in terms of trading opportunities, but also among his most troublesome.

- Once the French (and then the English) had been forced out of Egypt, the struggle to control the country became a three-way fight between the Ottoman Turks, a separate group of Albanian military units whom the Ottomans sent to Egypt, and the former ruling power of the Mamluks. The Mamluks—descendants of Eurasian stock—were, after more than 500 years in Egypt, the closest we get to a native Egyptian interest in this civil war.

### Muhammad Ali

- As an ethnic Albanian, Muhammad Ali hailed from yet another far-flung corner of the Ottoman Empire. And instead of Arabic, he relied, according to eyewitnesses, on his native Albanian language as well as Ottoman Turkish.

Muhammad Ali

- It was actually as early as 1805 that the Ottomans recognized Muhammad Ali as the country's viceroy. But it took another six years for him to get a firm grip on power. And in the decade between 1801 and 1811, a bafflingly complex series of political and military moves had ensued before Muhammad Ali managed to come out on top.

- Ultimately, Muhammad Ali's success came about because of two things: One, he was able to beat his political rivals through a combination of diplomacy and battlefield victories; and two, after years of skilful public diplomacy, he won over the Egyptian people.

- Born in 1769, in Kavala, Macedonia—part of modern-day Greece—Muhammad Ali was the only one of his father's 17 sons—by several wives—to survive to adulthood. His father died while the boy was still young.

- Ali went to live with an uncle—a local Ottoman official—who eventually employed him to collect taxes in their home district. Muhammad Ali's early exposure to both trade and bureaucracy would later prove central to his ability to rule Egypt.

- Another family connection first took him to Egypt, as a junior officer in his cousin's Albanian volunteer army unit. Effectively a mercenary force under the nominal control of the Ottoman sultan, Muhammad Ali's unit was part of a much larger force that was sent in 1801 to restore order, in the wake of the French withdrawal from Egypt.

- Over the next four years, Ali—then in his early 30s—played different warring factions against one another, whilst working hard to win the support of the Egyptian people themselves. In 1805, these same people demanded that Ali be made *wali*—the viceroy or governor—of Egypt. The sultan agreed.

### Muhammad Ali Breaks Away

- Following the Mamluk massacre, Muhammad Ali began to pull away from his Ottoman masters. Between 1811 and 1840, Muhammad Ali embarked on a series of military actions that we can divide into two types: those undertaken at the behest of the sultan, and those he carried out on his own initiative for his own gain.

- The first of these was his campaign on the behalf of the sultan to restore order in western and central Arabia. A minor tribe there had rebelled. It managed to capture the cities of Mecca and Medina, central symbols of Islamic authority to the Ottoman Caliphate. It took two of Muhammad Ali's sons, leading two separate campaigns, to eventually crush the troublesome rebellion in 1818.

- Muhammad Ali installed one of his victorious sons as governor of the newly subdued western Arabia, which is the history-laden territory otherwise known as the Hijaz.

- He then turned his attention to conquering Sudan. He undertook this latter campaign without the sultan's approval. He was in search of gold and slaves whom he could press into service in the Egyptian army. Soon, he had Sudan under Egyptian control, more than doubling the size of his de facto personal empire.

- The next major campaign Muhammad Ali undertook was to quell rebellions in Crete, Cyprus, and mainland Greece between 1824 and 1828. These were carried out on the sultan's orders. Before restoring order on Crete and Cyprus, Muhammad Ali first was able to get the sultan to promise the governorship of Syria and the Levant in the Mediterranean as his reward. His personal empire looked set to grow even more powerful.

- Once again, Muhammad Ali's army was successful. However, his continuing progress on Crete, Cyprus, and the Greek mainland now won him the close scrutiny of certain European powers.

## Military Modernization

- Even before he'd slaughtered the Mamluks in the Citadel, Muhammad Ali had started to transform the Egyptian army. He transformed his forces from disparate, and ethnically distinct, foreign units into an indigenous, national army, whose soldiers were drawn from the peasant class (just as Napoleon had done in France). Muhammad Ali thus developed a distinctly Egyptian professional army. An additional, long-term consequence of this policy was that—for the first time in the modern era—a spirit of "Egyptian-ness" and national pride was fostered in the nation state.

- Muhammad Ali was also industrializing Egypt, creating a military-industrial complex that allowed for more domestic production of arms.

- Many of Europe's more powerful nations were no allies of the Ottomans, nor of the Egyptians, and rather liked the status quo. As a result, the Europeans didn't like the looks of the ambitious Muhammad Ali.

- In October 1827, on the Bay of Navarino—off the coast of Greece—an Anglo-Franco force destroyed the fleet that Muhammad Ali had spent years and a great deal of money building up. In spite of the disaster at Navarino, Muhammad Ali retained power in Egypt and extended his control. He went on to rule for another 20 years, until the year before his death in 1848. He was able to do so in large part because of the administrative reforms he introduced to Egypt.

## Muhammad Ali's Reforms

- Whenever Muhammad Ali instituted reforms—in the army, agriculture, industry, and other areas—they were always based on a vision of modernization. And this, in turn, was based on his understanding of popular economic theory of the day, which arose from his family background in trade.

- The foundation stone of mercantilist economics is the principle that a country had to export more than it imported. Muhammad Ali was keen to see Egypt start producing materials for export, whether cash crops or industrial manufactures.

- With land now being the property of the state, he could tell the peasant farmers what to grow, and he did. Peasant farmers in Egypt before Muhammad Ali had strictly limited their production to the level of subsistence. It's reckoned that after Muhammad Ali, the people had more money, but less freedom and less choice.

- The switch from growing basic foodstuffs to producing food and cash crops didn't happen overnight. But it was a revolution to those who worked the land. Cotton was the new cash crop that had the biggest impact. Around this same time, cotton production in the United States was severely disrupted by the outbreak of the Civil War. And so Egyptian production had room to grow even more.

- As an unintended byproduct of Muhammad Ali's programm of military modernization and industrialization, young Egyptians were initially sent to Europe to study, before Egypt developed its own native schools and universities.

- Young Egyptians brought home—along with their newly acquired knowledge of engineering and new agricultural techniques—talk about political involvement and other potentially incendiary ideas.

- If, as some writers have stated, Muhammad Ali "Egyptianized" Egypt, he seems to have done so by accident more than design. But regardless of his intentions, it happened. If you speak to Egyptians today about Muhammad Ali, you are more likely to hear positive rather than negative opinions about the ethnic Albanian who broke the power of the Mamluks. He empowered

Egypt to become *Egypt* for the first time since the days of the pharaohs.

- When Muhammad Ali died, he had already bequeathed power to his son, Ibrahim. Muhammad Ali was buried in a mausoleum, inside a mosque that bears his name. It is situated in the heart of Cairo's Citadel, where our drama began.

- The longest-lasting legacy of Muhammad Ali's impressive 43-year reign was securing from the Ottoman sultan the right of dynastic succession for his heirs. Although Ibrahim governed for less than a year—and died before his father—Muhammad Ali's dynasty ruled in Egypt until 1952, when it was overthrown by its own army.

### Suggested Reading

Gelvin, *The Modern Middle East*.

Hodgson, *The Venture of Islam*, volume 3, book 6.

Hourani, *A History of the Arab Peoples*, chapter 16.

Marsot, *History of Egypt*.

Rodenbeck, *Cairo*.

Rogan, *The Arabs*, chapter 3.

### Questions to Consider

1. Considered by many to be the founder of modern Egypt, how does Muhammad Ali's pursuit of dynastic succession square with the at least nominal democratic urge of modern nationalism, Arab or otherwise?

2. What was happening to the Ottoman Empire that meant it was no longer strong enough to exert control over one of its wealthiest and most important territories? In what ways and to what extent was Napoleon's 1798 invasion of Egypt responsible for the power vacuum that Muhammad Ali filled?

# French Invasion of Algeria—1830

Lecture 31

The French invasion of Algeria in 1830 marks the moment when European nations took the momentous step of invading the Ottoman Empire, with a goal of permanent conquest and settlement. It should also be seen as the opening salvo in the infamous Scramble for Africa, when certain European powers—meeting in Berlin, in 1884—divided among themselves the entire continent of Africa. The French invasion of Algeria was the real start of this process, and was every bit as brutal and bloody as later colonial activity in Africa and elsewhere.

## Algeria

- Let's look at Algeria at the beginning of the 19th century. Algeria's population was about one-tenth of France's 35 million at the time. It had been a province of the Ottoman Empire since the legendary admiral Oruç Reis—known as Barbarossa, or Red Beard—conquered it, in 1516.

- The distance between the Ottoman capital of Constantinople—Istanbul, today—and the Algerian capital of Algiers is about 1,400 miles. That made Algeria the most westerly of the Ottoman domains.

- The main consequence of Algeria's remoteness from Constantinople was that it didn't take long before an ambitious Ottoman appointee inserted his family into the place of Algeria's hereditary rulers.

- A succession of these families rose and fell over time, and while the Ottomans might have wanted more control over who was appointed to rule the court in Algiers, for the most part there was little they could do about it. By the early 1700s, Ottoman sultans had very little real influence in the country, at all.

- From the Atlantic coast of North Africa east into the Mediterranean, the modern states of Morocco, Algeria, Tunisia, and Libya became known in Europe as the Barbary Coast. Throughout the 1700s, the Barbary Coast was famous for piracy.

- What the Europeans referred to as *piracy* was, in reality, *privateering*. The distinction is this: Pirates act independently of any government, whereas privateers operate with permission from one government or another. Algiers, when still an Ottoman province, had grown rich through privateering, including from the sometimes-lucrative trade in European slaves, sailors, and others captured at sea.

**Agriculture**

- Algeria, before the French invasion, was agriculturally very rich. It was the very fertility of northern Algeria that led to the French invasion of 1830, although its roots went deeper.

- In 1796, during his Italian campaign, Napoleon bought large quantities of grain, on credit, from a pair of Algerian merchants. By the 1820s, long after Napoleon's fall from power, the French government had paid only a portion of the debt. Complaining that they'd been overcharged—a little late, considering that the deal had been entered into 30 years earlier—the French government now refused to settle the bill.

- Unfortunately for the two merchants—and, as it turned out for Algeria—they, in turn, owed money to the Ottoman ruler in Algeria, Hussein Dey. In April 1827, Hussein Dey ordered the French consul to explain the situation.

- In what developed into a heated argument, Hussein Dey touched—some accounts say struck—the French consul with a fan. It became known as the Fan Affair, and was considered sufficiently insulting for King Charles X of France to demand an apology—and to blockade Algiers.

**French Invasion**

- In demanding an apology and ordering the blockade, King Charles certainly meant to convey to Algiers and the Ottomans a message about French naval strength and no doubt sought to redeem his personal honor. Deeply unpopular with the majority of his own people, Charles saw the invasion of Algeria as an opportunity to boost his standing at home.

- Unfortunately, the French attempt to impose economic sanctions against the Algerians backfired, and had a much more detrimental effect on French merchants than it did on the Algerians.

- By 1829, with French merchants complaining loudly, Charles X decided to send a negotiator to rectify the situation. In response, the Algerians fired a warning shot across the bows of one of the French ships blockading the harbor. For the French, this was provocation enough.

- In June of 1830, France invaded Algeria. This fateful step would lead to France occupying Algeria for 132 years, until it gained independence in 1962.

- Using an invasion plan that had originally been devised by Napoleon, a French armada of some 600 ships approached the Algerian coast. On the June 14, 1830, it landed 34,000 troops 17 miles west of Algiers. Although a sizeable defensive force of about 40,000 Algerian and Ottoman Turkish troops was sent out to engage the invaders, superior French artillery and training quickly saw them overrun.

- Within three weeks, the French were in Algiers, and Hussein Dey was forced to surrender, but not until he'd secured his own freedom—and the right to keep his personal wealth.

- Leaving the country to its fate, the Ottoman ruler sailed away to Naples, and a comfortable exile with his family. The Ottoman Turkish troops were likewise allowed to leave, and sailed back to

Constantinople. With this, 313 years of Ottoman rule in Algeria was over.

## Further Happenings

- Just a month later, in July 1830, a popular uprising in France, known as the July Revolution, ousted Charles X. The new regime saw the continued occupation of Algeria as an embarrassment. The masses thought otherwise, and were caught up in the patriotic fervour that followed the invasion.

- In Algeria, French troops were soon engaged in looting and plundering on a massive scale. Algerian men, women, and children were burned alive by French forces. Severed heads became trophies. By some estimates, between 1830 and 1870, 850,000 Algerians died as a result of the French invasion. Not all of these were murdered outright. Many starved to death, as the French expropriated farmland, forcing the locals to leave. Famines followed.

- One immediate result of French conduct, coupled with the sudden removal of existing Ottoman governmental and power structures, was a power vacuum. This led to further outbreaks of disorder and anarchy across the land. Increased violence and unrest meant the French had to commit ever greater numbers of troops to quell the disturbances.

- One byproduct of all this was the creation of the French Foreign Legion as a place to put foreign fighters previously inspired by Napoleon but with no role in the new France following his downfall.

## Abd al-Qadir

- In 1834, France formally annexed the northern portions of Algeria, and declared a military zone, with a French governor holding executive power. That meant he held virtually unlimited civilian and military authority. From 1848 forward, the country was declared part of metropolitan France. It became simply French Algeria.

- But fierce resistance to the French occupiers continued with vigor, which brings us to the life and legend of Abd al-Qadir. Born in the western Algerian city of Mascara, Abd al-Qadir was a noted Sufi and Islamic scholar (as was his father, who had been imprisoned by the Ottomans for organizing resistance to their rule in Algeria).

- Five years before the arrival of the French, father and son left Algeria to make the *hajj* pilgrimage to Mecca. From Mecca, Abd al-Qadir travelled on to Damascus and Baghdad. His travels inspired him to lead a more religious life. An energized and excited Abd al-Qadir returned home to Algeria just months before the French invasion began, in June 1830. He was 22 at the time.

- Algeria's second largest city, Oran, is where the war of resistance now really got started. Then, in 1832, a group of Islamic partisans declared a religiously sanctioned war of resistance—or *jihad*—against the French, and elected Abd al-Qadir as the Emir al-Mu'mimeen, or Leader of the Faithful. Private French accounts and official reports attest to his chivalry and ethical conduct, on and off the battlefield.

- One order he issued stated that anyone who captured a French soldier alive would be given a cash reward, but—to claim the reward—the captor had to bring the prisoner to him. Additionally, if the prisoner complained about any mistreatment, the reward would not be paid. Asked what reward his men could expect for a severed French head, Abd al-Qadir replied, "Twenty-five blows with a baton on the soles of your feet."

**Abd al-Qadir in Exile**

- Despite organizing a tenacious, indigenous defense, Abd al-Qadir's resistance movement came to an end after 15 years.

In December 1847, he was forced to surrender to the French, agreeing to terms that he would be exiled in the Middle East.

Abd al-Qadir

- He eventually settled with his family in Damascus, the Syrian capital. In July 1860, a long-simmering dispute about rights, taxation, and the threat of expulsion led to violence breaking out between Syrian Druze and Christian Maronites.

- This violence spread along sectarian lines. Amid the threat of a massacre by Muslims of the city's largely foreign, Christian population, Abd al-Qadir—with his sons and his men—rode out in the midst of rioting. They rescued Christian nuns, priests, merchants, entire families, and even consuls from the United States, Britain, France, and elsewhere.

- Thousands were kept safe in the Citadel of Damascus—a large, medieval palace—while Abd al-Qadir also kept some families in his own house. And when a mob came to his door demanding that he hand over the Christians, he refused, telling them that they should be ashamed, and that if they were true Muslims they'd know that God forbids the killing of innocent people. The crowd dispersed.

- It's reckoned that Abd al-Qadir saved about 10,000 people over the course of the rioting. For his efforts, he was honored, and received gifts from numerous European governments, including even rivals, such as Greece and Ottoman Turkey, and the Pope.

- The British government presented him with a gold-inlaid shotgun, on behalf of Queen Victoria. France, in a remarkable turnaround, declared him a friend of France, and awarded the Legion of Honour along with an annual pension of 150,000 francs. President Abraham Lincoln sent Abd al-Qadir a pair of inlaid pistols and a thank you from a grateful country.

**Effects of the French Invasion**

- The French invasion of Algeria exposed the Ottoman Empire as the "Sick Man of Europe." From about 1800 on, this was reflected in the rise of nationalist movements in many parts of European and the Ottoman Empire.

- An uprising in Serbia, with Russia's aid, would lead to that country breaking away from the Ottomans in 1817. For most of the 1820s, Greece, with help from Britain, fought a war of independence that finished at almost the same moment the French were getting ready to invade Algeria.

- While the rise of those indigenous movements showed the Ottoman Empire was losing power in Central and Eastern Europe, the French invasion of Algeria showed another side of the equation. This was the rise in nationalism among Europe's great powers, as well as a shift in political direction that created an urge for greater imperial possessions—an itch that Britain, France, and others would spend the rest of the 19th century scratching in Africa, the Middle East, and elsewhere.

- The French invasion of Algeria also marks a major shift in European relations with the Middle East. For the first time in the modern era, a European state was inserting itself into the Middle East in what was meant to be a permanent fashion. This wasn't about mere conquest, but was ultimately intended to lead to the removal of local identity, rule, and language.

## Suggested Reading

Gearon, *The Sahara*.

Gelvin, *The Modern Middle East*.

Hodgson, *The Venture of Islam*, volume 3, book 6.

Hourani, *A History of the Arab Peoples*, chapter 16.

Kiser, *Commander of the Faithful*.

Sessions, *By Sword and Plow*.

Vikor, Knut. *The Maghreb Since 1800*, chapters 2 and 3.

## Questions to Consider

1. The Islamist guerrilla leader Abd el-Qadir became known as the "defender of the Christians," and was praised by President Abraham Lincoln in the United States and Queen Victoria in Britain, among others. How might his war against French occupation be seen today?

2. How far was the French invasion of Algeria driven by domestic political concerns, as opposed to the start of an effort to build an empire in Africa?

# East India Company in Yemen—1839

Lecture 32

For millennia, the Middle East has been a crossroads of trade. And the early 19th century British seizure of the port of Aden revolves—first and foremost—around trade. Those who captured Aden were not representing the British government. Instead, they were acting at the behest of the East India Company—an English joint stock company—and its shareholders. Yet there's no example more illustrative of the ties between trade and empire than the story we're about to consider.

## The British East India Company

- The British East India Company was established during the reign of Queen Elizabeth I in 1600, and came to trade in many items, including tea, silk, cotton, salt, saltpetre (which is used to make explosives), and opium. It would eventually grow to become the world's largest company. It was responsible for half of Britain's global trade at one time.

- The East India Company also had its own schools, factories, and—most importantly—private army, which made possible the muscular expansion (and enforcement) of its terms of trade around the world.

- Indeed, the East India Company maintained the most powerful armed force in Asia. By the time it turned its sights to Aden in the early 19th century, the East India Company's armed forces would number more than 260,000—more than twice the size of the British army.

- Acting on orders from company officers and the board, East India Company troops took control of Bombay, in India's extreme northeast, in 1756. In short order, the company controlled much of the subcontinent from Mughal's capital, Delhi, all the way to its southern shores.

Ship approaching Bombay, India

- From its founding, the East India Company had used sailing ships to ply its wares on long journeys around the globe. By the early 1800s, steam was replacing sailing ships. Goods from India typically were unloaded in Egypt's Port Suez, then transported overland to Alexandria, on the Mediterranean coast. From there, the goods were loaded onto another ship that steamed on to England.

- For this service to function, the East India Company needed coal—and coaling stations—en route. Each steamship required 700 tons of coal in order to make the 7,400-mile round trip voyage between Bombay and Port Suez. The port of Aden is equidistant between Bombay and Port Suez. And so this is where its problems began with the East India Company.

### Aden's Status

- Aden's location, 100 miles east of the Red Sea, and its large, natural harbor—situated within the crater of an extinct volcano—were ideal. Consequently, the town was a crucial location for seaborne trade between the Arabian Peninsula and the entire east coast of Africa, India, and the Far East.

- Western Europe came late to the party, when the Portuguese explorer Bartholomeu Dias became the first European to sail around the southernmost tip of Africa—and into the Indian Ocean—in 1488.

- The Portuguese and Ottomans each occupied Aden for a time, although by 1839—when our story takes place—Aden was an independent principality: part of the Arab Sultanate of Lahej.

- To put this into further context, the 18-year-old British Princess Victoria ascended to the throne as queen of the United Kingdom and the wider British Empire only two years earlier. And at the time of her accession, her overseas territories didn't yet include India, even after the East India Company had taken much of it. These territories remained the purview of the company (although 40 years later, a much-older Victoria would finally acquire the title Empress of India.)

### The Seizure of Aden

- At the time our story takes place, the Arabian Peninsula port had been part of the independent Muslim Lahej sultanate for just over 100 years. And yet, it didn't take East India Company officials long to persuade the local ruler, the sultan, to cede Aden to them.

- The sultan's son was against the deal, however, setting the stage for a confrontation. Then one of the company's sailing ships ran aground while making its way past Aden. Abandoned by the ship's captain and crew, the stricken vessel was plundered by locals.

- In effect, this dispute gifted the East India Company an excuse for military intervention. East India Company administrators demanded compensation from the luckless sultan.

- Under the command of Captain Stafford Bettesworth Haines, three East India Company ships reached Aden on January 16, 1839. They were accompanied by two vessels of the Royal Navy, with 700 British army infantry and Royal Marines in tow. The vast majority of arms were commanded by Indian troops belonging to the East India Company.

- Captain Haines silenced Aden's limited onshore defenses with a short bombardment, and then landed with his forces to take possession of the port. The action saw 165 dead, of whom 150 were the poorly equipped defenders.

- Although taking Aden hadn't been an official objective of British foreign policy, the port was now officially under British rule in the form of the Bombay Residency (a government within a government, still controlled at the time by the East India Company).

- The seizure of Aden marked the first territory occupied during Queen Victoria's 63-year reign, and the first of what would become a significant number of British territories, dependencies, and protectorates across the Middle East.

- The British compensated the local sultan for his loss with an annual payment of 6,000 riyals, which was a bargain. The sultan's son, however, refused to accept the deal, and led more than one attempt to retake Aden by force.

- While British and Indian forces were able to fight off these attempts, the East India Company realized that its long-term security—and Aden's prosperity—relied on friendly relations with the local tribes. So it paid them off too, signing treaties of "friendship and protection"—more like carrot and stick—with the nine tribes whose territories surrounded Aden.

- The newly conquered province of Aden was not very impressive, covering only about 75 square miles. It was little more than a derelict village, with a population of not more than 600. People lived in huts made from reeds and little else. Still, it was an important possession. Captain Haines—who'd surveyed Aden years before, as a possible coaling station—now became its first colonial governor.

- Aden soon became indispensable to the East India Company and the British Empire—to the point where the border between the two was blurred. Yet, for all of its importance, Aden also ended up being neglected to a shocking extent.

**Captain Haines**

- Born in southern England in 1801 or 1802, Captain Haines was energetic, ambitious, and single minded. He was given a great deal of responsibility, and—beyond the backing of company soldiers—very little support.

- Upon being appointed political agent for the territory, he was, in effect, the dictator of Aden. In addition to being responsible for law and order in the territory, Haines was also in charge of relations with local tribes. He was responsible for the maintenance of all official records, including company accounts, and the colony's defense.

- His first task was to build up the port's defenses before instituting a more general building program. He laid out a plan for the town, made it a free-trade zone, and offered cheap rent to anyone who built in stone. Between 1839 and 1854, Haines turned a small and dusty village of 600 into a thriving center with, eventually, a 42-fold increase in population.

- As Aden became a prosperous port, the Ottoman Turks in Constantinople argued that they retained sovereignty over the whole of Arabia, including Aden and the rest of Yemen. Britain felt otherwise.

- The Ottoman authorities in Constantinople eventually gave their tacit approval to the agreements the British signed with the various tribal rulers in and around Aden—in large part because there was precious little they could do to alter the reality of the situation on the ground.

- Haines served loyally and unflinchingly for 15 years. It would be a rare individual who could carry out every one of his distinct responsibilities with equal skill and success. Alas for Haines, he was not that man.

- To the contrary, Haines wrote an endless steam of letters asking his bosses at the East India Company for help in running the fast-growing city. But he was forced to muddle through. How big of a muddle it all was became clear when company auditors finally arrived in February 1854. Haines's bookkeeping skills—or lack of them—let him down to disastrous effect.

- When the East India Company auditors finished going through a decade-and-a-half of accounts, they found a deficit of 28,000 pounds, roughly equivalent to $10 million today. Haines was relieved of his duties and shipped back to Bombay to face trial on charges of embezzlement.

- Initially found guilty, he was later acquitted on two separate occasions, and was almost universally believed to be innocent of wrongdoing. Extremely careless, yes, but a thief, no. In spite of the not-guilty verdicts, the company held him responsible for the lost funds. He spent time in a debtors' prison in Bombay.

- Six years later, his case was re-examined a third time. He was cleared of all guilt and released from prison. A week after that—

aboard a ship in Bombay's harbor—Haines died at the age of 58, waiting to set sail for England. The harsh life he'd endured as the East India Company's political agent in Aden, and as its prisoner in Bombay, had clearly taken a toll.

### Haines's and Aden's Legacy

- In spite of the tragedy of his untimely death, Haines must be thought of as highly successful in making Aden a port of literally global importance, and in helping to establish Britain as a naval power in the region.

- It was in Aden that the Royal Navy and the navy of the East India Company would launch anti-piracy operations across the waters off the Arabian Peninsula, and around the horn of Africa, a story that retains a remarkably contemporary feel to it.

- While it amounts to no consolation for Haines, some of the East India Company's various excesses rebounded against it, when large numbers of the company's native troops revolted during the Indian Rebellion of 1857. It was this violent uprising that led the British government to nationalize and dissolve the East India Company, effectively taking over both the company and the Indian subcontinent by the following year, 1858.

- Yet let's consider again what the East India Company's capture of Aden led to. Seized on January 19, 1839, the port, town, and province remained a British possession until 1967—almost 130 years later.

- Less than a century after Captain Haines and a private army of the East India Company landed at Aden, Britain would also have control over Oman, the United Arab Emirates, Qatar, Bahrain, Kuwait, Iraq, and the then British-mandated states of Transjordan and Palestine, encompassing what would later become the state of Israel. They also controlled Egypt and the Sudan—quite a haul.

## Suggested Reading

Gavin, *Aden Under British Rule*.

Hawley, *The Trucial States*, chapters, 3, 4, 5 and 6.

Hourani, *A History of the Arab Peoples*, chapters 16 and 17.

Robbins, *The Corporation That Changed the World*.

Waterfield, *Sultans of Aden*.

## Questions to Consider

1. Consider the seizure of Aden by the East India Company as an example of Britain acquiring an empire by accident. What was the East India Company's primary motivation?

2. If the Ottoman Empire had been strong enough to retain possession of Aden before the arrival of the East India Company, it's safe to assume they would have done so. How important was this as a sign of Ottoman decline, taking place as it did in a Muslim-majority country, rather than in Christian-majority Eastern Europe?

# Egypt, Europe, and the Suez Canal—1869

Lecture 33

The story of the Suez Canal combines engineering, trade, politics, power, and ultimately, debt and downfall. In this lecture, we'll first look at the idea of uniting the Mediterranean Sea and Red Sea, an aspiration with an ancient pedigree but that needed the drive of a modern visionary—Ferdinand de Lesseps—to make it become a reality. Then, we'll turn to the construction of the canal itself, which was a building project on an incredible scale. Ultimately, the construction and opening of the Suez Canal is a story of foreign debt that would cost Egypt its independence.

### Early Canals, Early Challenges

- After Napoleon's invasion of Egypt in 1798, members of the scientific team that accompanied him uncovered traces ancient canals. This discovery, coupled with Napoleon's limitless drive, started him thinking about digging a canal more or less where the Suez Canal is today.

- Unfortunately for Napoleon's ambitions, one of the surveyors responsible for an initial survey made a serious miscalculation. His report concluded erroneously that the Red Sea was 33 feet higher than the Mediterranean. Had this been accurate, locks would have to have been added to the canal, making the project prohibitively expensive. As a result, no further action was taken during the Napoleonic era.

- In truth, the difference in height between the two seas is much less—about four feet—as another surveyor reported to the British government in 1830. However, in spite of concluding that no locks were needed, the British government refused to discuss any canal building project. As an alternative, it built a railway from Alexandria to Cairo, and another line from Cairo to Port Suez.

- The British never let up in their complaints and objections from the moment when the great French engineer Ferdinand de Lesseps won the concession in 1854 to create a company to build the Suez Canal, until it opened 15 years later.

- The problem wasn't a British failure to grasp that the Suez Canal would benefit its interests, but rather that Great Britain recognized the canal would benefit *other* countries' interests, as well. That included Britain's rivals France and Russia.

**Ferdinand de Lesseps**

- So, who was Ferdinand de Lesseps? Born in Versailles in 1805, de Lesseps was a diplomat in his first career. In this role, he spent much of the 1830s based in Egypt. And we can point to two incidents during this period that would alter the course of his life.

Ferdinand de Lesseps

- The first event took place even before he set foot in Egypt. As the ship he sailed on approached Alexandria, passengers and crew had to spend a period in quarantine, during which time he read an account of Napoleon's military adventures in Egypt. In this book, he first learned about the possibility of a canal, an idea that struck him powerfully and remained in his mind.

- The second detail was de Lesseps's subsequent friendship with the Egyptian leader, Muhammad Ali, and with Muhammad Ali's fourth son. The fourth son struggled with his weight and faced ridicule as well as forced exercise and starvation diets. De Lesseps took pity, giving him plates of pasta and other treats in secret.

- In time, a sequence of accidental and premature deaths in the Muhammad Ali line saw this son become khedive of Egypt. This son was Sai'd Pasha. Later, when de Lesseps came looking for permission to build the canal, Sa'id Pasha—a Francophone—was on the throne. He hadn't forgotten the kindness de Lesseps had shown him.

- Although Sa'id Pasha ruled for only nine years—dying in 1863, at the age of 40—he is perhaps best remembered today for having given his name to Port Sa'id, the Suez Canal's northern terminus. He's also remembered for running up an enormous national debt, which debt his nephew and heir inherited before adding to it in an equally profligate fashion.

**Building the Canal**

- The Suez Canal cost more to build than the original estimate—twice as much, as it turned out. Responsible for paying were the shareholders of the Universal Suez Ship Canal Company, which de Lesseps formed in 1858, four years after obtaining a 99-year concession to build and operate a canal. Egypt, in the form of Sa'id Pasha, held 22 percent of the shares of the Universal Suez

Ship Canal Company, while the remainder were made available to investors.

- Groundbreaking took place at Port Sa'id on 25 April 1859. Work was completed exactly a decade later. A total of 1.5 million people worked on the project. During the first four years, the manual toil was performed by forced labor—mainly Egyptian peasants pressed into service by the khedive. There were never fewer than 30,000 men employed on the project. The death toll stood as high as 100,000.

- Britain—keen to score political points, and delay progress of the canal—objected to the use of compulsory labor. This prompted de Lesseps to write to the British government, reminding them that they'd not been too bothered about using forced labor when they'd constructed the Egyptian railway just a few years earlier. Concerned about European public opinion, the khedive nevertheless brought to an end this ready resource, which was another reason why the costs rose as steeply as they did.

- Halfway along the canal, the entirely new town of Isma'ilia was built to house Suez Canal Company workers. Isma'ilia takes its name from Sa'id Pasha's nephew and successor, Isma'il.

- Said's son and presumptive heir died in an accident, drowning when in a railway carriage that fell into the Nile as it was being ferried across. Said's death meant that Isma'il became the fifth of the Muhammad Ali dynasty to rule Egypt. Like his uncle Sa'id Pasha, Isma'il was a great supporter of the Suez Canal project. And, like his grandfather Muhammad Ali, Isma'il was a keen modernizer.

### The Canal Opens

- The Canal's dimensions have increased over time—including again, very recently—but in the beginning it was 102 miles long. Since then it has grown to a length of 120 miles, a depth of 79 feet, and a width across of almost 700 feet across.

- Yet the most important figure is as true today as it was on opening day in 1869. That's the fact that the Suez Canal cut almost in half the sea voyage from India to Britain, slicing 4,500 miles from a single trip.

- For the official opening on November 17, 1869, Isma'il made sure to spare no expense. Royalty, aristocracy, government officials, cultural icons, and the biggest celebrities of the day were all invited to Egypt for three weeks of festivities, all of which were paid directly by the khedive Isma'il. Isma'il also commissioned the construction of an 850-seat opera house in Cairo to celebrate the canal's opening.

- The construction of the canal was obviously the major cause of Egypt's growing debt, though hospitality on this scale certainly didn't help the country's increasingly precarious financial footing.

**The Canal's Traffic**

- Within a couple of years of its opening, Britain had not only stopped grumbling, but was one of the canal's biggest users. By the early 1870s, 35,000 British troops passed back and forth through the canal every year.

- Not only did this man-made passage greatly reduce the journey to and from India—the jewel in the crown of the British Empire—but in the age of the steamship, journey times were reduced even further.

- In 1854, the year de Lesseps got the concession to build the Suez Canal, *Lloyd's Register of Shipping* recorded 10,000 ships, of which just 187 were steamers. By the 1890s, some 5,000 ships were passing through the canal every year—70 percent of them British, and every one of them a steamship.

**Egypt's Debt**

- By 1875, Egypt's financial crisis had come to a head. Khedive Isma'il sold what he could to raise money in a hurry. One asset that could readily be converted to cash was Egypt's shares in the Suez Canal.

- British Prime Minister Benjamin Disraeli quickly saw the importance of Britain increasing its stake in the canal, and so he agreed to pay £4 million in sterling for the shares, which translates to about £90 million today, or $140 million. French investors—including the government and individuals—remained the largest bloc. But overnight, Britain had gotten its hands on 44 percent of the canal's ownership.

- The sale of Egypt's shares in the Suez Canal produced a tidal wave in Egypt. Egypt's sale wasn't enough to clear state debts. And so, after investigations by a series of commissions in Britain and France, the hapless Isma'il was forced to accept joint Anglo-French control over Egypt's finances and government.

- After another inquiry in 1878, this one by Lord Baring—later, the Earl of Cromer—Isma'il was forced to hand over his personal estates to Anglo-French control. He had to accept a reduced and humiliating status of a constitutional monarch.

- Matters got even worse. Many Egyptians were upset by Isma'il's incompetent handling of the economy and the ward status of their country in the hands of France and Britain. The result was a serious revolt starting in 1879, led by the disaffected Egyptian Army colonel Urabi Pasha.

- What was the result of Urabi's revolt to save his country? Military intervention by Britain, and the removal from power of Isma'il, who was replaced by his more pliant son. Egypt would go on to be fully occupied and ruled by Britain until the 1950s.

**The Canal's Impact**

- It would be many, many years before the Egyptian economy realised the financial promise that de Lesseps had envisioned for the canal. Until then, if anyone were a winner, it was the British Empire.

- The 20th-century history of the Suez Canal represents yet another fascinating story. In 1956, the Egyptian president Gamal Abdel Nasser announced that he was going to nationalize the Suez Canal. He viewed the canal as an economic lifeline. This led to yet another British invasion, accompanied by French and Israeli forces.

- The ultimate withdrawal of Britain and France from Egypt in 1956, at the behest of the United States and the Soviet Union, was a colossally embarrassing moment, reinforcing their dwindling power in the Middle East. But it was the making of President Nasser, who became a hero throughout much of the Arab World.

- In 1962, the Egyptian government finally paid off its debt for the canal's construction to the Universal Suez Ship Canal Company. That company still exists today, although after a series of mergers, it's now called GDF Suez. The Suez Canal Authority, a wholly state-owned, Egyptian entity, now operates the canal.

- In 2014, the Egyptian government embarked on a grand building project to widen parts of the Suez Canal, and add a new, 45-mile lane to run parallel with a stretch of the existing canal. This $4 billion investment aims to to double the canal's shipping capacity, and provide a big boost to the economy.

- One unintended consequence of the Suez Canal was the inward migration of non-indigenous marine life into the Mediterranean. Scientists reckon that about 350 non-indigenous species have established themselves in the Mediterranean since 1869. Two examples of concern are the toxic, silver-cheeked pufferish and the nomad jellyfish.

- It's unlikely that environmental impacts were a prominent concern for the man behind the canal. Nevertheless, scientists today remember his name. They've dubbed movement of non-indigenous species through the Suez Canal the *Lessepian migration*.

## Suggested Reading

Hodgson, *The Venture of Islam*, volume 3, book 6.

Hourani, *A History of the Arab Peoples*, chapter 17.

Marsot, *A History of Egypt*.

Owen, *The Middle East in the World Economy, 1800-1914*.

Rodenbeck, *Cairo*.

## Questions to Consider

1. Consider the role international trade has played in the political and economic life of the Middle East. How different might this have been without the construction of the Suez Canal?

2. How far were Anglo-French interests and rivalries responsible for Egypt's debt and subsequent status as a British Protectorate?

# Discovering Middle East Oil—1908

Lecture 34

It's hard for people to think about the Middle East in any capacity without oil lurking somewhere in the back of their mind. Why should this be the case? Quite simply because, since it was discovered in what was then called Persia, in 1908, oil has had such an enormous impact on the region that it's virtually impossible to quantify. Nothing has had anything like a comparable influence—for good or ill—in the region in the past 100-plus years.

## George Reynolds's Discovery

- On May 26, 1908, a man named George Reynolds was assailed by a strong smell of sulphur. The whole camp reeked of it. He knew the smell of sulphur was a sure sign of natural gas. Where there's gas, oil is often right behind. Reynolds couldn't contain his excitement. He instructed his men to keep drilling.

- Reynolds and his team were working in Persia, drilling near a town called Masjed Soleyman, in the Zagros Mountains. Starting north of Iran—in Iraqi Kurdistan—the Zagros range runs south for almost 1,000 miles, roughly following the course of the Iran-Iraq border, and south to the Strait of Hormuz, in the Gulf.

- Reynolds and his team had permission from the shah, or king, for their prospecting activities. But they'd been ordered to stop work a week earlier, by the man who was funding this expensive exploration. Their boss was a man named William Knox D'arcy, and while he'd made a fortune from gold mining in Australia, he was on the edge of insolvency after funding eight dry years of prospecting.

- Then again, D'Arcy was in London, a long ways away from Masjed Soleyman. And so Reynolds, ever the optimist—at least with someone else's money—ignored his boss, and kept drilling.

- A week later, in the early hours of May 26, the smell of sulphur filled the camp. At 4:00 am—at a depth of just under 1,200 feet—Reynolds struck oil. A fountain of black gold began spewing into the first light of dawn. Five days later, when his triumphant telegram bearing the good news arrived back in London, D'Arcy is said to have remarked, "If this is true, all our worries are over."

- It was, indeed, true. Under a deal struck with the shah in 1901, known as the D'Arcy Concession, the Englishman possessed—for the next 60 years—the exclusive right to explore, drill, produce, and export petroleum from almost all of Persia (excluding the regions abutting Russia).

- In exchange for this concession, across 490,000 square miles—an area larger than Texas and California combined—the shah received £30,000 in cash, £30,000 in shares, and the promise of 16 percent of annual profits. For D'Arcy and his shareholders—who soon would be dominated by the British government—this was the deal of the century.

- Now that he'd discovered oil, D'Arcy co-founded the Anglo-Persian Oil Company, known as APOC. In time, APOC would be renamed British Petroleum—and later still BP. D'Arcy and his APOC team started work by laying a pipeline from Masjed Soleyman to Abadan, at the head of the Gulf. That is near today's Iran-Iraq border. APOC's refinery at Abadan would be the largest in the world for the next 50 years.

### Overproduction and War

- APOC was exporting oil by 1912. Yet, now it had a new problem: overproduction. D'Arcy's enterprise was on the point of ruin in 1914 because it lacked a market for the vast reserves of petroleum it was accumulating.

- Not only did supply exceed demand—remember, this was before cars were ubiquitous—but also other major supplies of oil were available elsewhere, not least in Russia and the United States.

And other companies had been in the business of selling oil for decades before the first strike in the Middle East.

- This is when good fortune again favored D'Arcy. Britain's Royal Navy was in the process of changing its fleet from coal to oil-powered vessels. The government bureaucrats hadn't accounted for a guaranteed source of oil, however.

- Winston Churchill, as First Lord of the Admiralty at the time, got a proposal before Parliament for Britain to buy a secure source of oil. And so the British government bought about 56 percent of the shares of APOC for £2.2 million—equivalent to about $400 million today.

- Exactly eight weeks later, in July 1914, the First World War broke out. Now, oil was a strategic concern for the first time.

**After the War**

- The Ottoman Empire collapsed in the war's aftermath. Now, new borders and new countries were emerging in the former Ottoman domain, including in the Middle East. Among these was the state of Iraq. It was a British Mandate, under the legal protection and direction of the British government.

- What's more, Winston Churchill—during a rare period out of political office—was in 1923 hired by Burmah Oil to lobby the Iraq government to grant exclusive exploration and drilling rights to APOC. (Burmah Oil was an APOC shareholder.) Iraq granted these rights two years later, and a massive oil discovery followed in Kirkuk, northern Iraq, in 1927.

- A lack of qualified petroleum geologists typically made prospecting in the Middle East a little like looking for a needle in a haystack. One believer, however, was a British–New Zealander by the name of Frank Holmes. Although not a petroleum engineer per se, he had sufficient experience of mining and knowledge of geology to become convinced there was oil in the region.

- Holes set up the Eastern and General Syndicate Limited in London in 1922. He was in Arabia the following year, and entered into direct negotiations with the territory's chief leader, Ibn Saud. Although Britain's high commissioner advised Ibn Saud not to give Holmes the concession, the British stopped paying their annual stipend to him in 1923, and Saud felt entitled to grant Holmes the concession.

- Ibn Saud and his fellow rulers across the Arabian Peninsula were delighted to meet anyone who would pay cash in return for the right to dig in the sand. Financial boons were hard to come by in the climatically and economically harsh area.

- Unfortunately for Holmes—although he found traces of oil—he couldn't find a financial backer in London. As his syndicate started to run out of money, he decided to try his luck in Bahrain, which was then a British protectorate.

- Holmes had a nose for oil. He also had a combination of charm and bluster. Between 1922 and the outbreak of the Second World War in 1939, Holmes was welcomed by the leaders of Saudi Arabia, Bahrain, Qatar, Kuwait—where he had major success—and in the United Arab Emirates.

## Exploration and Dissatisfaction

- After the discovery of oil in modern-day Iran in 1908 and in Iraq in 1927, the 1930s saw a flood of prospecting activity in and around the Arabian Peninsula. Commercial quantities of oil were discovered in Bahrain in 1932; in Kuwait and the United Arab Emirates in 1937; in Saudi Arabia in 1938; and in Qatar in 1939.

- By the 1950s, there wasn't a single state in the region that didn't feel dissatisfied (at best) or cheated (at worst) by the deals they'd signed. In Iran, where oil had been discovered much earlier, the dissatisfaction also came much earlier.

- Representatives of the Iranian government—which was known as Persia until 1935—spent much of the 1920s and early 1930s negotiating with APOC, before signing a new deal in 1933. This new contract gave the government a greater share of profits, and reduced the size of the company's concession. But it was still most favorable to APOC.

- The revised compact allowed company officials to chose where they drilled. It extended their concession by 32 years. And, most carelessly, it exempted them from all import and customs duties, costing the government untold millions in revenue.

- By 1950, Iran was getting just 17 percent of the profits from Iranian oil. The following year, in 1951, the Iranian parliament voted to nationalize the country's oil reserves. Iran also elected the highly regarded statesman and champion of nationalization, Muhammad Mossadeq.

- A 1953 coup ousted Mossadeq. Jointly orchestrated by the CIA and Britain's MI6, the removal from power of a poular, democratically elected prime minister sent a very clear message to rulers of the region's other oil-producing nations: Be very careful about getting any ideas of oil nationalization.

- After 1953, seven petroleum companies dominated the world's oil industry, and often they could do pretty much whatever they pleased. But in a wave that could not be turned back, countries began to shop around for partners. Just 20 years later, the big seven were joined by more than 300 independent and 50 state-owned firms. The stranglehold that Middle Eastern states felt was loosened.

- These new agreements gradually shifted leverage, power and profits from the companies to the governments. Among the first Middle Eastern countries to adopt such a policy were Iran, initially in 1951, and again in 1979; Iraq, in 1961; and Egypt, in 1962.

- In most instances, countries were careful not to talk about nationalization, but rather about *enhanced partnerships* and *sharing*. The reality was, of course, nationalization. Today, major international oil companies frequently must defer to the National Oil Companies, or NOCs, as they're called.

- Based on proven energy resources—oil and gas—the top five NOCs in the world are all in the Greater Middle East. As of recent count, Saudi Arabia's Aramco was number one, followed by the National Iranian Oil Company, Qatar Petroleum, Iraq National Oil Company, and the Abu Dhabi National Oil Company.

**Oil's Impact and Curse**

- Before the discovery of oil in Iran in 1908, the principal strategic importance the Middle East enjoyed was principally geopolitical rather than geological. How times have changed. Every major oil-producing country is important in the geopolitics of the modern world, which goes far beyond their own national borders.

- From Britain's strategic goal of protecting Iran during the First World War to the U.S.-led coalition that went to war against Saddam Hussein's regime following his 1990 invasion of Kuwait, the presence of large quantities of oil and gas in the Middle East has come to play what some think of as a disproportionate role in global politics.

- Yet this lecture must discuss something called the *oil curse* before concluding. The central concept behind the oil curse theory is that countries and regions with an abundance of non-renewable natural resources—such as oil and gas—tend to be less democratic, and have less economic growth, than countries with fewer natural resources. Is this true? And if so why?

- It is true is that the petroleum industry relies on skilled labor, much of which traditionally has come from the West. This does little to alleviate more local and regional employment and income disparities.

- Another problem is that while oil-rich countries have provided free health care and education, the rulers have little or no need to generate income from taxes. That sounds good, but it can also mean that Arab leaders don't feel compelled to consult with their citizens on how they are governed. In that way, it's sometimes argued, while there's plentiful oil revenue to be had, it's hard to see democracy getting well established.

**Suggested Reading**

Al-Rasheed, *A History of Saudi Arabia*, chapter 3.

Esposito, *Islam*, chapter 5.

Gelvin, *The Modern Middle East*, chapter 16.

Sardar, *Mecca*.

Yergin, *The Prize*.

**Questions to Consider**

1. The societal changes that have impacted the oil-rich nations of the Middle East since the discovery of oil in the 20th century are without parallel. However, it has also been argued that the wealth generated by oil has also prevented similar political developments. Consider the so-called oil curse as a force for political stagnation.

2. To what extend have vast oil revenues in Saudi Arabia and elsewhere in the Arabian Peninsula fostered the spread of "Wahhabi" Islam, as well as radical, Islamist-inspired terrorist groups?

Lecture 35

# World War I in the Desert—1914

The Ottoman Empire, which politically dominated much of the Middle East at the start of World War I, is the dominion on which we will focus our attention in this lecture. Among the questions we'll consider are: Why did the Ottoman Empire in Constantinople join the war? And why did it enter the war on the side of Germany and the Austro-Hungarian Empire? We'll also consider the scope of the conflict in the Middle East, and look at the role of religion in the war—specifically Islam. And then we will focus on the Arab Revolt, which unfolded in modern-day Saudi Arabia and Jordan.

## Before the War

- For much of the 19th century, Britain, France, and other European powers had been wrestling with the so-called Eastern Question, i.e., what to do about the weakening Ottoman Empire.

- Britain's policy, by and large, had been to support the Ottomans' territorial integrity. Why? Because many bits of Ottoman territory bordered—or were close to—Russia, which was Britain's greatest imperial rival in the late 19th century.

- The Ottomans straddled other areas of enormous geo-strategic importance, as well, including the Mediterranean Sea, the Black Seas, and the Bosphorus strait, which connects these bodies of water.

- Britain, France, and Germany had all looked for some form of alliance with the Ottomans. But the First World War laid to rest the Eastern Question, and saw Britain scramble to pick up what bits of the Ottoman Empire it could at war's end.

## Ottoman Turmoil

- In Sarajevo—the capital of Bosnia—on June 28, 1914, a Serbian nationalist assassinated the heir to the Austro-Hungarian Empire, Archduke Franz Ferdinand, and his wife. In response, Austria-Hungary declared war on Serbia a month later. Because of a system of alliances then in place, much of Europe took up arms.

- The Ottomans and Germany entered into their own secret treaty on August 2, 1914. There's more to the picture than meets the eye. The very last thing the Ottoman Empire wanted in 1914 was to go to war. It was close to collapse economically and in a state of political upheaval thanks to the so-called Young Turk Revolution of 1908. That revolution had led to the restoration of the Ottoman parliament by Sultan Abdul Hamid II.

- The following year, Abdul Hamid II tried—and failed—to pull off a countercoup. He was instead ousted, and replaced by his brother, Mehmet V. Then, in 1911, the Ottomans lost Libya (the last of their North African possessions) to the Italians.

- In 1912–13 they also lost the so-called Balkan Wars, in which they were beaten by a union of the newly independent states of Montenegro, Greece, Serbia, and Bulgaria. This devastating defeat cost the Ottoman Empire more than 80 percent of its remaining European territory. And in 1913, the Ottomans' possession of Kuwait—supported by the British—declared its independence.

## Need for an Ally

- The Ottoman Empire still ruled much of the Middle East. But in the autumn of 1914, it needed a European ally to act as insurance for its very survival. And that is the answer to our next question: Why did the Ottomans join forces with the German and Austro-Hungarian Empires?

- This was far from an obvious choice, not least because the Austro-Hungarian (or Hapsburg) Empire had been the Ottoman main European foe for hundreds of years, battling for dominance over much of Eastern and Central Europe.

- Throughout much of 1914, representatives from the Ottoman government had also lobbied the French and British to enter into an alliance with them. Paris and London rejected these overtures. In essence, neither Britain nor France wanted to be weighed down by a weak and clearly ailing partner.

- Germany, on the other hand, was very keen to have Constantinople on its side. For one thing, Germany was building a railway from Berlin to Baghdad, which ran straight through the Ottoman Middle East. The Ottomans had little choice but to enter into an alliance with the Central Powers, that is, Germany and Austro-Hungary.

- For his part, the new sultan—Mehmet V—wanted to remain neutral, and refused to sign the alliance. However, the Young Turk Revolution meant that the sultan had lost much of his political power. And so the German-Ottoman alliance was ratified by senior government officials—among them the minister of war, Enver Pasha.

- Even then, the Ottomans argued with the Germans—through diplomatic channels—to try and stay neutral, which Germany would never allow. The Ottomans entered the war on October 29, three months after it started.

**Conflict in the Middle East**

- Most historians agree that the Middle Eastern theater of war consisted of five major campaigns and several minor campaigns. The various Middle Eastern campaigns made up the largest geographical area of any theater of war. The major campaigns were in the Sinai, Palestine, Mesopotamia, the Caucasus, Persia, and Gallipoli.

- As we're about to see, the Arab Revolt—which began in Mecca and Medina, in modern Saudi Arabia—would arguably be the most important of all clashes waged in the Middle East during the war, even though it also is considered a minor campaign.

- Pitting more than one trans-national empire against another meant that the ethnic makeup of those fighting for the Ottomans included Turks, Arabs, Berbers, Persians, Kurds, Chechens, as well as Central Asian Turcomen and European Circassians.

**Islam in the War**

- The question of the possible role of Islam in the First World War had taxed British and German military and civilian intelligence agencies even before the conflict. What role would the Islamic faith play?

- The British author John Buchan wrote a novel, *Greenmantle,* published in 1916. It revolves around German attempts to foment a jihad against Britain. For the British, the very scenario Buchan outlined in *Greenmantle* articulated one of their greatest fears—that a call to arms, based on religious duty, would spread to British India, which was then home to one of the world's largest Muslim populations.

- The Ottomans did indeed declare a jihad, on November 14, 1914. The sultan Mehmed V was also the caliph during this period in Ottoman history, and thus nominally the highest religious authority for all Sunni Muslims. At the same time, he was far from universally beloved across the Muslim world.

- British fears were calmed as Indian Muslims failed to heed the call. Where there were plots against British and other interests, more often than not they were based on nationalism rather than faith.

## The Arab Revolt

- Now we come to the Arab Revolt, where competing Islamic religious and political claims come clashing together. Hussein bin Ali—the custodian of Mecca and Medina, the two holiest cities in Islam—had grown tired of serving at the pleasure of the Ottomans, and worried they might soon replace him with another more pliant leader. In June 1916, he declared his own holy war against the Ottoman Empire, and the person of the sultan.

- The disappointed Germans now saw that their plans to incite a global Muslim uprising against Britain had failed. Instead, Hussein bin Ali was taking direct aim at a German ally, in alleging that the Ottoman rulers had strayed from the true path of Islam and that all good Muslims owed it to their faith to rise up and defeat the Turks and their allies.

- Hussein bin Ali's uprising—which came to be known as the Arab Revolt—was driven not by Islam, however, but by a thirst for power. Backed by Britain and France, Hussein bin Ali saw an opportunity to throw off Ottoman control and become king of all Arabs in an independent, post-war state.

- Without the Arab Revolt, the small but strategically important port of Aqaba—in modern Jordan, at the head of the Red Sea—wouldn't have fallen to British military liason T. E. Lawrence (Lawrence of Arabia) and the Arab army he advised.

- This surprise attack against the Ottoman-controlled port of Aqaba was a small affair in strictly military terms. But the ease with which Lawrence and his Bedouin allies took the port understates the long-term value of having it as a staging post for the remainder of the Arab Revolt and the First World War.

- Even as Hussein bin Ali was throwing in his lot with the British, they were betraying him in a secret deal known as the Sykes-Picot Agreement. Under the terms of this agreement, Britain and France agreed that after the war they would divide up the

Ottoman-controlled Arab lands, thereby thwarting the creation of any Arab state that Hussein hoped to rule.

- On October 3, 1918, Arab troops who'd been fighting the Arab Revolt entered Damascus with Lawrence, and in the process, ended 400 years of Ottoman rule over the city and Syria. The Arab army took Damascus, expelling the Ottoman Turks, only to have the entire region taken away from them by the wilier—and more powerful—imperial powers of Britain and France.

**Fallout and Arab Nationalism**

- The best available estimates put the total of Ottoman dead at approximately five million men, women, and children. The largest single loss of life within the Ottoman Empire during the war was not strictly related to the European conflict, but rather to a more domestic one known as the Armenian genocide. This was the Ottoman government's attempt to eliminate its Christian

The flag of the Arab Revolt flies from the Aqaba Flagpole in Jordan.

Armenian minority population, which was viewed as a potential fifth column.

- Ethnic Armenians died in staggering numbers as the result of executions, combat, famine, and disease. Current best estimates of Armenian dead range from 800,000 to 1.5 million, with the higher figure seemingly closer to the truth.

- Nationalism, as a broader force to be reckoned with, was the spark that ignited the First World War, in Sarajevo. And it spread through the Balkans to the great empires and beyond, including the Middle East. World War I marks the globalization of local conflagrations that persist to present day.

- Anti-Ottoman unrest would also be one of the principal inspirations for Arab nationalism. Small Arab elites, some of them gathering together while studying in Paris or London—or while reading political theory at home in Damascus, Beirut, Jerusalem, and Cairo—were soon organizing political movements along explicitly Arab lines.

- In the midst of the collapse of the Turkish-Ottoman Empire, a sense of Arab-ness grew from Morocco to the Arabian Peninsula. After all, they shared a common language— albeit with different dialects—and shared cultural and historical ties.

- Yet when Arab nationalism was first discussed, religion—Islam—wasn't a leading consideration, not least because some of the earliest proponents of Arab Nationalism were local Christian intellectuals. Religious tension emerged only later, after the war, in response to Western influence (or interference).

- Arab nationalism became the region's dominant political force for another half a century, until it was snuffed out in 1967, during the wake of the much more local Six-Day War. Israel's crushing defeat of a coalition of Arab nations led by Egypt, Jordan, and

Syria highlighted both a military imbalance in the region and a disastrous lack of unity among putative allies.

**Suggested Reading**

Coates Ulrichsen, *The First World War in the Middle East*.

Fromkin, *A Peace to End All Peace*.

Gelvin, *The Modern Middle East*.

Lawrence, *Seven Pillars of Wisdom*.

Rogan, *Fall of the Ottomans*.

Yergin, *The Prize*.

**Questions to Consider**

1. The first World War in the Middle East was the single most traumatic event in the region's modern history. When we consider the post-war peace settlements, the impacts of that war are still being felt in the region. Consider the possible outcomes for the region if the Ottomans had sided with Britain and France in 1914.

2. Considering the post-war settlements, should we see the activities of T.E. Lawrence and the Arab Revolt a success or a failure?

Lecture 36

# The Last Caliphate Falls—1924

Our focus in this lecture is on the end of the Ottoman Empire in 1922, and the abolishment of the Ottoman caliphate two years later by the government of the newly constituted Republic of Turkey. In 1924, when the news of the caliphate's abolition broke, it sent shockwaves throughout the world. For the first time in 1,300 years, the Sunni Muslim faithful had no caliph—no formally designated successor—to Muhammad. This event was one of the most important consequences of the First World War.

## Treaties and Resistance

- When Muslims fought for one side or another in World War I, the demands and entreaties of various Muslim religious authorities made little difference. People fought for a variety of reasons, but typically Islam wasn't one of the important ones.

- Exactly five years after the assassination of Archduke Franz Ferdinand, the Allied European powers and Germany signed the Treaty of Versailles outside Paris on June 28, 1919. The most famous of the post-war treaties, Versailles assigned fault for the war to Germany; limited the size of its future army; took away certain territory in Europe and in its overseas colonies; and set such an enormous bill for reparations that many historians see it as a catalyst leading to the rise of Adolf Hitler.

- But there were other treaties after Versailles. The first of these to deal mainly with the breakup of the Ottoman Empire was the Treaty of Sevres. Signed by the Ottoman government in August 1920, it was never ratified. Its terms were so severe that we can say it was ultimately responsible for the snuffing out of the Ottoman Empire.

- To begin with, the Treaty of Sevres envisioned cutting away all Arab lands from the Ottoman Empire, and made

Constantinople—and the land on either side of the Bosporus—a demilitarized zone under international control. Had it been implemented, the treaty would also have carved away huge chunks of Anatolia (the Turkish heartland), leaving little more than a rump state. Naturally, the beneficiaries would have been the victors: Britain, France, Italy, and Greece.

- This was entirely unacceptable for Turkish nationalists led by Mustafa Kemal, the Turkish revolutionary later known as Ataturk. They rejected the treaty. What followed was the Turkish War of Independence, which went on until October 1922.

- By its end, the country had been fighting for more than a decade, including the Italo-Turkish war in North Africa of 1911, the Balkan Wars of 1912–1913, and the First World War. And now the Allied powers were back at the negotiating table. But this time, there was no negotiating with the Ottoman Empire, because it no longer existed.

- Instead, the talks were between the Allies and Ataturk, along with other representatives of Turkey's new government, the Grand National Assembly. The Treaty of Sevres was torn up, replaced by the Treaty of Lausanne, signed in the summer of 1923. Three months later, on October 29, 1923, the Republic of Turkey came into being.

**The Mandate System**

- An important part of remapping the region beyond the borders of Anatolia was the mandate system, introduced by the Allied-dominated League of Nations. The League of Nations was formed at U.S. President Woodrow Wilson's insistence, in June 1919. It enabled the victorious powers of Britain and France to have their way with the Middle East.

- The League administered three different classes of mandates—A, B, and C. With this international seal of approval, the class A mandates dealing with former Ottoman territories more or less authorized Britain and France to add them to their Middle Eastern empires, under the guise of foreign assistance.

- In other words, Britain and France were were solely responsible for deciding when—or if—full sovereignty would be granted.

**The New Republic**

- With the mandates in place, let's go back to the newly constituted Republic of Turkey. While the Ottoman Empire was abolished in November 1922 by order of the Grand National Assembly of Turkey, the Ottoman caliphate had about another year to go before it, too, would be consigned to history.

- One reason the empire and the caliphate weren't dismantled at precisely the same time is that it might've sparked a civil war—something the Turkish leader Ataturk was naturally keen to avoid. So, he first abolished the sultanate, and then appointed the man who would become the last caliph.

- A symbolic appointment by this time, the lot fell to Abdulmecid, a man whose heart was in scholarship and the fine arts, rather than politics. Abdulmecid placed Islam alongside—rather than above—other religions. He said he looked forward to a world where "all human beings will call one another brothers, racial and religious considerations will disappear, and people will live obeying the true word of God as it was brought to them by His prophets, Moses, Christ, Confucius, Buddha and Mohammad."

- On March 3, 1924, Ataturk signed the decree that abolished the position of caliph. An institution that had been in place for more than 1,300 years was no more. The order went out to treat Abdulmecid with utmost courtesy—but he had to be out of Turkey before dawn. All male descendants of the Osmans were given 24 hours to leave the country. Female family members had a week. And their passports were stamped to prohibit them from ever returning.

- At the same time, no Osman was to take up residence in a Muslim-majority country, in case the family was tempted to try and re-establish the caliphate or the sultanate.

**The Change**

- One way of understanding what had changed over the course of six centuries of Ottoman rule is to look at a partial list of the names of the states that they had conquered, and then compare this to a list of the states that emerged following the dissolution and breakup of the Empire.

- In 1299—which marked the start of the Ottoman era—the world was a collection of empires, kingdoms, principalities, and even a couple of crusader states.

- In 1922, the world had few kingdoms, and those few were more likely to be constitutional rather than absolute monarchies. Those aside, the political landscape was about to become dominated by republics and similar representative state systems.

**Two Questions**

- A frequent question today is, "Why is the Middle East in such a mess?" Coupled with this, there's often a sense that the Middle East has always been at war, and that the countries of the region will never get along.

- Let's tackle the idea that the Middle Eastern countries have never gotten along. Most of these states were created in the wake of the First World War, and a majority of them gained independence only after the Second World War.

- Oman—an absolute monarchy—is the longest-standing independent country in the Middle East, having gotten rid of the Portuguese in the 17th century. Egypt obtained independence by right in 1922. But not until 1952 did it become a republic, no longer subject to British orders.

- Likewise, Iraq became independent of Britain in 1932, but had to wait until the 1940s to exercise meaningful freedom. It was also in 1932 that the Kingdom of Saudi Arabia was established.

- France gave Lebanon its independence in 1943, and extended it to Syria in 1946. Jordan became independent from Britain in 1946, while Israel came into being in 1948. Libya didn't exist as a formal state until 1951.

- While Morocco and Tunisia both gained independence from France in 1956, Algeria had to wait—and fight the French—until 1962. And it wasn't until 1971 when Bahrain, Qatar, and the United Arab Emirates became independent states. Before independence, these states had been under British military protection, having signed the General Maritime Treaty, in 1820. A united Yemen came into being as recently as 1990.

- Now let's rephrase the question, and ask: "Is it always going to be like this in the Middle East?" Of the 16 countries mentioned above, it'll be about the year 2050 before a majority have had even a century of independence. The American Civil War—which left more than 600,000 dead—began just 85 years after the United States declared independence from Britain. When we remember that, we begin to understand just how radically things can change.

### Islam's Continuing Role

- To many outsiders, Islam remains the central social and political force in the Middle East. However, even if such a claim is taken at face value, it's important to see and understand the immense and very real differences of opinion as to what this means.

- Let's take two examples to illustrate the point. One is the Saud-Wahhab pact that fused state power and the Muslim religion in the land we know of today as the Kingdom of Saudi Arabia. The other is the last Ottoman: Ertugrul Osman, who moved to New York in 1939 and lived in exile until his death in 2009.

- In the example of Saudi Arabia, we see an oil-rich state where the authorities appear wholly resistant to the sort of democracy that most of the world either enjoys, or aspires to. Yet when asked, it turns out that a majority of Saudi Arabians want greater political freedoms and representation.

- On the other hand, Osman was perfectly content to see the end of the Ottoman sultanate in Turkey. Later in life, he thought democracy worked well in Turkey. At the same time, while holding out no false hopes that he might be restored to the posititions held by his ancestors—as titular head of a Muslim empire and the Muslim faithful—he did express the view that some form of a non-governing caliphate might not be a bad thing. As Osman saw it, such an institution could bring greater unity to Islam in the setting of the modern world.

- To close a course that has examined almost 1,400 years of history, the following story is appropriate for two reasons. First, it's taken from the life of Islam's founding prophet, Muhammad. Second, it challenges the stereotype of Muslims as wholly fatalistic.

    - The story goes like this: One day Muhammad saw a Bedouin leaving his camel unattended. Muhammad asked the man, "Why don't you tie up your camel?"

    - The Bedouin answered, "I place all my trust in God."

    - Muhammad's response: "Trust in God, but tie up your camel!"

**Suggested Reading**

Finkel, *Osman's Dream*.

Fromkin, *A Peace to End All Peace*.

Gelvin, *The Modern Middle East*, chapter 11.

Hodgson, *The Venture of Islam*, volume 3, book 6.

Hourani, *A History of the Arab Peoples*, chapter 19.

Lewis, *Islam in History*, chapter 17.

Rogan, *Fall of the Ottomans*.

Yergin, *The Prize*.

**Questions to Consider**

1. In the modern, post-Ottoman era, nation states have become the norm across the Middle East. With this in mind, is there any possibility of an internationally recognized caliphate, with both religious and political authority, emerging across national borders?

2. Looking back over the 14 centuries that have passed since the emergence of Islam in Arabia, in 622, what events or individuals have had the greatest significance in their own day, or lasting legacy down the years?

Al-Ghazali, Abu Hamid Muhammad. *The Incoherence of the Philosophers*. Translated by Michael Marmura. Provo, UT: Brigham Young University Press, 2002. This is arguably the single-most important text in the history of Islamic theology, by Sunni Islam's most influential theologian.

———. *Al-Ghazali's Path to Sufism: His Deliverance from Error*. Translated by R.J. McCarthy, SJ. Louisville, KY: Fons Vitae, 2000. Al-Ghazali's spiritual autobiography is a fascinating insight into the mind of Islam's most influential thinker after Muhammad, and far more accessible than *The Incoherence of the Philosophers*.

Al-Hassani, Salim, ed. *1001 Inventions: The Enduring Legacy of Muslim Civilisation*. Washington DC: National Geographic, 2012. A delightful, colourful, and easy to read book, as one would expect from National Geographic. Written to accompany an exhibition of the same name. A great resource for all ages, and for teachers.

Al-Jabarti, Abd al-Rahman. *Napoleon In Egypt: Al-Jabarti's Chronicle Of The French Occupation, 1798*. Translated by Shmuel Moreh. Princeton, NJ: Markus Wiener, 2005. A fascinating, first-hand account of life in Egypt after Napoleon's invasion, and written by a native, Egyptian man of letters.

Al-Khalili, Jim. *The House of Wisdom: How Arabic Science Saved Ancient Knowledge and Gave Us the Renaissance*. New York: Penguin Press, 2011. What have the Arabs ever done for us? Here are some of the answers, from the Islamic Golden Age.

Al-Rasheed, Madawi. *A History of Saudi Arabia*. Cambridge: Cambridge University Press, 2002. The standard, single volume introduction to the history of Saudi Arabia. The best place to start for anyone interested in facts instead of sensationalism.

Al-Tabari, Ibn Jarir. *The History of al-Tabari*. Translated by Gautier Juynboll. Albany, NY: SUNY, 1989. A polymath of great renown, this is al-Tabari's most famous work. An attempt at a universal history, it is still an important source of information on the period.

Armstrong, Karen. *Muhammad: A Prophet for Our Time*. New York: Harper Collins, 2006. A sympathetic, considered, and accessible biography of Islam's founding prophet.

Bennison, Amira. *The Great Caliphs: The Golden Age of the Abbasid Empire*. New Haven, CT: Yale University Press, 2009. A useful account of the Abbasid caliphates. Detailed and scholarly, this is a serious, but not dry, read.

Bennison, Amira, and Alison Gascoigne, eds. *Cities in the Pre-Modern Islamic World: The Urban Impact of Religion, State and Society*. London: Routledge, 2007. This book is full of insights and ideas that one would not readily find written up elsewhere.

Bovill, Edward William. *The Golden Trade of the Moors: West African Kingdoms in the Fourteenth Century*. 2nd ed. Princeton, NJ: Markus Wiener, 1995. One of those joyous finds in one's reading life. Although writing about a specialist and rather arcane area of expertise, Bovill's book is a genuine classic that will make you think on every page.

Brett, Michael, and Elizabeth Fentress. *The Berbers: The Peoples of Africa*. Oxford, England: Blackwell, 1996. Too often overlooked in general histories of North Africa, this is the best single-volume treatment of the region's indigenous peoples.

Brown, Nancy Marie. *The Abacus and the Cross: The Story of the Pope Who Brought the Light of Science to the Dark Ages*. New York, NY: Basic Books, 2010. The fascinating story of Pope Sylvester II and his legacy. Possibly the only pope fluent in Arabic, he studied in Morocco and introduced much Arabic mathematical wisdom to Europe.

Bulliet, Richard. *The Camel and the Wheel*. New York, NY: Columbia University Press, 1990. Like Bovill (above), this book is a great find and a must read. Why do some societies favor pack animals over the wheel? And why after trying the wheel did some societies abandon it?

Canfield, Robert, ed. *Turko-Persia in Historical Perspective*. Cambridge: Cambridge University Press, 1991. Deals with the important impact that Persian and Turkic cultures on Arabic ones.

Coates Ulrichsen, Kristian. *The First World War in the Middle East*. London: Hurst 2014. Readable history of this important period in Middle Eastern history.

Cole, Juan. *Napoleon's Egypt: Invading the Middle East*. New York, NY: Palgrave Macmillan, 2007. A great account of Napoleon's doomed Egyptian adventure, and the many unintended consequences.

Collins, Roger. *The Arab Conquest of Spain: 710–797*. Oxford: Basil Blackwell, 1989. Very good account of the conquests themselves.

Crawford, Michael. *Ibn 'Abd al-Wahhab*. London: Oneworld Publications, 2014. One of the most controversial figures in modern Middle Eastern history, this is a good introduction to the man who is responsible for the ultra-radical face of Islam in today's Saudi Arabia.

Crone, Patricia. *God's Rule: Government and Islam: Six Centuries of Medieval Islamic Political Thought*. New York: Columba University Press, 2005. A great book by one of her generation's greatest scholars of this period in history. Crone was sometimes controversial, not least because she was an original thinker.

———. *God's Caliph: Religious Authority in the First Centuries of Islam*. Cambridge: University of Cambridge Press, 2003. A great book by a great scholar. Deep, thoughtful, challenging and brilliant.

Dabashi, Hamid. *Shi'ism: A Religion of Protest*. Cambridge, MA: Belknap Press of the University of Harvard, 2011. The idea of protest, and martyrdom, remain central in Shia Islam. This is a good treatment of these ideas and much more.

Daftary, Farhad. *A History of Shi'i Islam*. London: IB Tauris, 2013. A useful and readable introduction to the history of Shia Islam.

De Villiers, Marq and Sheila Hirtle. *Timbuktu: Sahara's Fabled City of Gold*. New York: Walker and Company, 2007. A book full of amazing tales of the Sahara, and those who went in search of the legendary city of Timbuktu.

Donner, Fred. *Muhammad and the Believers: At the Origins of Islam*. Cambridge, MA: Belknap Press, University of Harvard, 2010. An excellent book about earliest Islam and possible roots or sources of inspiration.

Bearman, PJ, Th. Bianquis, C.E. Bosworth, E. van Donzel, W.P. Heinrichs, et al., eds. *Encyclopaedia of Islam (Second Edition)*. Leiden: EJ Brill, 1960–2005. A must-have reference for anyone with even a passing interest in one of the world's major religions.

Esposito, John. *Islam: The Straight Path*. Oxford: Oxford University Press, 2011. This is the best introduction to Islam in the contemporary setting. Esposito's scholarship is peerless, and his tone honest but non-dogmatic. Start your reading on Islam here.

———. *Oxford Encyclopaedia of the Islamic World* (4 volumes). Oxford: Oxford University Press, 2009. An essential reference work, edited by one of the world's foremost scholars of Islam.

Esposito, John, ed. *Oxford History of Islam*. Oxford: Oxford University Press, 1999. A standard, one-volume reference work, this hefty volume offers something a little bigger than an introductory history to the subject.

Finkel, Caroline. *Osman's Dream: The History of the Ottoman Empire*. New York: Basic Books, 2007. A really good, easy-to-read introduction to Ottoman history.

Freely, John. *Istanbul: The Imperial City*. London: Pengiun Books, 1998. This is a pleasure to read: a biography of one of the most important cities in human history.

Fromkin, David. *A Peace to End All Peace: Creating the Modern Middle East, 1914–1922*. New York: Henry Holt, 1989. A detailed but not dull account of the post–World War I peace conferences. (And what a great title!)

Gabrieli, Francesco, ed. and translator. *Arab Historians of the Crusades*. Oakland, CA: University of California Press, 1984. It is fascinating and important to read Arabic sources, rather than relying just on European voices to tell us about this important period in Middle Eastern history.

Gavin, RJ. *Aden Under British Rule: 1839–1967*. New York: Barnes and Noble Books, 1975. A good account of the time when Britain first took possession of a bit of the Middle East.

Gearon, Eamonn. *The Sahara: A Cultural History*. New York: Oxford University Press, 2011. Modesty prevents one from praising this book too highly, but it's the only single volume history of the whole of the Great Desert available, and written for the general reader, not the specialist.

Gelvin, James. *The Modern Middle East: A History*. Oxford: Oxford University Press, 2011. A brilliant book about the last 500 years of regional history, which is a must read.

Gibbon, Edward. *History of the Decline and Fall of the Roman Empire*. London: Penguin Classics, 1996. This is one of the greatest books of history ever written in any age. Everyone should read this once in a lifetime. It's not always easy, but it's always exceptional (and don't skip the footnotes).

Goodwin, Jason. *Lords of the Horizons: A History of the Ottoman Empire*. New York: Henry Holt, 1998. Very good narrative history of the Ottoman Empire. Easy to read and well written.

Hawley, Donald. *The Trucial States*. London: George Allen & Unwin, 1971. The history of the smaller Gulf nations before modernity is a really interesting one, and this is a good treatment of the period.

Hitti, Philip. *History of the Arabs*. 10th ed. London: Palgrave Macmillan, 2002. One of the greatest Middle East scholars who ever lived. This was the standard text for decades; still a great place to start, for those who want a long introduction to the area.

———. *Capital Cities of Arab Islam*. Minneapolis, Minnesota: University of Minnesota Press, 1973. Six chapters; six cities; six brilliant long essays covering Mecca, Medina, Damascus, Baghdad, Cairo and Cordova during their periods of rule.

———. *Makers of Arab History*. New York: Saint Martin's Press, 1968. A series of scholarly, accessible, long essays on a dozen of the most important men in the history of Arabic world.

Hodgson, Marshall. *The Venture of Islam* (3 volumes). Chicago: University of Chicago Press, 1974. If one were to have access to just one book on the history of Islam and the Middle East, this should be it, in all three incomparable volumes.

Hopkins, JFP, and Nehemia Levtzion. *Corpus of Early Arabic Sources for West African History*. Princeton, NJ: Markus Wiener, 2000. Important and does what it sets out to do; provide sources on West African history.

Houben, Hubert. *Roger II of Sicily: A Ruler between East and West*. Translated by Graham A. Loud and Diane Milburn. Cambridge: Cambridge University Press, 2002. An account of one of the most interesting figures in medieval history, the brilliant king who ruled the Kingdom of Sicily at its most brilliant moment.

Hourani, Albert. *A History of the Arab Peoples*. 2nd ed. Cambridge, MA: Belknap Press, 2002. Like Hitti's history (above), this remains an excellent and important introduction to Middle Eastern history, packed with knowledge and insight.

Ibn Khaldun. *The Muqaddimah: An Introduction to History*. Princeton, NJ: Princeton University Press, 1967. Like Gibbon (above), but far broader in scope, this is one of the most important books in human history, in its scope, originality and inspiration for three or more fields of study.

Ibn Shaddad, Baha ad-Din. *The Rare and Excellent History of Saladin*. Translated by D.S. Richards. Saladin remains one of the most famous Arab (actually Kurdish) generals in the West, who taught Richard the Lionheart more than a little about chivalry and proper conduct in war.

Institute of Egypt. *Description de l'Egypte*. Cologne, Germany: Taschen, 2001. The outcome of Napoleon's invasion of Egypt, this massive work of scholarship covers in words and pictures, every Ancient Egyptian monument and more the French scholars encountered. Formidable!

Irwin, Robert. *The Middle East in the Middle Ages: The Early Mamluk Sultanate 1250–1382*. ACLS History E-Book Project, 1999. The Mamluks remain one of the most interesting, non-dynastic periods of rule in history, and this book by the brilliant Robert Irwin does them justice.

———. *The Alhambra*. Cambridge, MA: Harvard University Press, 2011. What a companion Irwin would be for a week wandering around the Alhambra. In lieu of his company, this is the next best thing. A small treasure of wit and erudition.

Issawi, Charles. *An Arab Philosophy of History: selections from the Prolegomena of Ibn Khaldun of Tunis (1332–1406)*. London: John Murray, 1950. There aren't anough books about Ibn Khaldun and his work in English, but this helps plug the gap.

Jackson, Peter, ed. *Cambridge History of Iran* (7 volumes). Cambridge: Cambridge University Press, 1986. A brilliant work of scholarship, this may not be light reading, but it is vital reading. After reading this volume, especially on the Safavids (volume 6), everything else on the subject will be easy to follow.

Kasaba, Resat, ed. *Cambridge History of Turkey* (4 volumes). Cambridge: Cambridge University Press, 1996–2012. The best, academic history of Turkish history, ancient to modern.

Kennedy, Hugh. *The Prophet and the Age of the Caliphates: The Islamic Near East from the Sixth to the Eleventh Century*. London: Longman, 1986. A great book about early Islamic rule by the prolific and always entertaining Hugh Kennedy.

———. *Muslim Spain and Portugal: A Political History of al-Andalus*. New York: Longman, 1996. If you want to read one book about Muslim Spain and Portugal, this is the one to get.

———. *The Great Arab Conquests: How the Spread of Islam Changed the World We Live In*. Cambridge, MA: Da Capo Press, 2007. The story of the early Arab conquests told with all the excitement and pace of events themselves. A great read.

———. *When Baghdad Ruled the Muslim World*. Cambridge, MA: Da Capo Press, 2005. Like Kennedy's other works, this is a great read that really does bring alive on the page that which otherwise might seem distant and alien.

Kiser, John, *Commander of the Faithful: The Life and Times of Emir Abd el-Kader*. Monkfish Book Publishing, 2008. Rightly celebrated in both the West and the East, this is the story of the man who led the guerrilla war of resistance to the French invasion of Algeria, after 1830.

Lane-Poole, Stanley. *Saladin and the Fall of the Kingdom of Jerusalem*. New York: GP Putnam's Sons, 1898. Although a 19th-century work, with all that implies, this remains a readable account of the life and times of Saladin. A modern work it is not: a classic from its time it remains.

Lapidus, Ira. *A History of Islamic Societies*. 2nd ed. Cambridge: Cambridge University Press, 2002. This is a book to make any aspiring scholars green with envy: No other book matches Lapidus for this inspiring work on Islamic societies around the world and throughout history.

Lawrence, T.E. *Seven Pillars of Wisdom: A Triumph*. New York: Anchor Books, 1991. (Countless editions available.) This book set in Arabia during WWI continues to capture the imagination. As the subtitle says, a triumph. Read it as Lawrence's dramatic, almost poetic account, and not as a straightforward history.

Lewis, Bernard. *The Middle East: A Brief History of the Last 2,000 Years*. New York: Scribner, 1995. A concise and clearly written introductory history that covers all the main elements of Middle Eastern history.

———. *Islam in History: Ideas, People, and Events in the Middle East*. London: Alcove Press, 1973. An interesting book, full of useful and sometimes surprising observations and ideas, all presented in clear prose.

Lings, Martin. *Muhammad: His Life Based on the Earliest Sources*. New York: Inner Traditions International, 1983. A very useful biography of Muhammad that makes extensive use of original source material, which makes this a uniquely practical work.

Loud, Graham. *Roger II and the creation of the Kingdom of Sicily*. Manchester, England: Manchester University Press, 2012. The glory of the Norman Kingdom of Sicily, and its greatest monarch, are revealed in this well researched, clearly written book.

Lyons, Jonathan. *The House of Wisdom: How the Arabs Transformed Western Civilization*. New York: Bloomsbury Press, 2009. The Islamic Golden Age produced some of the greatest scholarship in human history, as this book explains in a most engaging style.

Lyons, Malcolm Cameron and D.E.P. Jackson. *Saladin: the Politics of the Holy War*. Cambridge: Cambridge University Press, 1984. An important, detailed, academically inclined study of Ayyubid Egypt, and the man behind the dynasty.

Maalouf, Amin. *The Crusades Through Arab Eyes*. London: Al Saqi Books, 1984. One of the best books available on the Crusades, mainly because it presents great insight from the viewpoint of local, Arab opinion. Full of surprises, which challenge Western approaches to the subject.

Marsot, Afaf Lutfi Al-Sayyid. *A History of Egypt: From the Arab Conquest to the Presen*t. Cambridge: Cambridge University Press, 2007. A standard text for students coming tot he study of Egyptian history. A good read, full of detail.

Norwich, John Julius. *The Kingdom in the Sun, 1130–1194: The Normans in Sicily*. London: Faber & Faber, 2010. A thoroughly engaging and entertaining history of one of the gems of Mediaeval Mediterranean history, Norman Sicily.

Owen, Roger. *The Middle East in the World Economy, 1800–1914*. Don't be put off by the word *economy* in the title. This is an important and rightly acclaimed book that considers regional economic history, which helps enormously in making sense of political history from the same period.

Riley-Smith, Jonathan Simon Christopher. *Oxford History of the Crusades*. Oxford: Oxford University Press, 1999. A readable, short introductory history, which gives you most of the facts you could need about the subject.

Robbins, Nick. *The Corporation That Changed the World: How the East India Company Shaped the Modern Multinational*. London: Pluto Press, 2012. The riotous story of the East India Company told in all its glory and infamy.

Robinson, Chase, ed. *New Cambridge History of Islam* (6 volumes). Cambridge: Cambridge University Press, 2010. This is an amazing work of scholarship that brings together the world's greatest scholars of Islamic history. An essential reference.

Rodenbeck, Max. *Cairo: The City Victorious*. London: Picador, 1999. A great narrative history of one the world's greatest cities, by long-term Cairo resident and *The Economist*'s Middle East editor.

Rogan, Eugene. *The Arabs: A History*. London: Penguin, 2011. A brilliant political history of the region from 1517, the year the Ottomans conquered Cairo, this is not only a good read, but wears its learning lightly. Full of good vignettes that make the subject come alive.

———. *The Fall of the Ottomans: The Great War in the Middle East, 1914-1920*. London: Allen Lane, 2015. The best book about the First World War in the Middle East, not least because of the author's pains to offer the story from both the Ottoman and Western points of view.

Runciman, Steven. *The Fall of Constantinople 1453*. Cambridge: Cambridge University Press, 1990. A dramatic history of the end of the Byzantine Empire from the master of Crusader history.

———. *A History of the Crusades* (3 volumes). London: Folio Society, 1994. The standard "complete" history of the Crusades for decades. There are newer titles available, but few that have the same breadth of knowledge. Especially good on the view from Byzantium.

Ruthven, Malise. *Islam: A Very Short Introduction*. Oxford: Oxford University Press, 2012. Probably the best, short introduction to Islam available. Obviously an important subject, Ruthven draws on a deep, wellspring of knowledge, and manages to synthesise this in an accessible yet scholarly work in less than 200 pages.

Sardar, Ziauddin. *Mecca: The Sacred City*. London: Bloomsbury, 2014. A useful book about Mecca, not least because there are few others worth reading in English, and lots of good stories, and anecdotes from the author, including his *hajj* journeys to the city.

Schacht, Joseph and C.E. Bosworth, eds. *The Legacy of Islam*. 2nd ed. Oxford: Oxford University Press, 1974. Although a little dated, this is a beautiful book full of considered insights into the many and varied cultural impacts and achievements to come out of the Middle East.

Sessions, Jennifer. *By Sword and Plow: France and the Conquest of Algeria*. Ithaca, NY: Cornell University Press, 2011. Good books about French Algeria in English are in short supply; this does a good job of telling this important period of North African history.

Strathern, Paul. *Napoleon in Egypt: The Greatest Glory*. New York: Bantam, 2009. Napoleon's invasion of Egypt is one of the more colourful episodes in a Technicolor life, which this book captures perfectly.

Streusland, Douglas. *Islamic Gunpowder Empires: Ottomans, Safavids, and Mughals*. Boulder, CO.: Westview Press, 2011. A great comparative study of the three so-called gunpowder empires, it does a good job of highlighting broader Middle Eastern history of the period.

Stoye, John. *The Siege of Vienna*. London: Collins, 1964. A little dated, this remains a good read about a truly dramatic story.

Twitchett, Denis, and John K. Fairbank, eds. *Cambridge History of China* (volume 3). Cambridge: Cambridge University Press, 1976. Like all of Cambridge University's multi-volume histories, this is a milestone in national and area studies. The indispensable source.

Vikor, Knut. *The Maghreb Since 1800*. London: Hurst, 2013. One of the best introductory volumes to Maghrebi history now available in English.

Walker, Paul. *Exploring an Islamic Empire: Fatimid History and Its Sources*. London: IB Tauris, 2002. Fatimid history is one of the most interesting periods in all Islamic history, and this is a good place to start the journey to find out more.

Waterfield, Gordon. *Sultans of Aden*. London: John Murray, 1968. A short narrative account of the period when, in the first half of the 19th century, Britain began acquiring Middle East possessions.

Yergin Daniel. *The Prize: The Epic Quest for Oil, Money, and Power*. 1990. This remains the best single volume history of the discovery and exploitation of oil. Written for the general reader, it's full of anecdote and dramatic stories, which are much more exciting than the subject might suggest.

# Image Credits

**Page No.**

4 .......... © eFesenko/Shuttershock.
12 .......... © Zurijeta/Shutterstock.
21 .......... © Sam Robinson/Photodisc/Thinkstock.
33 .......... © David Hlavacek/Shutterstock.
40 .......... © BrooklynMuseumBot/Brooklyn Museum/Wikimedia Commons/Public Domain.
45 .......... © Omar2788/Wikimedia Commons/Public Domain.
53 .......... © The British Library.
62 .......... © GifTagger/Wikimedia Commons/Public Domain.
71 .......... © Zereshk/Wikimedia Commons/Public Domain.
78 .......... © Khonsali/Wikimedia Commons/CC BY-SA 3.0.
88 .......... © Christopher Halloran/Shutterstock.
96 .......... © Migel/Shutterstock.
107 .......... © Georgios Kollidas/Hemera/Thinkstock, Georgios Kollidas/iStock/Thinkstock.
115 .......... © Misa123a/Wikimedia Commons/Public Domain.
118 .......... © Gryffindor/Wikimedia Commons/Public Domain.
122 .......... © sedmak/iStock/Thinkstock.
126 .......... © Bakanov~commonswiki/Wikimedia Commons/Public Domain.
132 .......... © Alex Yeung/Shutterstock.
146 .......... © Алексей03/Wikimedia Commons/Public Domain.
153 .......... © Bilinmiyor/Wikimedia Commons/Public Domain.
160 .......... © Westend61 Premium/Shutterstock.
171 .......... © Kassus~commonswiki/Wikimedia Commons/CC BY-SA 3.0.
178 .......... © Neuceu/Wikimedia Commons/CC BY-SA 3.0.
182 .......... © JM Travel Photography/Shutterstock.
187 .......... © Dal89/Wikimedia Commons/Public Domain.
195 .......... © Murat/Wikimedia Commons/Public Domain.
201 .......... © Osmanlı98/Wikimedia Commons/Public Domain.
210 .......... © Maurice Flesier/Royal Collection Trust/Wikimedia Commons/Public Domain.
219 .......... © Austriacus/Wikimedia Commons/Public Domain.
233 .......... © Morphart Creation/Shutterstock.
243 .......... © BomBom/Wikimedia Commons/Public Domain.
254 .......... © Cropbot/Wikimedia Commons/Public Domain.

258.................................................................................................© Photos.com/Thinkstock.
266.......................................................................................................... © lynea/Shutterstock.
285...............................................................© Aviad2001/Wikimedia Commons/Public Domain.

# Notes

Notes

Notes